Essentials of Marketing Communications

We work with leading authors to develop the
strongest educational materials in marketing,
bringing cutting-edge thinking and best learning
practice to a global market.

Under a range of well-known imprints, including
Financial Times Prentice Hall, we craft high quality
print and electronic publications which help readers
to understand and apply their content, whether
studying or at work.

To find out more about the complete range of our
publishing please visit us on the World Wide Web at:
www.pearsoned.co.uk

Jim Blythe
University of Glamorgan

Essentials of Marketing Communications

Third Edition

FT Prentice Hall
FINANCIAL TIMES

An imprint of **Pearson Education**
Harlow, England • London • New York • Boston • San Francisco • Toronto
Sydney • Tokyo • Singapore • Hong Kong • Seoul • Taipei • New Delhi
Cape Town • Madrid • Mexico City • Amsterdam • Munich • Paris • Milan

Pearson Education Limited
Edinburgh Gate
Harlow
Essex CM20 2JE
England

and Associated Companies throughout the world

Visit us on the World Wide Web at:
www.pearsoned.co.uk

First published 2000
Second edition 2003
Third edition published 2006

ISBN-13: 978-0-273-70205-4
ISBN-10: 0-273-70205-X

British Library Cataloguing-in-Publication Data
A catalogue record for this book is available from the British Library

Library of Congress Cataloging-in-Publication Data

Blythe, Jim.
    Essentials of marketing communications / Jim Blythe.
        p. cm.
    Rev. ed. of: Essentials of marketing. 2nd ed. 2001.
    Includes bibliographical references and index.
    ISBN 0-273-70205-X
    1. Marketing. I. Blythe, Jim. Essentials of marketing.. II. Title.

    HF5415.B485 2006
    658.8--dc22

                                                                2005054965

10 9 8 7 6 5 4 3 2
09 08 07 06

Typeset by 30 in Palatino 10/12.5pt
Printed by Ashford Colour Press Ltd, Gosport, UK

The publisher's policy is to use paper manufactured from sustainable forests.

Brief contents

Contents

Supporting resources

Visit **www.pearsoned.co.uk/blythe** to find valuable online resources

For instructors
- Complete downloadable Instructor's Manual, including sample answers for selected material in the book
- Customisable PowerPoint slides, including key figures and tables from the main text

For more information please contact your local Pearson Education sales representative or visit **www.pearsoned.co.uk/blythe**

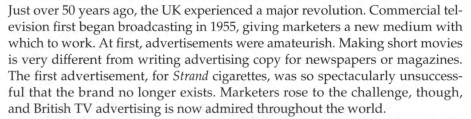

Preface

Just over 50 years ago, the UK experienced a major revolution. Commercial television first began broadcasting in 1955, giving marketers a new medium with which to work. At first, advertisements were amateurish. Making short movies is very different from writing advertising copy for newspapers or magazines. The first advertisement, for *Strand* cigarettes, was so spectacularly unsuccessful that the brand no longer exists. Marketers rose to the challenge, though, and British TV advertising is now admired throughout the world.

The ability of marketers to adapt, re-create, and make their own any new form of communication is astounding. Engineers and designers use new technologies to develop new ways of doing things, lawyers are presented with new legislation or new case law to which they must adapt and accountants agree new ways of presenting corporate results. But of all the business disciplines, marketers are easily the most competitive in making innovative use of new opportunities.

This is partly because of the often-quoted idea that people are 'bombarded' with advertising messages, implying that marketers need to produce something extremely interesting to cut through the clutter. Partly it is because of the intense competitive activity in most markets, putting pressure on marketers to improve the 'cutting edge' of their communications. Partly it is simply because communicating is fun.

Of all human activities, communication is the most obvious. More than any other animal (as far as we can tell) human beings love to communicate. We talk, write, text, e-mail, wave our arms, send Morse code, and even use our faces as complex signalling devices – anything, as long as we are communicating! Marketers are no exception. They have become communicators *par excellence*, so much that people outside the profession believe that communication is all that marketers do. Like anybody else, marketers communicate in order to inform, persuade, advise, warn, and entertain: they also listen (through marketing research) to other people's communication, and are often better at this than most people, if the truth be told.

Purpose of this book

This book aims to provide the reader with some insights into the ways marketers approach their own communications activities. Starting with the theoretical background to marketing communications, the book moves into the mechanics of producing marketing communications, describing the various techniques marketers have for telling their story. The final chapter looks at new developments in marketing communications: the new possibilities inherent in the technological revolution.

New to this edition

This edition has been fully revised with new case studies and examples throughout. Chapter 12 has been rewritten to take account of the most recent available research regarding the Internet and other new media, and Chapter 1 has been substantially revised to include the latest thinking on communication theory.

All the chapters have been updated to include recent research from academics worldwide.

Acknowledgements

I'd like to thank my friends and colleagues at the University of Glamorgan for their help and advice, my students for asking me awkward questions, and for making me explain things more clearly. I also thank my wife, Sue, for helping me to see what is important and what is not.

In addition, I'd like to thank the following reviewers who provided insightful feedback for this third edition:

Marylyn Carrigan, University of Birmingham

Claudia Muller, NHH Norwegian School of Economics and Business Administration

Sheila West, University of Westminster

Ifan D H Shepherd, Middlesex University Business School

Thanks also to Thomas Sigel, Senior Acquisitions Editor and Mary Lince, Senior Editor, at Pearson Education for their help in making this edition happen.

Viewers in 1955, watching their black and white TV sets, could little imagine the communications possibilities available in the early twenty-first century. Mobile telephones, holographic window displays, the Internet, literally hundreds of TV channels, FM radio stations catering to local or minority audiences, text messaging, e-mail, and even direct mail advertising were unknown in 1955. Yet all of these media have been adopted, adapted and developed by marketers for their own communications. Marketing revenues subsidise (or even pay entirely for) all of these communications media, but more importantly it is the business of marketers to make their communications interesting, informative, and valuable in themselves to the people who use those media. This book has been written in the hope that future marketers will continue to enrich our communications.

Jim Blythe
August 2005

Publisher's acknowledgements

We are grateful to the following for permission to reproduce copyright material: Figure 1.5 from Kahneman, Daniel, *Attention and Effort*, 1st edn, © 1973. Adapted by permission of Pearson Education, Inc., Upper Saddle River, NJ; Figure 1.7 from *The Theory of Buyer Behaviour*, John Wiley & Sons, Inc. (Howard, J.A. and Sheth, J.N. 1969); Figure 1.8 reprinted with the permission of Scribner, an imprint of Simon & Schuster Adult Publishing Group, from *The Nine American Lifestyles: Who we are and where we are going* by Arnold Mitchell. Copyright © 1983 by Arnold Mitchell; Table 4.1 reprinted by permission of Sage Publications Ltd. from *The Media In Western Europe* by Euromedia, copyright (© The Euromedia Research Group 1992, 1997); Table 5.2 and 5.3 based on Ambient media: advertising's new media opportunity? (Shankar, A. and Horton, B. 1999) reproduced with permission from *International Journal of Advertising* 18(3), 305–322; Figure 6.2 from 'Stakeholder theory and internal marketing communications: A framework for analysing the influence of new media' in *Journal of Marketing Communications* 9(3), 147–161, Taylor & Francis Ltd. http://www.tandf.co.uk/journals (Debussy, N.M., Ewing, M.T. and Pitt, L.F. 2003); Table 8.1 from 'Dimensions of trade show exhibiting management' in *Journal of Marketing Management*, 9(1), January, 55–63, Westburn Publishers Ltd (Shipley, D., Egan, C. and Wong, K.S. 1993); Table 8.2 from 'Assessing trade show functions and performance: an exploratory study' in *Journal of Marketing*, 51, July, 87–94 (Kerin, R.A. and Cron, W.L. 1987) reproduced with permission from the American Marketing Association; Table 11.5 from 'From key account selling to key account management' in *Journal of Marketing Practice: Applied Marketing Science*, 15(1), 9–21, © MCB University Press www.emeraldinsight.com/jmpams.htm (Millman, T. & Wilson, K. 1995).

We are grateful to Ostrich.com Incorporated for permission to reproduce material from their website www.ostrichesonline.co.uk.

In some instances we have been unable to trace the owners of copyright material, and we would appreciate any information that would enable us to do so.

1 Theories of communication

Objectives

After reading this chapter you should be able to:

- explain the main theories of communication
- explain how attitudes are formed
- explain how perception and cognitive dissonance theories affect communication
- contrast theories of motivation
- explain how culture affects communication

INTRODUCTION

Marketing communication is an ever changing field. New theories, new techniques, cultural changes and technological advances all combine to create a dynamic environment within which marketers try to ensure that their messages get through to their target audiences.

This chapter is about the main theories surrounding marketing communication. With the next chapter, it gives an overall view of the current thinking on marketing communications, and an overview of the tools and techniques of marketing communications.

COMMUNICATION

Communication is one of the most human of activities. The exchange of thoughts which characterises communication is carried out by conversation (still the most popular form of entertainment in the world), by the written word (letters, books, magazines and newspapers) and by pictures (cartoons, television and film). People enjoy communicating, and in fact people often expect and welcome marketing communications (Madden and Perry 2003). This is also true in business-to-business markets, where communication is crucial in developing and maintaining relationships (Holden and O'Toole 2004).

Communication has been defined as a transactional process between two or more parties whereby meaning is exchanged through the intentional use of symbols (Engel *et al*. 1994).

The key elements here are that the communication is intentional (a deliberate effort is made to bring about a response), it is a transaction (the participants are all involved in the process), and it is symbolic (words, pictures, music and other sensory stimulants are used to convey thoughts). Since human beings are not telepathic, all communication requires that the original concepts be translated into symbols which convey the required meaning.

This means that the individual or firm issuing the communication must first reduce the concepts to a set of symbols which can be passed on to the recipient of the message; the recipient must decode the symbols to get the original message. This means in turn that the participants in the process must share a common view of what the symbols involved actually mean. In fact, the parties must share a common field of experience. This is illustrated in Figure 1.1.

The sender's field of experience and the receiver's field of experience must overlap, at least to the extent of having a common language. The overlap is likely to be much more complex and subtle in most marketing communications; advertisements typically use references from popular culture such as TV shows, from proverbs and common sayings, and will often make puns or use half-statements

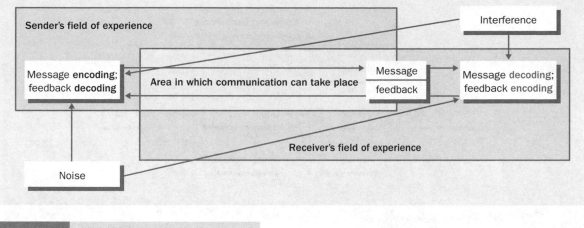

FIGURE 1.1   Model of the communication process

which the audience will be able to complete because they are aware of the cultural referents involved. This is why foreign TV adverts are often unintentionally humorous, or even incomprehensible.

Noise is the surrounding distractions present during the communications process, and varies from children playing during the commercial break, through to arresting headlines in a magazine. **Interference** is deliberate attempts to distract the audience's attention with intelligent communications. For example, a car driver may be distracted away from a radio ad by another car cutting in (noise) or by seeing an interesting billboard (interference). For most marketing purposes the difference is academic.

The above model, based on the work of Schramm (1948, 1971) is in essence a one-step model of communication. This is rather oversimplified; communications do not necessarily occur in a single step in this way. Katz and Lazarsfeld (1955) postulated a two-step model in which the messages are filtered through opinion leaders, and in most cases the message reaches the receiver via several routes. Sending the same message by more than one route is called **redundancy**, and is a good way of ensuring that the message gets through. Figure 1.2 shows this diagrammatically.

In the diagram, the sender sends almost identical messages via different routes. The effect of noise and interference is to distort the message, and the opinion leader will moderate the message, but by using three different routes the meaning of the message is more likely to get through than if only one or two routes were used. This is the rationale behind the integration of marketing communications.

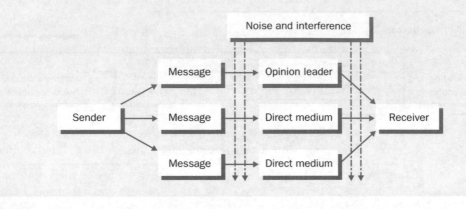

FIGURE 1.2   Redundancy in communication

An alternative view

In recent years, an alternative view of the communications process has emerged, largely as a result of the work of communications theorists Deetz (1992) and Mantovani (1996). For these authors, the Schramm model omits several important factors, the first of which is the fact that the receiver of the communication is not passive in the process. The person who receives a communication will think about it and interpret it, but more importantly is unlikely to be listening very closely to it in the first place. Human conversations are not necessarily the reasoned affairs that the Schramm model implies: more often, people talk past each other, each one eager to make his or her point without really wanting to absorb what the other person is saying (Varey 2000).

In this model, the communicators might be seen as individuals standing on different sides of a pool of knowledge. Each is contributing something to the pool, and each is taking something from the pool, in an attempt to develop a single view of reality.

In fact, the Schramm model is not only widely taught but is also widely accepted instinctively as the way communications work. People imagine that what they say will be taken at face value, even when it has in fact been said for effect. People (and especially marketers) frequently overstate the case, exaggerate, omit negative facts and otherwise distort messages in order to persuade people to accept the speakers' own view of reality.

For example, a bank might send out a mailing to promote a new credit card. The intention of the mailing is to inform people and persuade them to apply for the card, so the bank will emphasise the low introductory interest rate but is unlikely to mention the large penalties for late payment or exceeding the credit limit on the card.

Recipients of the mailing might respond in any of the following ways:

- Throw the mailing away. (Reality for the receiver: These people are stupid, they are wasting my time yet again with their inappropriate mailings.)

- Respond to the mailing, on the basis that six months' interest-free credit will help nicely. (Reality for the receiver: These people are stupid, I will take advantage of their offer and then switch back to my existing card or to another freebie.)

- Respond to the mailing, because it looks like a good deal. (Reality for the receiver: These people are clearly looking after the customer. I'll give them a try.)

- Examine the exact wording of the address to work out which mailing list has been used. (Reality for the receiver: These people can't fool me. I know how they are doing this.)

For the bank, all of the above outcomes, except for the third one, are negative. Except for the third one, all the above outcomes lie outside the scope of the Schramm model.

Information is therefore not a fixed thing; it cannot be transferred from one mind to another. Information is subject to interpretation. In the alternative view, it is unrealistic to talk about transmitters and receivers. A more accurate view would be to speak of initiators, apprehenders and appreciation. Acceptance of a communication arises from the apprehender's choice, not from the initiator's intentions (Varey 2000).

If this alternative view is correct, it has wide-reaching consequences not only for marketing, but for management in general, since all organisations operate by communicating with their stakeholders.

Whichever perspective is adopted, whether the Schramm view or the alternative view, marketers need to consider the effects of their communications in terms of the recipient's pre-existing ideas, attitudes and capacities. Customers and consumers are also consumers of information: in either model, they will decode and encode responses which are based (at least in part) on what they already know, and on what they believe about the communication from the marketer. The overall effect may or may not be a change in the customer's world view.

The hierarchy of communication effects

Communication does not necessarily create all its impact at once. A series of communications will move the recipient up a 'ladder' of effects, as shown in Figure 1.3. At the bottom of the ladder are those consumers who are completely unaware of the product in question; at the top are those who actually purchase the product.

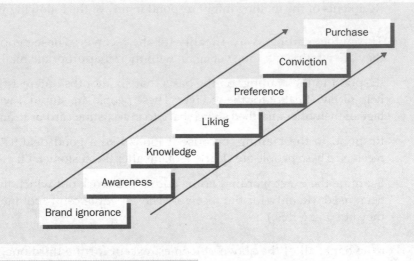

FIGURE 1.3   The hierarchy of communication effects

One of the problems with the hierarchy of communication effects is that it implies that the process is invariably linear. This is not necessarily the case; an individual can become aware of a product and form an instant liking for it without having detailed knowledge of the product. Equally, it is perfectly possible for a consumer to buy a product on impulse and form an opinion about it afterwards.

Having said that, the hierarchy of effects model is helpful in planning communications campaigns, since different communications methods and styles can be used according to the consumer's level on the hierarchy. For example, when a new product is first introduced (or a product is introduced into a new market), few of the target audience will know anything about it. Establishing the brand name in the market is therefore a realistic first move in the communications process.

Signs and meaning

A **sign** is 'anything that stands for something (its object) to somebody (its interpreter) in some respect (its context)' (Pierce 1986). Signs fall into three categories, as shown in Table 1.1.

TABLE 1.1	Categorising signs

Type of sign	Definition	Example
Icon	A sign that looks like the object, or represents it visually in a way that most people would relate to	A drawing of someone relaxing on a beach would signify a holiday to most people, even if this were not their own favourite type of holiday
Index	A sign that relates to the object by a causal connection	A sweaty athlete coming into a locker room relates to a drink; most people are familiar with the idea of being thirsty after playing sport, even though the drink itself is not shown
Symbol	An artificial sign which has been created for the purpose of providing meaning	Most people are familiar with the intertwined arrows used to denote recyclable or recycled materials. This conveys an image of 'greenness' to the products it appears on

The most obvious symbols are, of course, words. Words only have meanings as they are interpreted by people – and over long periods of time, even words change their meanings. For example, 'nice' has come to mean polite, pleasant or enjoyable, yet 150 years ago it meant 'precise'. Meanings of words can be **denotative** (having the same meaning for everybody), or **connotative** (having a meaning which is unique to the individual). Although everybody knows what 'strawberries' are (denotative), some individuals are allergic to them and might associate the word with the allergy (connotative).

Because connotative meanings vary among individuals, marketers need to develop empathy with their target audiences. This is easiest when the marketer and the audience are as similar as possible in terms of background and outlook. Semiotics, syntactics and semantics are fields of study which enable us to ensure that the correct meanings are attributed to symbols.

Semiotics

Semiotics is really more of a theoretical approach than an academic discipline (O'Sullivan *et al.* 1983), and uses spoken language as the prime example of a sign system (although it is not limited to language). Semiotics pays attention to the reader (or observer) since meaning can only be derived socially; it is an interaction between the reader and the text. In the first instance, texts are created by reworking signs, codes and symbols within the particular sign system in order to generate myths, connotations and meanings. The social process involved generates pleasure as well as cognitive (or rational) activities.

For example, a film (or indeed a TV advert) uses the sign systems of the spoken word, the actions of the actors, the music of the soundtrack, and the conventions of direction and production to generate its meaning. The viewer will then filter the information and add it to his or her pre-existing attitudes, knowledge and prejudices in order to create a meaning. In this sense all communication is interactive to the extent that the observer edits and mutates the meanings offered.

Semiotics is an attempt to show how meaning is produced within a social context, implying that meaning is not produced by an individual but is subject to power plays, struggle and interpretation, much like any other social interaction. In the context of the alternative view of communications described earlier, semiotics studies the ways in which social contexts affect the recipient of a communication. This in turn affects the world view that the recipient creates, or the mutual pool of understanding from which the recipient draws meaning.

Syntactics

Syntactics is about the structure of communications, how the symbols and signs are arranged relative to one another. Symbols and signs change their meanings according to the syntax, or contexts, in which they appear. For example, a road-safety poster showing a 10-year-old girl holding her father's hand to cross the road has a different meaning from that of the same 10-year-old holding her 4-year-old brother's hand. The girl means something different in each poster. In the first instance she is the protected person, in the second she is the protector, but there are greater connotations of vulnerability in the second example, which might make this poster more effective in alerting drivers to the dangers of children crossing the road.

Equally, the same word can have different meanings in different sentences, or the whole advertisement can acquire a different meaning when seen in different locations.

Semantics

Semantics is concerned with the way words relate to the external reality to which they refer. It is not actually about the study of meaning (although this is a common misconception), but is really only concerned with the appropriateness of the words themselves. For example, advertisers often use probability markers such as 'probably', 'may', or 'could' in advertising copy in order to 'hedge' their claims. In general, the target audiences for these advertisements regard such hedges negatively (in other words they do not trust them), so that the message the advertiser intended is actually changed by the interpretation the recipient gives it (Berney-Reddish and Areni 2005).

In fact, communication is carried out in many other ways than the verbal or written word. Only 30 per cent of communication uses words; people (and companies) communicate by pictures, non-verbal sounds, smell, touch, numbers, artefacts, time, and **kinetics**. Many of these media are used by marketers – for example, women's magazines sometimes have scratch-and-sniff cards which contain new fragrances, and charities sometimes send out free pens to prospective donors so that they can more easily fill in direct-debit contribution forms.

Table 1.2 shows some of the ways these silent communications methods are used by marketers.

TABLE 1.2	Silent communications

Medium	Example
Numbers	The Porsche 911: there is an implication that the car is the latest in a long series (although Americans might associate 911 with the emergency telephone number)
Space	An image of a man and a woman standing close together implies that they are lovers; likewise an image of wide open spaces implies freedom
Artefacts	Images of what people own imply their social status. Also, small gifts and free samples convey a small obligation to the recipient
Time	Images of people in a hurry might imply success and energy to north Europeans and Americans; to an African it would imply somebody who has no time for other people and is arrogant
Kinetics	People who are walking (or running) imply a fit and active lifestyle; those who are gesticulating with their hands imply intellectual discussion or heated argument

A brand is a type of sign; the brand name, logo and image of the brand convey information to the observer. Conveying the brand image to the consumer is one of the major roles of marketing communications (there is more on the subject of branding in Chapter 7).

Culture

The main problem with silent languages is that they are not culturally universal. Most body language does not transfer well to other cultures, even when the cultures are otherwise close. Well-known examples are the two-fingers sign which is highly insulting to British people but which can denote merely 'two' in the rest of Europe; the thumb and index finger circle which denotes 'OK' to Americans but which is a rude gesture in Brazil; and showing the soles of the feet to Thais, which is again insulting. Other examples are more subtle. Japanese people tend to show their emotions less in public than do Americans; Indians tend to regard shabby or torn clothes as denoting poverty, whereas north Europeans often associate this with independence and freedom; and numbers which are considered lucky in some cultures are neutral in others (Costa and Pavia 1992).

The problem arises because of **ethnocentrism**, which is the practice of assuming that others think and believe as we do. Ethnocentrism is one of the few features of human behaviour that belongs to all cultures: the tendency is for people to believe that their own culture is the 'right' one and everybody else's is at best a poor copy (Shimp and Sharma 1987). This easily leads to misunderstandings and outright rejection of the communication, and is remarkably common. Very few marketing communications can be applied worldwide, although adverts for jeans and music CDs are exceptions as the global youth market responds to these in a fairly consistent manner (Steen 1995).

Sometimes national cultural characteristics can be identified. Hofstede (1984) carried out a transnational survey in 66 countries, with over 6,000 respondents, and was able to identify four dimensions of national characteristics:

1 *Individualism vs collectivism*. The degree to which the culture values individualism and individual freedom above allegiance to the group.

2 *Uncertainty avoidance*. The degree to which the culture adheres to rules and customs to reduce uncertainty.

3 *Power distance*. The degree to which power is centralised in the culture.

4 *Masculinity–femininity*. The degree to which the culture exhibits 'masculine' qualities of assertiveness, achievement and wealth acquisition rather than the 'feminine' attributes of nurturing, concern for the environment and concern for the poor.

While these categorisations are interesting and useful when planning the approach to a mass market, it would be dangerous to make assumptions about individuals from another culture based on these broad generalisations. Individuals from within a culture differ more from each other than do the cultures from each other; in other words, the most individualistic Taiwanese is a great deal more individualistic than the most conformist American.

Astute marketers ensure that their messages are tailored to each culture. For example, Stella Artois lager is promoted in Britain as a premium lager, whereas in its native Belgium it is promoted as a mass-market beer. Interestingly, the UK adverts are written entirely in French (which is presumably intended to move the brand upmarket, since the observer would need a certain minimum education to understand the advertisement), but the beer is actually brewed in Leuven, a Flemish-speaking part of Belgium.

Symbols differ from one culture to another. British marketers might use a lion to symbolise patriotism, whereas French marketers would use a cockerel and Americans would use a bald eagle. Advertisements transfer cultural meanings into products (McCracken 1986).

INFORMATION PROCESSING

There are several models of information processing, one of the simplest of which is the AILA model shown in Figure 1.4.

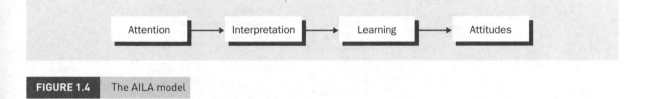

FIGURE 1.4   The AILA model

The AILA model is in fact rather too simplistic to be of real use. It implies that, having attracted the attention of the observer, the rest of the process will follow naturally. This further propagates the fallacy that the consumer is someone to whom things are done, rather than someone who actively participates in the communications process.

In fact, most marketing communications operate below the conscious level. We are aware of brands, but in most cases cannot remember when we first became aware of them. Kahneman's (1973) model, shown in Figure 1.5, takes account of the capacity of the individual to process information.

Kahneman's model is an attempt to show how the individual's limited capacity for processing information can be allocated to the task at hand. The model takes account of the individual's long-term attitudes (enduring dispositions) and immediate impulses (momentary intentions) in allocating attention to a particular communication. The available capacity is further determined by a subconscious evaluation of demands on the individual's capacity.

For example, a person might have an enduring disposition to be interested in foreign travel. Passing a travel agent's the individual might be attracted by a special offer in the window and might normally allocate attention to the offer, but at the same time have his or her attention capacity reduced by having a screaming 2-year-old to look after. This would affect the individual's allocation policy at that moment. This problem is of course subjective to the individual and is impossible for marketers to predict.

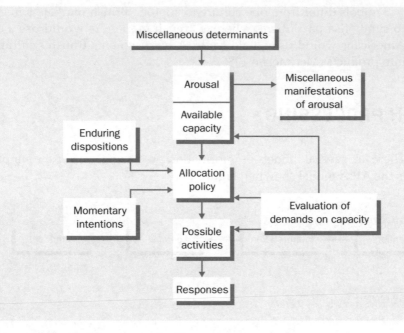

FIGURE 1.5	Capacity model of attention

Source: Kahneman, Daniel, *Attention and Effort*, 1st edn, © 1973. Adapted by permission of Pearson Education, Inc., Upper Saddle River, NJ

Assuming that the individual is able to pay attention to the communication, he or she will need to process the information received. McGuire's (1976) model of information processing is shown in Table 1.3.

TABLE 1.3	McGuire's information processing model

Stage	Explanation
1 Exposure	The consumer must have proximity to the message; in other words, the consumer must not only see the message (or hear it) but must also experience it in some way
2 Attention	The consumer must be aware of the message and must allocate information-processing capacity to it
3 Comprehension	The consumer must understand the message, interpreting it to get the meaning that the sender intends it to have

TABLE 1.3	Continued
4 Acceptance	The message must be absorbed into the consumer's existing set of beliefs and knowledge. If existing attitudes and beliefs are changed during this process then persuasion has also occurred
5 Retention	The message becomes part of the individual's long-term memory

Source: Based on McGuire (1976)

If McGuire's model is correct, then clearly marketing communications involves much more than merely placing as many adverts as possible in as many places as possible. The message must key into the consumer's existing thought patterns and patterns of belief. This has major implications for policy; it may be worth spending more money on creating the right message than on buying media space to expose the message to the public. There are many examples of high-impact communications which have been achieved with small media expenditure – the Benetton series of billboard advertisements being one of them. Benetton uses controversial, even offensive, images in its advertising to create maximum impact, and also gains considerable press exposure as the advertisements themselves create controversy which is reported as news.

A further complication arises because people have differing strengths and weaknesses in receiving information. Some people receive and process information primarily through vision, others hearing, and others through touch. Neurolinguistic programming is an emerging discipline for studying the information-processing preferences of individuals, and has been shown to have considerable effects on people's responses to advertising (Skinner and Stephens 2003). There are three key elements in attracting attention in advertising: the pictorial element, the brand itself, and the text or spoken element (Pieters and Wedel 2004). In general, the pictorial element is superior in capturing attention whatever the size of the picture; the text element captures attention in proportion to its size; and the brand element transfers attention to the other elements.

Involvement and perception

The degree to which consumers respond to advertisements is also related to **involvement**. This is the degree of perceived personal importance and relevance accompanying product and brand choice within a specific situation or context (Antil 1984). Involvement is a function of perceived risk of negative outcomes (fear of making a mistake), social sanctions (fear of looking stupid, or the desire to look good), and ego-relatedness (degree of fit with self-image) (Laurent and Kapferer 1985).

Involvement creates the obstacle of **selective perception** under which the consumer rejects information which is not relevant or which conflicts with existing ideas. **Perception** is the process by which individuals select information from the surrounding environment and synthesise it into a world view. Because there is so much going on around us at any one time, we usually select only that which is most immediate or interesting. Inevitably this means that there are gaps in each individual's view of the world, and these gaps are usually filled in by using either previous experience or analogies drawn from elsewhere. Each individual's world map differs from every other individual's because it is, in part, a construct of the imagination.

Mapping is affected by the following factors:

- **Subjectivity**. The existing world view within the individual, and unique to that individual.

- *Categorisation*. The pigeonholing of information and the pre-judging of events and products. This can happen through the process of **chunking**, whereby the individual organises information into chunks of related items (Miller 1956).

- *Selectivity*. The degree to which the brain is selecting from the environment. For example, colour can have a dramatic effect in attracting attention and cutting through the clutter which surrounds the average person (Jansson *et al.* 2004).

- *Expectations*. These lead individuals to interpret later information in a specific way.

- *Past experience*. Sights, smells or sounds from the past will often trigger responses. For example, the smell of baking bread might trigger a memory of a village bakery from twenty years ago, but in fact the smell might have been artificially generated by an aerosol spray near the supermarket bread counter (Davies *et al.* 2003).

Part of the function of marketing communications is to ensure that the product occupies the right place in the consumer's world view. If the product is a high quality, high priced product then it needs to be mapped next to other premium products; this affects the type and style of the communications. If, on the other hand, the product is a cheap, serviceable version then it needs to be mapped next to other everyday products. In this connection, individuals often use surrogates to judge quality – for example, price is often used as an indicator of quality in circumstances where other clues are not available.

Message interpretation is influenced by personal factors, by social factors and by psychological factors. Each of these pushes the individual in different directions, so that the message which was originally formulated by the marketer might well be interpreted in an entirely different (and sometimes inappropriate) manner. Figure 1.6 illustrates the influences.

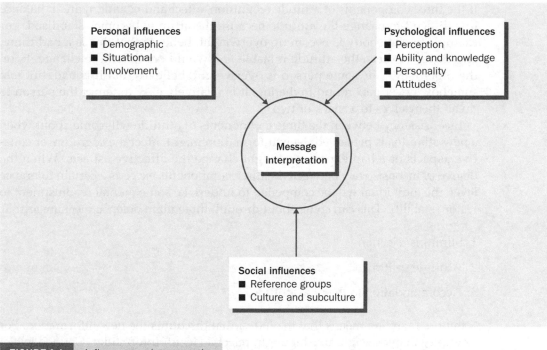

FIGURE 1.6 Influences on interpretation

ATTITUDE FORMATION

Attitude is a learned tendency to respond to an object in a consistently favourable or unfavourable way (Onkvisit and Shaw 1994). Attitudes are formed as a result of translating needs into motivation to process information, and consequent exposure to stimulus. The processing of this information leads to **cognitive** (thought) responses and to **affective** (emotional) responses, which then may lead to conation, or intended behaviour.

During the process, consumers acquire **salient beliefs** about products. Because the cognitive system can only hold a relatively small number of facts in mind at once, the salient beliefs are the most important ones and are the ones which the consumer will use in making the judgement.

There are three ways of changing attitudes:

1 Add a new salient belief.

2 Change the strength of a salient belief. If the belief is a negative one, it can be discounted or played down. If it is a positive one, it can be given greater importance.

3 Change the evaluation of an existing belief.

If the three components of attitude (cognition, affect and **conation**) are in balance it is difficult to change the attitude because the attitude becomes stabilised. For example, if somebody is becoming overweight, believes that this is a bad thing, and therefore diets, the attitude is stable and would be difficult to change. If, on the other hand, the same person is overweight, believes that it is bad, but just somehow never gets round to dieting, it is relatively easy to tempt the person to 'treat' themselves to a snack or two.

Inconsistency between the three components of attitude will come about when a new stimulus is presented. New information might affect the cognitive or conative aspects or a bad experience might change the affective aspects. When the degree of inconsistency between the three components exceeds a certain tolerance level, the individual will be compelled to undertake some mental readjustment to restore stability. This can come about through three main defence mechanisms:

1 Stimulus rejection

2 Attitude splitting

3 Accommodation to the new attitude

Stimulus rejection means that the individual discounts the new information. For example, an overweight person might reject a Health Information Council leaflet saying that slim people live longer than fat people, on the grounds that the research does not examine people who used to be fat but are now slim and have kept the weight off. By rejecting the new information, the individual is able to maintain the status quo as regards the cognitive element of attitude.

Attitude splitting involves only accepting that part of the information that does not cause an inconsistency. Here, the individual might accept that the new information is basically true but believe that his or her own circumstances are exceptional. For example, consider an individual who is averse to a particular car company because he once owned a car of theirs that rusted very quickly. He may see an advert that explains that the company now rustproofs all the cars, and while he accepts that is true and that the cars would not now generally rust badly, he lives near the sea and therefore believes that the cars would rust anyway.

Accommodation to the new attitude means, in effect, changing the attitude to accommodate the new information. The fat person may switch to a low-fat diet, the smoker may cut down or give up altogether, the car buyer may just go ahead and buy the car.

The three elements are so closely related to each other that a change in one element will usually cause a change in the others (Rosenberg 1960). New information causing a change in cognition will change the consumer's feelings about the product, which in turn is likely to change the consumer's intentions about the product.

Changing attitudes

The *elaboration likelihood model* (Petty and Cacioppo 1983) describes two routes by which attitude might be changed. The *central route* involves an appeal to the rational, cognitive element; the consumer makes a serious attempt to evaluate the new information in some logical way. The *peripheral route*, on the other hand, tends to involve the affective element by associating the product with another attitudinal object. For example, if a pop star appears in an advert for a soft drink this might cause the star's fans to change their attitudes towards the drink. This has nothing to do with the attributes of the drink, but everything to do with the attributes of the star. Peripheral cues such as this are not relevant to a reasoned evaluation, but because of the interdependence of the components of attitude, change will occur. In effect, the affect felt towards the star 'rubs off' on the product.

Changing existing attitudes relies heavily on market research, but in particular the teasing out of the factors which go to make up the attitude can be a demanding task. This is because of **halo effect**. Halo effect is the tendency for attitudes about one salient belief to colour attitudes about another. For example, if a consumer had a bad meal at a restaurant, this is likely to lead to a view that everything else about the restaurant was bad, too. Likewise, a favourable view of some factors often leads to respondents reporting a favourable view of other factors.

Often the most effective ways of changing attitudes can be based on emotion rather than logic. For example, studies have shown that campaigns to discourage smoking among teenagers work best on boys if they use emotional, 'cosmetic' appeals (for example, telling boys that the smell of smoke on their clothing is repellent to girls) whereas long-term health appeals (a logical, cognitive approach) work better on teenage girls (Smith and Stutts 2003).

Cognitive dissonance theory states that if an individual holds two conflicting cognitions, he or she will experience discomfort and will seek to reduce the dissonance either by changing one or other of the views held, or by introducing a third view which will account for, and reduce, the discrepancy (Festinger 1957).

The most interesting aspect of dissonance theory was that attitudes could apparently be changed more easily by offering low rewards than by offering high ones. Festinger and Carlsmith (1959) induced students to lie to other students (by telling them it was part of a psychological experiment) and offered them payment varying from $1 to $20. The students who were offered the lower amount actually began to believe the lie; those offered the higher amount tended not to. The higher-paid students were able to justify lying on the basis that they were receiving a substantial reward (at 1959 prices). The lesser-paid students had no such external justification, and therefore had to revert to believing the lie themselves in order to resolve the dissonance.

The reason for the power of cognitive dissonance in attitude formation is that the arousal of dissonance always contains personal involvement; therefore the reduction of dissonance always involves some form of self-justification (Aronson *et al.* 1974). Self-justification is necessary because the individual usually feels that the dissonance has arisen through an act or a thought that is immoral or stupid. In the marketing context, cognitive dissonance shows up most frequently as post-purchase dissonance. Here, the new owner of a product finds that the information previously gathered about the product turns out to be inaccurate; the cognition based on the pre-purchase information search conflicts with the direct experience of using the product. In these circumstances, the consumer can take one of four general approaches to reducing the dissonance:

1 Ignore the dissonant information and look for positive (consonant) information about the product.

2 Distort the dissonant information.

3 Play down the importance of the issue.

4 Change the behaviour or the situation.

For example, a car buyer who is disappointed with the performance of a new car might just accept the poor acceleration (ignore the dissonant information), might pretend that the car actually performs quite well, but was affected by the weather or the road conditions (distort the information), might seek other benefits of the car, concentrating on how comfortable it is or how easy to drive (play down the information) or might trade the car in for a more lively model (change the behaviour or the situation).

If post-purchase dissonance does occur, the consumer may take action against the vendor. These responses fall into three categories: voice responses (complaints to the vendor), private responses where the consumer generates negative word-of-mouth by talking to friends, family and colleagues about the product, and third-party responses where the consumer complains to a trade body or consumer rights organisation (Singh 1988).

MODELLING CONSUMER BEHAVIOUR

Models are simplifications of reality intended to make the world more comprehensible and, indeed, manageable. The problem is, of course, that models almost always lose some of the detail. There is therefore a trade-off between, on the one hand, creating a model that is detailed enough to be a good surrogate for the total picture and, on the other hand, keeping it simple enough to be comprehensible.

AIDA

AIDA is a simple model of consumer response to marketing communications. AIDA stands for Attention, Interest, Desire and Action, and implies that gaining the consumer's attention and interest will automatically lead to desire for the product and action in purchasing it. In fact, attention and interest are more likely to come about as a result of consumer need; an individual who feels the need for a new hi-fi system will probably seek out information on new models, but the attention and interest in the manufacturers' adverts and brochures are generated by the need, not the adverts.

AIDA is still widely used, but the implication that the consumer is a mere recipient of marketing communications does not recognise the interplay between the communication and the target audience. Even when the communication is one way, there is a degree of interaction between the recipient and the message: the message is interpreted in the context of the recipient's pre-existing attitudes and beliefs. This is not part of the AIDA model.

Consumer purchase behaviour may follow a sequence of five steps:

1 Need recognition

2 Pre-purchase activities or search

3 Evaluation and purchase decision

4 Act of purchase and consumption

5 Post-purchase evaluation

Although this model is almost self-evidently an accurate outline of what happens, it is also very much oversimplified. It does not describe the mechanisms by which need is recognised, or by which need can be activated; it does not describe what types of pre-purchase activity might be undertaken; and it does not describe methods of evaluation. Nonetheless, it offers a useful guide to the types of communication that might be most appropriate at each stage of the process.

The Howard–Sheth model

The Howard–Sheth model shown in Figure 1.7 is a simplified version of the full model, but it does provide a much fuller picture of the consumer decision-making process, particularly in terms of the factors which are involved in the process.

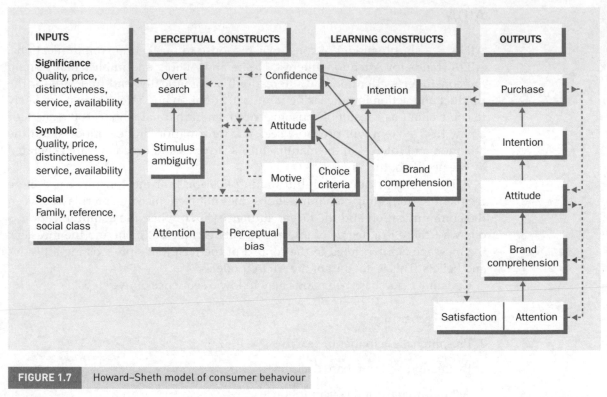

FIGURE 1.7 Howard–Sheth model of consumer behaviour

Source: Adapted from Howard, J. A. and Sheth, J. N. (1969) *The Theory of Buyer Behaviour*. Copyright © 1969 John A. Howard and Jagdish N. Sheth. This material is used by permission of John Wiley & Sons, Inc.

In the diagram, the solid arrows show the flow of information, while the dotted arrows show the feedback effects. In essence the model shows the way the inputs are processed by and into perception and learning, and eventually become outputs which feed back to further perceptions. The areas in which marketing communications play a significant part are as follows:

- *Significance factors*. Quality is often conveyed by means of brochures and press releases which emphasise the physical characteristics of the product. Price is also advertised. The distinctiveness of a product can be conveyed by pictures and words, and the service and availability issues are also covered by advertising. All these factors are conveyed during an information search, when the individual is actively looking at marketing communications.

- *Symbolic factors*. The list is the same as for significance factors but this time the issues relate less to the usage of the product and more to the image the product conveys both in terms of the respect of others and in terms of self-esteem and self-actualisation issues. These factors are conveyed prior to the information search, in marketing communications that are basically unsought; most of this type of communication operates below the conscious level.

- *Learning constructs*. The areas of developing choice criteria and of brand comprehension are also subject to influence by marketing communications. The unsought communications which surround all of us will affect the selection of a decision set, and will often affect the features that the consumer will look for in the new purchase. A consumer's understanding of the features and benefits of each brand will have come largely from marketing communications (although friends and family will also have some input into the decisions).

Inbound marketing communications (surveys, returned guarantee cards, customer helplines and so forth) will come into play as the consumer uses the product and may affect the consumer's attitude to repeat purchases by encouraging a positive post-purchase evaluation.

Much of the influence on a consumer's purchasing behaviour is outside the marketer's direct control. Some of the information about a major purchase will have come from friends and family, and the importance of these groups cannot be overstated. **Reference groups** are frequently used in marketing communications as models; for example, if a product is to be aimed at a typical working-class family, an advert for the product might show people from an idealised form of such a family. For many years this was the promotional approach for the UK's Oxo cubes and for Mars Bars.

The second way in which marketing communications use reference groups is to imply that use of the product will enable the consumer to join a better group (an **aspirational group**). For example, advertisements for sportswear might show someone on the winning team in a football match.

A third way of using reference groups is to have an authority figure endorse the product. This can range from a TV doctor recommending a painkiller through to world-class athletes recommending running shoes.

The effectiveness of the **role model** in modelling behaviour will depend on the personal characteristics of the model. Attractive role models will usually be imitated more than unattractive ones, successful-looking models are given more credence than unsuccessful-looking ones, and a model who is perceived as being similar to the observer is more likely to be emulated (Baker and Churchill 1977).

The Howard–Sheth model is complex but fairly comprehensive; the purpose of a model is to simplify reality rather than to recreate it, and the model does this reasonably successfully. Note that most of the processes involved in consumer decision making happen below the conscious level and in relatively short periods of time in most cases, as most people are not aware of the influences on them.

Needs and motivation

Because motivations may come from many sources, and because it is often impossible to satisfy all one's emotional and physical needs at once, researchers have considered the possibility that needs can be both categorised and prioritised. An early attempt to classify psychological needs was made by Henry Murray, result-ing in a list of twenty basic needs. These are: succorance, nurturance, sentience, deference, abasement, defendence, infavoidance, harmavoidance, achievement, counteraction, dominance, aggression, affiliation, autonomy, order, rejection, sex, understanding, exhibition and play (Murray 1938).

Virtually all of these needs have marketing implications. The need for rejection is used by companies which urge consumers to reject own-label brands in favour of the 'genuine article'. The need for nurturance is emphasised in advertisements for cold cures and soups. The need for sentience is appealed to in advertisements for adventure holidays.

Murray's list is probably not exhaustive. Nor will all the needs he lists apply to everybody, and the needs may have different priorities for different people. Also, some of the needs on the list conflict with each other; for example, dominance and deference. It should also be pointed out that Murray's list was developed as a result of his clinical experience rather than as the result of a research programme, so much of the evidence for the list is anecdotal rather than empirical.

Researchers have therefore tried to establish whether there are certain needs that everyone has in common, and which can be prioritised for most people. The best-known example of this approach is Maslow's hierarchy of needs.

Abraham Maslow (1954) hypothesised that needs would be met in a specific order of importance. For Maslow, survival needs such as food, water and shelter would be met first, followed by security needs. Next would come the social needs of belonging and esteem, and finally the personal psychological needs of aesthet-ics and self-actualisation.

The hierarchy of needs does not necessarily imply that each need must be met before the higher needs can be addressed, merely that the individual's main pre-occupation will be with the lower needs until they are met. This means that a tramp may be more interested in spending time with his mates than in finding shelter for the night, or a sales rep may be more interested in winning the sales competition than in earning enough commission to pay the mortgage, but the theory is close enough to the true state of affairs for it to be useful. It should also be noted that circumstances can cause the individual to move down the hierarchy as well as up; the model is intended to demonstrate the relative importance of each need at a given time, rather than show a life's progression.

Certainly it is clear that people with a low income are usually less interested in the arts and the aesthetic life, having more important and immediate concerns; but the exceptions (the starving artist in a garret) are numerous, so although in many cases the theory is useful, there are many other cases in which it does not apply.

Maslow's theory adds weight to the development of the VALS structure shown in Figure 1.8. This diagram describes nine lifestyle options that the researchers at Stanford Research Institute (now SRI International) found in the USA. The same basic lifestyle patterns have also been identified among UK consumers (McNulty 1985). At the lower levels, which correspond to Maslow's survival, security and belonging needs, the consumers are controlled by their basic needs. After these very basic needs have been met, there is a divergence; some consumers become outer directed, or concerned with the opinions of others, whereas others become inner directed, concerned with their own internal drives. Ultimately, Mitchell theorises that consumers adopt an integrated position, where concern and respect for others is combined with a knowledge of their own needs and desires.

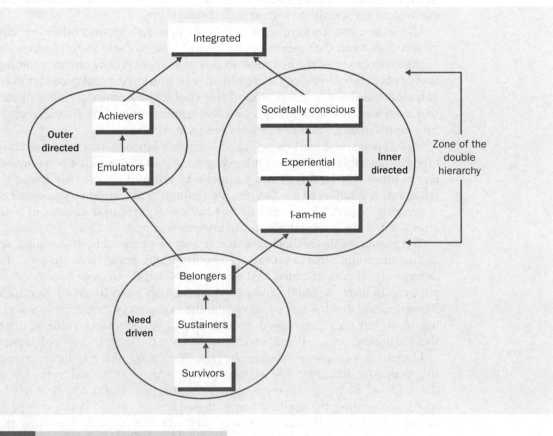

FIGURE 1.8   VALS (values and lifestyles) structure

Source: Adapted from Mitchell (1983)

A different approach was taken by Herzberg (1966). Herzberg started out as a medical researcher and became interested in the possibility that some factors might be motivators, whereas others might be demotivators, and the two groups might not necessarily overlap. As a medical man, he called the second group the 'hygiene' factors, since their absence would cause the 'disease' of demotivation.

Translating this into consumer behaviour, some factors in a purchase are basics that every buyer would expect (in other words, the **core benefits** of the product). For example, people expect a car to get them from A to B and be reliable. These are hygiene factors, not motivators, since these would be expected by every buyer.

Motivators would tend to be subjective, that is, specific to the individual. Some examples for a car might be extra performance, extra comfort, attractive styling. In other words, hygiene factors tend to be common to all consumers, whereas motivators are specific to segments and subgroups.

Motivation may be simple, of course; budget airlines and other low cost businesses operate on the basis of providing only the hygiene factors, and using price as the main driver of the business. In this case, there is only one motivating factor, that of cheapness. In theory there can only be one lowest cost provider in the marketplace, but the airlines get round this problem by offering different routes, so that each low cost airline flies a different combination of destinations and departure points in order to differentiate the service further.

Motivation should not be confused with avoidance. Adverse outcomes (pain or other undesirable effects) will not necessarily lead to a positive behavioural activity; in other words, threatening somebody will not necessarily make them do what you want them to do. Despite the frequency of 'cautionary tale' advertising, where the adverse outcomes of not taking a particular course of action are stressed, the motivational effects are uncertain at best.

The reason for this is that rewards can only be obtained by following a specified course of action, whereas there are usually many ways to avoid pain. Burris F. Skinner (1953) demonstrated that rats could be taught to push buttons in complex patterns in order to obtain food, and could also learn to avoid electric shocks. Skinner found that the rats performed in the expected or desired way when obtaining food, but they performed in unexpected ways when avoiding the electric shocks. In other words, the rats were inventive in the ways they avoided the shocks.

Human beings are, of course, not rats. People are likely to be far more inventive than a rat would be. For example, when a law was passed in the UK making the wearing of car seatbelts compulsory, the threat of a £50 fine led to some motorists holding the seatbelt across their chests to avoid being stopped by the police – the threat did not always result in drivers actually fastening the belts. The result of this was that drivers were even more likely to have accidents and be injured since many were driving one-handed. Avoidance of the consequences of the law does not necessarily mean obedience to the law.

One way in which marketers can use pain avoidance in motivating consumers is by **modelling** the bad consequences. For example, the London Underground ran a series of advertisements showing commuters who had been prosecuted for fare-dodging, complete with a detailed account of the consequences of the action ('It was the embarrassment of having to stand up in court and admit fiddling a £1.30 fare. And I lost my job'). Another example might be a housewife whose washing powder 'can't shift those greasy stains'. In each case, the consumer is invited to see the possible negative consequences of fiddling the fare or of using the wrong washing powder.

The problem with any model of consumer behaviour is that many forces influence the consumer's thinking, and all consumers are individuals so that it becomes extremely difficult to take account of all the possible factors. In particular, the consumer may not identify with the model used; a young unemployed woman may not identify with a middle-aged male executive used in the fare-dodging advertisements.

MISCOMMUNICATION

Failure to communicate can arise from several different causes. In essence, these can be categorised under the following headings:

- *Implication* – the meanings that are 'read into' communications by the recipient.

- *Distortion* – changes in the message generated by outside influences.

- *Disruption* – damage to the message caused by circumstances and by (sometimes deliberate) misconstruction of the message.

- *Confusion* – often arising from the ambiguity of the message.

- *Agreement/disagreement* – disagreement arises from a lack of perceptual commonality between the sender and the recipient.

- *Understanding/misunderstanding* – differences between the sender's and recipient's respective codes of understanding often arise through cultural differences (particularly differences of language).

- *Personal transformation* – this depends on the recipient's receptivity to change.

Each of these sources of miscommunication is present in marketing communications, as they are in interpersonal communications. The marketing implications of each are outlined in the following sections.

Implication

The implications of a communication are the meanings that are placed on it by the recipient. Miscommunication often arises between individuals because the communication raises painful implications, and therefore the message is not stated clearly enough. For example, a nurse telling relatives that their loved one is probably going to die soon might say, 'We don't hold out much hope, but there's always the possibility of a miracle.' The relatives might take this to imply that there is a possibility of survival.

Equally, marketing communications can fail because of implications. Marketers are usually dealing with people en masse, and therefore have to take a broad view of the implications as they apply to people at large. Frequently, these implications differ between individuals, even within the same target market. For example, an advertisement for an exotic holiday destination might appeal to many people who would enjoy such a trip, but to some people the fact that the destination has been widely advertised implies that it will be crowded with other tourists.

The main elements of implication are shown in Table 1.4.

TABLE 1.4 Elements of implication	
Element	**Explanation**
Assumption	If the recipient fails to understand the message, he or she is left to make assumptions about the sender or the message itself. These assumptions are subject to positive or negative slanting, may or may not be open to inspection and revision in future, and may turn out to be true or false when the recipient tries to act on them
Inference	The recipient may add extra ideas to the message as received, filling in what he or she sees as blanks in the message. This can happen even when the message itself is clear and no misunderstanding is involved, but the inferred element may well create a miscommunication
Expectation	Expectations about the communication may cloud the meaning even before the message is delivered. For example, many people have expectations about the message an unsolicited mailing will deliver, yet these expectations often bear no resemblance to the actual communication. Nevertheless, the expectation will colour the recipient's view of the real communication
Reflection	Consideration of past communications affects the recipient's behaviour towards future communications. For example, past experiences with mail order catalogues (whether good or bad) will affect the way the recipient responds to mail order in future
Attribution	In the case of interactive communications such as personal selling there is a problem of attributing responsibility for the jointly produced outcomes. For example, the salesperson may attribute a failed sale to the stupidity or perfidy of the customer, whereas the customer may attribute the failure to excessive praise of the product by the salesperson at the expense of concern about the customer's actual needs
Metacommunication	Shifting the focus from what is being said to how it is being said is the province of metacommunication. In marketing communications, this can appear in two ways: the style of the communication (for example, different styles of advert) and in the type of communication (press releases as opposed to corporate advertising, for example)
The search for common ground	As stated earlier, communications fail if there is no overlap between the sender's and recipient's fields of experience. In fact, both parties are likely to seek the common ground in which communication takes place – the sender because of the need for the message to get through, the recipient because of curiosity about the message content

Distortion

Internal distractions and external interference often lead to distortions in the meaning of the message. For example, an individual may have had a bad experience of a Japanese product, and from this conceived a dislike of all Japanese products. The messages conveyed by adverts for Japanese goods will be distorted by this internal distraction. Table 1.5 shows the main elements of distortion.

TABLE 1.5	Elements of distortion

Element	Explanation
Interference	To be able to comprehend the message, the recipient must be able to concentrate on it to some extent. Other incoming messages may be inadvertently included in the interpretation of the main message, or may distract the recipient so that pieces of the main message are omitted
Bias	This does not necessarily mean prejudice or bigotry; it can simply mean that the mindset of the recipient is such that the message is interpreted in a particular way. Ideological, ethnocentric or egocentric biases all contribute to distortion of messages
Miscalculation	Miscalculation occurs when the information presented is wrongly interpreted through a mistake in cognition. Sometimes this comes about through ignorance or mistakes; sometimes it comes about through a desire for an alternative truth to prevail. In marketing communication terms, a customer might misinterpret the terms of a special offer because he or she is unable to meet the true conditions and is hoping that other, simpler, conditions would be acceptable
Pseudo-communication	Some communications are carried out in order to cover up a true state of affairs, in order to preserve appearances. For example, a public relations exercise might be carried out in order to conceal bad practice on the part of a company. Without actually lying about the true state of affairs, the communication is nonetheless a distortion of the truth

Disruption

Disruption of communications can be caused by outside interruptions (not necessarily interference) or by internal misgivings on the part of the recipient. A typical example would be the breakdown of communication engendered when a prospective customer suddenly develops negative feelings about a salesperson and calls the presentation to a halt. Disruption is only possible in the case of dialogue; the communications must be two way, as in personal selling or mail order situations.

The elements of disruption are shown in Table 1.6.

TABLE 1.6	Elements of disruption
Element	**Explanation**
Unmanageable circumstance	The feeling that the situation is outside one's control can lead to disruption. For example, being approached by a forceful shop assistant may cause the customer to leave the shop. Likewise, an overcomplex mail order form may never be completed
Relational instability	The consistency of people's behaviour derives from the types of situations they choose for personal engagement. Someone finding themself in an unfamiliar or awkward situation may not be able to respond to the messages being offered
Conversational irregularities	Conversation normally involves statements, assessment of the meaning of the statements, and responses. If statements meet with inappropriate or undesired responses the communication breaks down and is disrupted. For example, if a customer writes to complain about a product and the response is a leaflet extolling the virtues of another product in the range, the dialogue breaks down
Lack of reciprocity	Life is a matter of give and take, and if, for example, a salesperson is clearly not prepared to give ground or allow the customer a chance to make a point, the dialogue will break down
Mutual misconstruction	This applies to personal encounters where the participants are unable to translate their interpretations of self and other into a coherent vocabulary. The root of the problem is our inability to understand why someone else's viewpoint appears sensible to them. This can cause problems when negotiating sales deals because there may be hidden agendas on both sides of the negotiation
Threat of dissolution	The knowledge that the relationship might end is one that can affect both parties. This is particularly relevant in business-to-business markets, where a disruption of supply can be as important to a customer as the disruption of income would be to the marketer. Without any stated threat by either party, the nature of the communications between them will be affected by the knowledge of their relationship. (See Chapter 9 for more on relationship marketing)

Confusion

Confusion arises from distortion, mistakes, disruption and conflict. Conflicting information about a product (for example, from an advertisement on the one hand and from a salesperson on the other) creates confusion in the mind of the recipient. Avoidance of confusion is one of the main driving forces behind the integration of marketing communications, since integration should (in theory at least) minimise the incidence of conflicting messages.

The elements of confusion are shown in Table 1.7.

TABLE 1.7	Elements of confusion
Element	**Explanation**
Conflict	Disputes between the parties will almost always create confused communications. Tension tends to result in overstatement of positions, and attempts to resolve the conflict can also cloud the issues which are the main object of the communication. In many marketing situations the existence of serious conflict will disrupt the communication rather than merely confuse it, however
Ambiguity	If the communication can be apprehended in two different ways at once it is ambiguous. This commonly happens in advertising, where the message is often so brief and so loaded with cultural connotations that it is easily misinterpreted
Equivocation	If two messages are received which conflict with each other, there is equivocation. This is the main reason for integrating marketing communications
Vagueness	There will always be some uncertainty in communications, but some communications are so vaguely constructed that the meaning is lost. As the level of uncertainty increases, the frames of reference need to be expanded and the individual becomes confused
Paradox	A paradox is a logical impossibility which creates confusion. For example, a special offer which must be taken up before a certain date is logical provided the goods concerned are available before the deadline date. If the goods will not be available, a paradox is created
Contradiction	Similar to equivocation and paradox, contradiction is the appearance of irreconcilable differences in the communications received. Again this can be overcome by integrating marketing communications

Agreement and disagreement

Disagreement occurs when the recipient understands but does not accept the message. The message might be discounted because of a bias against the source, or because of the style of the message, or because the recipient has a different frame of reference from the sender.

Table 1.8 shows the elements of agreement and disagreement.

TABLE 1.8	Elements of disagreement
Element	**Explanation**
Relational ties	If the relationship between the parties is not a close one, disagreement is more likely than if the relationship is close. This is part of the reason for the increasing emphasis on relationship marketing (see Chapter 9)
Commonality of perspectives	If there is a foundation of consensus between the parties there will be a common perspective applied to discussions. This greatly increases the likelihood of agreement between parties
Compatibility of values	If the personal value systems of the participants are close, there is less scope for disagreement. Salespeople are well aware that buyers buy from people as much like themselves as possible; this is why they try to establish common ground and go along with the buyers' expressed attitudes (see Chapter 11)
Similarity of interests	If both parties stand to gain from the encounter, and are perhaps aiming for a mutually beneficial goal, the interaction is likely to lead to more agreement. Common experience and common goals both lead to closer agreement on other issues
Depth of involvement	The importance of the issues under discussion will influence the degree to which the parties become involved; the greater the involvement, the greater the possibilities for both agreement and disagreement. However, a greater depth of involvement is more likely to lead to agreement in the long run, because the parties are less likely to withdraw from the discussions prematurely
Quality of interaction	The quality of interaction is affected by the levels of agreement or disagreement. Disagreement will make the interaction unpleasant, and therefore more likely to terminate early
Equality of influence	The party with the greatest power in the relationship will be able to enforce agreement from the other party. If the relationship is one of equals, then genuine agreement is more likely, and a more lasting relationship becomes possible

Understanding and misunderstanding

There is always a risk of misunderstanding; part of the problem is that it is often impossible for the recipient of a message to know that he or she has misunderstood it, at least until the time comes to act on the information. Minimising misunderstanding is clearly of importance to marketers, since misunderstandings are a common cause for complaints against firms.

Sometimes basic disagreements lead to misunderstandings, sometimes it is the other way round. It is certainly easier to determine whether the participants agree or disagree with each other than it is to determine whether they really understand each other: sometimes participants will act as if they understand each other in order to reach an agreement more quickly. Understanding is a construction of the mind; there are degrees of understanding, and the process of interpretation is (potentially) inexhaustible.

The elements of understanding are shown in Table 1.9.

TABLE 1.9   Elements of understanding

Element	Explanation
Recognition of intent	Although it is impossible to be sure about the intentions of the other party, knowledge of intent is essential for understanding
Multiple perspective taking	The more opportunity the recipient has to examine the information from different angles, the less likely it is that a misunderstanding will occur
Warrants and reasons	A warrant is an explanatory mechanism that connects acts of observation to a given conclusion. It is the reasoning process the individual goes through to arrive at an understanding. Reasons are the elements that serve as the basis for the warrant to operate on
Tests of comprehension	The true measure of understanding lies in whether the knowledge is effective when used to predict outcomes in the real world. Sometimes it is possible to test comprehension without making a commitment; for example, a consumer may call a helpline to check that the terms of a special offer are as they appear to be
Code switching	The ability to understand is greatly improved if the participants are able to switch from one style of communication to another. Again, the integration of marketing communications aids understanding because it allows the dialogue to continue in a different way. Code switching is an element in redundancy; sending the message via different routes and using different codes will usually improve comprehension

TABLE 1.9   Continued

Element	Explanation
Synchrony and alignment of communicative styles	Understanding is improved if both parties can remain synchronised and aligned throughout the exchange. Synchronisation means that both follow through the dialogue at the same pace; alignment means that they follow through each stage together without being diverted on to side issues or irrelevancies
Working through problematic concerns	More commonly found in personal selling situations, a preparedness to work through problems together is more likely to lead to mutual understanding. For this to happen, both parties must perceive a mutually beneficial outcome
Mutual struggle to minimise miscommunication	Where both participants are prepared to spend time on minimising misunderstanding, understanding is more likely to result

Personal transformation

The willingness of the recipient to be open-minded about the communication and to be prepared to change, is of paramount importance. If the recipient of the message has already decided that the communication is not going to make any difference, then (in effect) he or she will not be listening to the message.

Elements of personal transformation are shown in Table 1.10.

TABLE 1.10   Elements of personal transformation

Element	Explanation
Receptivity to change	An individual who is not prepared to change is unlikely to be receptive to communications; expressions of confusion are likely to result
Supportive communication	Communications which support a customer through a change of attitude are usually helpful; this is why salespeople will often leave information about the products with a customer

Perhaps the best way of minimising miscommunication is to ensure that the participants are motivated to seek understanding. Motivating the recipients to want to understand and learn from the communications is as important as (for example) motivating salespeople to go out and tell the story, or motivating creative people in advertising agencies to come up with a clever campaign.

CASE STUDY: OSTRICHES ON LINE

The ostrich is a remarkable bird. A member of the group of ratites (running birds) it is the largest living bird, and is known for its meat, feathers and leather. Although ostrich farming has been carried out for 150 years in South Africa, it is only in recent years that ostrich farming has become a growth industry in the rest of the world. Interest in the bird's cholesterol-free meat, its efficient conversion of food to meat, and its wide range of by-products has meant a rapid growth in ostrich farming: over 3,000 ostrich ranches exist in the USA alone. Ostriches can be farmed in almost any climate, from Arctic to tropical, and the demand for the meat seems to be insatiable – Fuddruckers Restaurants in the USA report selling over 4,000 ostrich burgers per week. In France, ostrich farming is also becoming more popular: in Corsica the Société Corse Autruche is dedicated to the promotion of ostrich farming as a way of improving the Corsican economy, and also (in typical French manner) offers recipes for the preparation of ostrich meat. The marketing of ostrich products has, as a result, huge potential worldwide.

Ostriches On Line is an Anglo-American company with offices in Manchester, Chicago and Ladybrand (South Africa). As the name suggests, the company deals in everything to do with ostriches – feathers, meat, ostrich leather, even cuddly ostrich toys. The company can supply all your ostrich-related needs, in ten countries on five continents.

The company's mission statement is simple yet comprehensive:

Mission Statement

Ostriches On Line are dedicated to the worldwide advancement of the ostrich industry through ethical agriculture, education, promotion and sound business philosophies which provide a fair and realistic approach to everyone with whom we come into contact.

Our mission comprises five interrelated parts which form the basis of our international operations. Fundamental to our mission is the necessity to discover new and creative ways of addressing all five parts whilst holding a deep respect for all individuals inside and outside the company.

To grow, distribute and sell the finest quality livestock, eggs, feathers, meat, leather and all affiliated products including reference material, incubators, feed, assorted paraphernalia and other ostrich items to an international and diverse clientele.

To operate the Company on a sound financial basis of profitable growth whilst creating career opportunities and financial rewards for all our employees, partners, agents, distributors, suppliers, representatives and re-sellers.

To educate the world to the phenomenal benefits of ethically farming ostriches in order to produce luxurious ostrich leather and heart-healthy ostrich meat together with the unequalled by-products of this unique animal.

To put ostrich meat onto the food tables of all the countries of the world.

To recognise the central role that Ostriches On Line plays in the structure of our environment and to initiate innovative ways to improve the quality of life of all those within our community on a local, national and international level.

The company has been operating since the 1990s, and is not only a retailer: it also advises on ostrich farming, owns and operates ostrich farms, sells machinery and equipment for ostrich farming and processing of ostrich products, will buy back the products of ostrich farms which it has helped to set up, and overall is a complete, vertically integrated business which does anything and everything to do with ostriches.

The company's business is largely conducted online: orders can be placed for everything from feather boas to minced ostrich meat, and deliveries are sent out from Chicago or Manchester. Shipping can be arranged to anywhere in the world, using courier services for small orders. Fresh meat is packed in cooler boxes, and express delivery options are available for a small extra charge. Wholesale shipments are also available, in large quantities if necessary.

The company's website is English-only, and clearly potential customers in, say, South America might not feel strongly inclined to buy fresh meat through the post. Eventually, Ostriches On Line hopes to expand worldwide and offer its products everywhere – but that day is still some way off. In the meantime, with demand outstripping supply, the owners of Ostriches On Line need have few worries about the future of their unusual company.

Questions

1 How is the company positioning itself in the minds of potential customers?

2 What needs does the company fulfil?

3 Why might the company be limiting itself to ostrich-related products?

4 What cultural issues might help (or hinder) the company's progress?

5 What methods other than the Internet might the company use for promoting and distributing its products?

SUMMARY

This chapter has covered some aspects of communications theory and consumer behaviour. Consumer behaviour is not straightforward, and marketing communications is not simply a matter of 'pushing the right buttons'. People are individuals and cannot be treated as if they were all alike.

The key points from this chapter are as follows:

- Ideas can only be transmitted indirectly, through symbols.

- Symbols do not have universally accepted meanings.

- Senders and receivers must have a common field of experience.

- Noise and interference detract from communications.

- Most communication is non-verbal.

- Ethnocentrism is a common cause of communications failure.

- Perception is both analytical and synthetic. Thus, each individual has their own view of reality.

- Marketing communications have a major role in positioning brands correctly in the consumer's world map.

- Attitudes can be changed by altering either cognition or affect.

- Halo effect colours all aspects of the attitudinal object.

- Most of the influences on decision making will be outside the marketer's control.

- Needs are the driving force in consumer behaviour, not marketers.

- Miscommunication has many causes, but motivation to seek understanding will reduce the incidence of miscommunication.

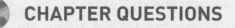

CHAPTER QUESTIONS

1 What is the difference between a symbol and an icon?

2 If ideas can be transmitted through symbols, why are there so many cases of misunderstood communications?

3 What are the factors in the success of Coca-Cola's global communications strategy?

4 Why are most advertisements ignored by consumers?

5 How does celebrity endorsement work?

FURTHER READING

Blythe, J. (1997) *The Essence of Consumer Behaviour*. Hemel Hempstead: Prentice Hall. This covers consumer behaviour in rather more detail than is possible here.

Varey, Richard J. (2002) *Marketing Communication: Principles and Practice*. London: Routledge. This book provides an excellent overview of the current debate in communications theory and critiques the current accepted wisdom on marketing communications.

REFERENCES

Antil, J. (1984) 'Conceptualisation and operationalisation of involvement', in Kinnear, T. (ed.), *Advances in Consumer Research*, vol. 11. Provo, UT: Association for Consumer Research, p. 204.

Aronson, E., Chase, T., Helmreich, R. and Ruhnke, R. (1974) 'A two-factor theory of dissonance reduction: the effect of feeling stupid or feeling awful on opinion change', *International Journal of Communication Research*, **3**: 340–52.

Baker, M. J. and Churchill, G. A. Jr (1977) 'The impact of physically attractive models on advertising evaluations', *Journal of Marketing Research*, **14**: 538–55.

Berney-Reddish, I. A. and Areni, C. S. (2005) 'Effects of probability markers on advertising claim acceptance', *Journal of Marketing Communications*, **11**(1).

Costa, J. A. and Pavia, T. M. (1992) 'What it all adds up to: culture and alpha-numeric brand names', in Sherry, J. F. and Sternthal, B. (eds), *Advances in Consumer Research*, vol. 19. Provo, UT: Association for Consumer Research, p. 40.

Davies, B. J., Kooijman, D. and Ward, P. (2003) 'The sweet smell of success: olfaction in retailing', *Journal of Marketing Management*, **19**: 611–27.

Deetz, S. A. (1992) *Democracy in an Age of Corporate Colonization: Developments in Communication and the Politics of Everyday Life*. Albany, NY: State University of New York Press.

Engel, J. F., Warshaw, M. R. and Kinnear, T. C. (1994) *Promotional Strategy*. Chicago: Irwin.

Festinger, L. (1957) *A Theory of Cognitive Dissonance*. Stanford, CA: Stanford University Press.

Festinger, L. and Carlsmith, J. M. (1959) 'Cognitive consequences of forced compliance', *Journal of Abnormal and Social Psychology*, **58**: 203–10.

Herzberg, F. (1966) *Work and Nature of Man*. London: William Collins.

Hofstede, G. (1984) *Culture's Consequences: International Differences in Work-related Values*. Beverley Hills, CA: Sage.

Holden, M. T. and O'Toole, T. (2004) 'Affirming communication's primary role in a manufacturer–retailer context', *Journal of Marketing Management*, **20**(9/10): 1047–73.

Jansson, C., Marlow, N. and Bristow, M. (2004) 'The influence of colour on visual search times in cluttered environments', *Journal of Marketing Communications*, **10**(3): 183–93.

Kahneman, D. (1973) *Attention and Effort*. Englewood Cliffs, NJ: Prentice-Hall.

Katz, E. and Lazarsfeld, P. (1955) *Personal Influence: The Part Played by People in the Flow of Mass Communications*. New York: Free Press.

Laurent, G. and Kapferer, J-N. (1985) 'Measuring consumer involvement profiles', *Journal of Marketing Research*, **12**(February): 41–53.

Madden, K.M. and Perry, C. (2003) 'How do customers of a financial services institution judge its communications', *Journal of Marketing Communications*, **9**(June), 2: 113–27.

Mantovani, G. (1996) *New Communications Environments: From Everyday to Virtual*. London: Taylor & Francis.

Maslow, A. (1954) *Motivation and Personality*. New York: Harper & Row.

McCracken, G. (1986) 'Culture and consumption: a theoretical account of the structure and movement of the cultural meaning of consumer goods', *Journal of Consumer Research*, **13**(June): 71–81.

McGuire, W. (1976) 'Attitude change and the information processing paradigm', in Hollander. E. and Hunt, R. (eds), *Current Perspectives in Social Psychology*, 4th edn. Oxford: Oxford University Press.

McNulty, W. K. (1985) 'UK social change through a wide-angle lens', *Futures*, August.

Miller, G. A. (1956) 'The magical number seven, plus or minus two: some limits on our capacity for processing information', *Psychological Review*, March: 81–97.

Mitchell, A. (1983) *The Nine American Lifestyles*. New York: Macmillan.

Murray, H. A. (1938) *An Exploration in Personality: A Clinical Experimental Study of Fifty Men of College Age*. London: Oxford University Press.

O'Sullivan, T., Hartley, J., Saunders, D. and Fiske, J. (1983) *Key Concepts in Communication*. London: Methuen.

Onkvisit, S. and Shaw, J. J. (1994) *Consumer Behaviour, Strategy and Analysis*. New York: Macmillan.

Pierce, C. S., in Mick, D. G. (1986) 'Consumer research and semiotics: exploring the morphology of signs, symbols and significance', *Journal of Consumer Research*, **13**(September): 196–213.

Petty, R. E. and Cacioppo, J. T. (1983) 'Central and peripheral routes to persuasion: application to advertising', in Percy, L. and Woodside, A. (eds), *Advertising and Consumer Psychology*. Lexington, MA: Lexington Books.

Pieters, R. and Wedel, M. (2004) 'Attention capture and transfer in advertising: brand, pictorial and text-size effects', *Journal of Marketing*, **68**(2): 36–50.

Rosenberg, M. J. (1960) 'An analysis of affective-cognitive consistency', in Rosenberg, M. J. *et al.* (eds), *Attitude, Organization and Change*. New Haven, CT: Yale University Press.

Schramm, W. A. (1948) *Mass Communications*. Urbana, IL: University of Illinois Press.

Schramm, W. A. (1971) 'The nature of communication between humans', in Schramm, W. A. and Roberts, D. F. (eds), *The Process and Effects of Mass Communication*. Urbana, IL: Illinois University Press.

Shimp, T. and Sharma, S. (1987) 'Consumer ethnocentrism: construction and validation of CETSCALE', *Journal of Marketing Research*, **24**(August): 280–9.

Singh, J. (1988) 'Consumer complaint intentions and behaviour: definitions and taxonomical issues', *Journal of Marketing*, **52**(January): 93–107.

Skinner, B. F. (1953) *Science and Human Behaviour*. New York: Macmillan.

Skinner, H. and Stephens, P. (2003) 'Speaking the same language: the relevance of neuro-linguistic programming to effective marketing communications', *Journal of Marketing Communications*, **9**(3): 177–92.

Smith, K. H. and Stutts, M. A. (2003) 'Effects of short-term cosmetic versus long-term health fear appeals in anti-smoking advertisements on the smoking behaviour of adolescents', *Journal of Consumer Behaviour*, **3**(2): 155–77.

Steen, J. (1995) 'Now they're using suicide to sell jeans', *Sunday Express*, 26 March.

Varey, R. (2000) 'A critical review of conceptions of communication evident in contemporary business and management literature', *Journal of Communications Management*, **4**: 328–40.

2

The communications mix

Objectives

After reading this chapter you should be able to:

- explain the main issues around planning a communications strategy
- describe ways of researching the effectiveness of the communications activities
- describe ways of dealing with agencies and the media
- explain how the integration of marketing communications can improve the effectiveness of communication
- describe some of the limiting factors on integration, and be aware of problems which might arise from adopting an integrated communications policy
- understand the main issues surrounding budgeting

INTRODUCTION

This chapter is an overview of the various elements that go to make up the communications mix. Chapter 1 described some of the problems of communication, and highlighted the risk of failure in communication; many marketing communications are misunderstood or misinterpreted because, of necessity, they tend to be brief. One way of overcoming this is to send the message by various routes, creating redundancy in the system so that a failure in one route does not prevent the message from getting through. This means in turn that an understanding of the strengths and weaknesses of different routes will be of prime importance in designing an integrated marketing communications strategy.

ELEMENTS OF THE COMMUNICATIONS MIX

Marketers have many tactics at their disposal, and the best marketers use them in appropriate ways to maximise the impact of their communications activities. A very basic taxonomy of promotional tools is the four-way division into advertising, public relations, sales promotion and personal selling. This taxonomy is really too simplistic; each of the elements subdivides further, and there are several elements which do not fit readily into these categories. For example, T-shirt slogans are clearly communications but they are not advertising, nor are they really public relations; yet T-shirts with brand logos on, or even adaptations of brand logos, are a common sight and can be considered as marketing communications.

Table 2.1 lists some of the elements of the mix. This list is unlikely to be exhaustive, and there is also the problem of boundary-spanning: some elements of the mix go beyond communication and into the realms of distribution (telemarketing and home shopping channels, for example) or even into new product development (as with the website which allows students to sell successful essays to other students).

Each of the elements in Table 2.1 is dealt with in more detail elsewhere in the book.

The range of possible tools at the marketer's disposal is obviously large; creating a good mix of communications methods is akin to following a recipe. The ingredients have to be added in the right amounts at the right time, and treated in the right way, if the recipe is to work. Also, one ingredient cannot substitute for another; personal selling cannot, on its own, replace advertising, nor can public relations exercises replace sales promotions. Figure 2.1 shows how the above elements of the mix relate to each other.

TABLE 2.1   Elements of the communications mix

Element	Explanation
Advertising	A paid insertion of a message in a medium
Ambient advertising	Messages placed on items such as bus tickets, stamp franking, till receipts, petrol pumps and so forth. Any message that forms part of the environment – for example, 'art installations' in city centres
Press advertising	Any paid message that appears in a newspaper or magazine
TV advertising	Commercial messages shown in the breaks during and between TV programmes
Radio advertising	Sound-only advertisements broadcast on radio
Outdoor advertising	Billboards, bus shelters, flyposters etc.
Inside transport advertising	Posters in stations and inside buses and trains
Outside transport advertising	Posters on buses, taxis and, in some countries, the sides of trains
Press releases	News stories about a firm or its products
Public relations	The planned and sustained effort to establish and maintain goodwill and mutual understanding between an organisation and its publics (Institute of Public Relations 1984)
Sponsorship	Funding of arts events, sporting events etc. in exchange for publicity and prestige
Sales promotions	Activities designed to give a temporary boost to sales, such as money-off coupons, free samples and two-for-the-price-of-one promotions.
Personal selling	Face-to-face communications between buyers and sellers designed to ascertain and meet customers' needs on a one-to-one basis

TABLE 2.1	Continued

Element	Explanation
Database marketing	Profiling customers on to a database and sending out personalised mailings or other communications to them
Telemarketing	Inbound (helpline, telephone ordering) or outbound (telecanvassing, teleselling) telephone calls
E-commerce	Use of websites to promote and/or sell products
Off-the-screen selling	Using TV adverts linked to inbound telephone operations to sell goods. Also home shopping channels such as QVC
Exhibitions and trade fairs	Companies take stands at trade fairs to display new products, meet consumers and customers, and to raise the company profile with interested parties
Corporate identity	The overall image that the company projects; the company's 'personality'
Branding	The mechanism by which marketing communications are coordinated.

The interconnections between the various elements shown in Figure 2.1 are only the main ones; in fact, every marketing communication impinges on every other in some way. The methods used will depend on the firm, the product and the audience.

THE MARKETING COMMUNICATIONS PLAN

The elements which need to be considered in the strategic planning process are as follows:

- *Situational analysis* – researching the current environment into which the marketing communications will fit.
- *Setting objectives* – means deciding what the communications are expected to achieve.
- *Strategic decision making* – setting the overall direction that the communications will take.

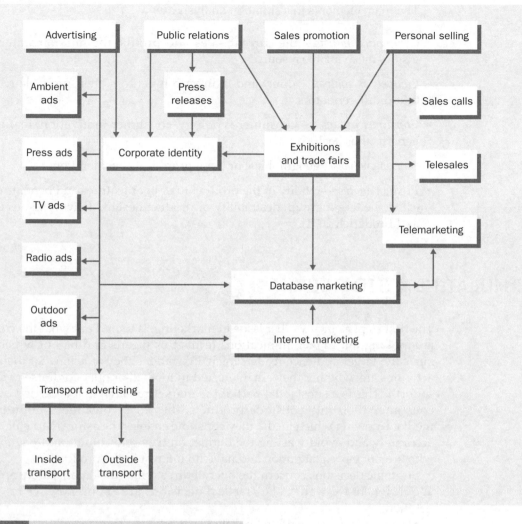

FIGURE 2.1   A taxonomy of marketing communications

- *Operational decision making* – tactics.

- *Campaign management* – the actions that are taken to ensure that the strategy and tactics are carried out.

- *Campaign evaluation* – methods for checking that the projected results have been delivered, and the application of control mechanisms to keep the campaign on track.

Some elements of the marketing communications plan will be discussed in more detail in other chapters.

The main elements in a situation analysis are:

- *Company analysis* – the current sales and profits, the mission statement or vision, the available resources.

- *Competitor analysis* – direct and indirect competitors, their probable resources, brand differentiators.

- *Consumer analysis* – consumer typology, consumer motivation, features and benefits they seek.

- *Market analysis* – geographical or demographical considerations.

- *Product analysis* – ability of the product to deliver features and benefits of interest to the target group, desirability of product design, delivery issues (Pickton and Broderick 2001).

FORMULATING A STRATEGY

The first step, as in any other issue in marketing, is to find out what the customers are looking for. In communications terms this means finding out which magazines the target audience reads, which TV stations they watch, what their leisure activities are, whether they are interested in football or opera or horse racing, and so forth. This is a substantial part of the market research that is carried out daily; consumers not only consume products, they also consume communications media. Knowing which media they consume enables the astute marketer to target accurately and avoid wasting the budget on trying to communicate with people who are not paying attention and have no interest in the product.

Strategic decisions concern the overall direction of the organisation. Strategy is about 'where we want to be'; tactical decisions are about 'how we're going to get there'.

Strategic decisions tend to be difficult to reverse. They usually involve a rejection of other strategic options, and they generally therefore involve a major personal commitment on the part of the decision maker. Tactical decisions are relatively easy to change, involve less commitment and can often run alongside other options (Table 2.2).

Strategy must be integrated across the whole range of marketing activities; it must be formulated in the light of good analysis of the environment; and it must include a feedback system so that the strategy can be adapted in the light of environmental changes. Strategy is influenced by organisational objectives and resources, competitor activities, the structure of the market itself, and the firm's willingness to make changes and take risks.

TABLE 2.2	Comparison of strategic and tactical decisions

Strategic decisions	Tactical decisions
• Concern overall direction	• Concern methods of achievement
• Difficult to reverse	• Relatively easy to change
• Involve rejection of alternatives	• Allow combination of alternatives

The communications environment

Communications are being revolutionised by computer-based and cell-based electronic systems. Computer-based communications include database systems and websites (see Chapters 9 and 12).

Databases can be merged to generate a profile of the consumers on them that is ever more accurate. This in turn leads to much more accurate targeting of mailings, so that an individual consumer is able to receive a mailing which is unique. At its simplest level, the mailing can be personalised, putting the individual's name in the appropriate places, but at the more complex and subtle level marketers are able to identify which individuals are likely to be in the market for a given product at a given time, and target them exclusively (Evans 1994). In recent years, concerns about privacy have led to legislation which limits the extent to which companies can merge information from different databases.

Internet marketing (e-commerce and e-tailing) uses websites and e-mail to communicate with existing and prospective customers. The number of Internet users has doubled every year since its inception. Estimates vary, but it is thought that approximately 13 per cent of the world's population are regular Internet users (Internet World Stats 2005).

In some countries, governments have actively encouraged their citizens and businesses to adopt the Internet. The UK government made a commitment in 2001 that everyone in the country would be online within five years. This is seen as crucial to national development, since it is expected to make education, work and business function much more efficiently. The growth of free or low cost servers has encouraged people to go online; previously, surfing the Net meant paying for use of the telephone line at a rate calculated by the minute – an expensive proposition for regular surfers. The phenomenal growth of the Internet in the USA has in part been fuelled by the fact that US telephone companies do not levy charges for local calls, so that surfing the Net is in effect free in the USA. Broadband access has also contributed to the growth in Internet usage in western

Europe: because telecommunications companies offer a broadband package which includes cable TV, telephone and unlimited Web access, many people find that their Internet access is in effect free.

There is more on the subject of websites in Chapter 12, and on database marketing in Chapter 9.

Push versus pull strategies

Two basic strategic alternatives exist for marketing communications, at least as far as promotional activities are concerned. **Push strategy** involves promoting heavily to the members of the distribution channel, that is, to wholesalers, retailers and agents on the assumption that they will, in turn, promote heavily to the end consumers. In this way the products are pushed through the distribution channel. **Pull strategy** involves promoting heavily to end users and consumers to create a demand that will pull the products through the distribution channels. The ultimate pull strategy was adopted by Levi Strauss when it launched Levi 501 jeans into the UK market; the firm ran a series of TV adverts before the product was available in the shops. This generated consumer demand, which led to the shops demanding that Levi supply the jeans as quickly as possible.

Push strategies tend to place the emphasis on personal selling and sales promotion, whereas pull strategies tend to emphasise mass advertising. The two strategies are not mutually exclusive, but rather represent opposite ends of a spectrum; most campaigns contain elements of both.

Table 2.3 shows the functions which need to be carried out when planning the communications campaign.

TABLE 2.3   Communications planning functions

Planning function	Explanation
Situation analysis	• *Demand factors* – consumer needs and decision-making processes, cultural and social influences on demand, product category and brand attitudes, individual differences between consumers • *Identify the target* – it is better to approach a small segment of the market than to try to use a 'scattergun' approach on everybody • *Assess the competition* – other products, possible competitor responses, etc. • *Legal and regulatory restrictions* that might affect what we are able to do
Defining the objectives	Deciding what the communications are supposed to achieve. It is essential here to give the advertising agency, PR agency, salesforce and indeed everybody associated with the campaign a clear brief. 'We want to raise awareness of the product to 50 per cent of the adult population' is a measurable objective. 'We want to increase sales as much as possible' is not measurable, so there is no way of knowing whether it has been achieved

TABLE 2.3	Continued

Setting the budget	This can be done in four basic ways (see also later in the chapter). • *Objective-and-task approach*, whereby objectives are set and an appropriate amount of money is put aside. This method is difficult to apply because it is difficult to assess how much will be needed to achieve the objective. • *Percentage of sales approach*, whereby the budget is set as a percentage of sales. This is based on the false idea that sales create advertising, and usually results in less being spent on marketing communications when sales fall, thus reducing sales further • *Comparative parity approach*, whereby the company spends the same as the competition, means that the firm is allowing its budgets to be set by its rivals • *Arbitrary approach*, whereby a senior executive (usually a finance director) simply says how much can be allowed within the firm's overall budgets. This does not take account of how the firm is to achieve the objectives • *Marginal approach*, in which the company continues to spend up to the point where further expenditure will not bring in any more business
Managing the elements of the mix	• *Media planning* – deciding which media will carry the communications. There are two main decision areas: the **reach** (number of potential consumers the communication reaches) and the **frequency** of coverage (number of times each consumer is exposed to the communication). In advertising, the decision is often made on the basis of cost per thousand readers/viewers, but this does not take into account the impact of the ad or the degree to which people are able to skip past it • *Briefing the salesforce* – deciding whether it is to be a push or pull strategy, choosing the public relations (PR) and support communications
Creating the platform	Deciding the basic issues and selling points that the communication must convey. This clarifies the agency briefings, or at least clarifies the thinking on producing the communications

Budgeting

Having decided the overall plan for the promotional campaign, the marketer needs to decide what the organisation can afford. The level of noise from advertising **clutter** means that (unless the creative people are very creative indeed) companies must spend a certain minimum amount to be heard at all, so there is likely to be a minimum level below which there is no point in spending any money at all. Table 2.4 illustrates some methods for setting budgets.

TABLE 2.4   Promotional budgeting methods

Method	Explanation	Advantages	Disadvantages
Objective-and-task method	Identify the objectives to be achieved, then determine the costs and effort required to achieve those objectives	Has a logical basis, and if carried out correctly will achieve the firm's strategic goals	Difficult to calculate the necessary spend to achieve the objective. Time consuming and expensive in terms of market research
Percentage of sales method	The planner simply allows a fixed percentage of the company's sales to be used for promotion. This promotional budget increases as sales go up, and decreases as sales go down. A very common method of budgeting	Simple to calculate; also ensures that, if sales drop off, costs also drop	Is based on the false premise that sales cause promotion, rather than promotion causing sales. Logically, if sales fall promotion expenditure should be increased to bring the customers back in
Comparative parity method	The marketer matches expenditure to that of the competitors. Thus the firm does not lose ground if a competing firm increases its budget	Ensures that the firm remains on a par with the competitors, and does not waste expenditure	Takes no account of changes in the market or opportunities that might arise; in other words it is not customer-orientated
Marginal approach	Marketer only spends up to the point where any further spending would not generate enough extra business to justify the outlay	This method would maximise profits since no excess spending would result	Extremely difficult to calculate, given the changing nature of markets
All-you-can-afford method	The marketer spends whatever money can be spared from other activities. Often used by small businesses when starting out	Company cannot become overcommitted or run into trouble by relying on sales which do not, in the end, materialise	Again, bears no relationship to the state of the marketplace. Also relies on the marketer being able to persuade other departments within the firm to give up expenditure on their own pet projects

In the real world, marketers usually adopt a combination strategy, using several of the above methods. Even an objective-and-task approach might begin by looking at what the competition are spending (**comparative parity** approach) if only to determine what the likely spend would have to be to overcome clutter. Likewise, a marketer may be part-way through a campaign and be told by the finance department that no more money is available (or perhaps that more than anticipated is available) and will switch to an all-you-can-afford policy.

PLANNING THE CAMPAIGN

Whether the planning stage comes before or after the budget-setting stage will depend on whether the marketer is adopting an objective-and-task policy or not. In most cases, though, planning the campaign in detail will come after the budget is known and agreed upon; few companies give the marketing department a blank cheque for promotional spending. Campaigns can be carried out to achieve many objectives; a new product launch is often an objective, but in most cases the products will be in the maturity phase of the product life cycle.

Image-building campaigns are designed to convey a particular status for the product, and to emphasise ways in which it will complement the user's lifestyle. For example, Volvo promotes the reliability and engineering of the car rather than its appearance, thus appealing to motorists who prefer a solid, reliable vehicle.

Product differentiation campaigns aim to show how the product is better than the competitors' products by emphasising its differences. In most cases this will take the form of the **unique selling proposition**, or **USP** for short. The USP is the one feature of the product that most stands out as different from the competition, and is usually a feature which conveys unique benefits to the consumer. Mature products often differ only very slightly from each other in terms of performance, so a USP can sometimes be identified in terms of the packaging or distribution, and is commonly generated by a prestigious brand (see Chapter 7). The USP will only be effective if it means something to the consumer – otherwise it will not affect the buying decision.

Positioning strategies are concerned with the way consumers perceive the product compared with their perceptions of the competition (see Chapter 1). For example, a retailer may claim 'lower prices than in other shops' or a restaurant may want to appear more upmarket than its rivals. Avis car hire said, 'We're Number Two, so we try harder', thus positioning its product as number two in size (behind Hertz) but emphasising the positive aspects of this.

Direct response campaigns seek an immediate response from the consumer in terms of purchase, or request for a brochure or a visit to the shop. For example, a retailer might run a newspaper campaign which includes a money-off coupon. The aim of the campaign is to encourage consumers to visit the shop to redeem the coupon, and the retailer can easily judge the effectiveness of the campaign by the number of coupons redeemed.

Putting it all together

To make the best use of the promotional effort it is worth spending time planning how it will all fit together. The recipe will need to be adapted according to what the product is and how the company wants to promote it.

The elements marketers need to consider are:

- size of budget
- size of individual order value
- number of potential buyers
- geodemographical spread of potential buyers
- category of product (convenience, unsought, shopping and so on)
- what it is the firm is trying to achieve

It is impossible to achieve everything all at once, so marketers often plan the campaign as an integrated package. For example, Table 2.5 shows a product launch strategy designed to maximise penetration of a new food product.

TABLE 2.5   Example of a promotional calendar

Month	Activity
May	Press release to the trade press and retailers
June	Sales campaign to persuade retailers to stock the product. The aim is to get 50 per cent of retailers stocking the product, so the salesforce tell them a big advertising spend is forthcoming. Begin a teaser campaign (see Chapter 5)
July/August	Denouement of teaser campaign. Promotion staff appear in major retail outlets offering free samples. Press releases to cookery writers, possibly reports on daytime TV if product is newsworthy enough
September/October	Once 50 per cent retailer penetration has occurred, start the TV campaign. Brief the advertising agency to obtain maximum brand awareness
January/February	Begin a new campaign to inform consumers about the brand. Possibly use money-off sales promotion, linked promotions, etc. Review progress using market research. Possibly issue some press releases, if the product is innovative enough, to the business/cookery press.

Carrying out this kind of planning needs the cooperation of all the members of the marketing team. It is no use having the PR people doing one thing and the salesforce doing something else that negates their efforts. If the campaign is to be effective it is important that all the team members are involved in the discussions so that unrealistic demands are not made of them.

Structuring the communications mix

Structuring the communications mix will differ from one firm to another, and indeed from one promotion to another within the same firm. Developing effective marketing communications follows a six-stage process:

1 *Identify the target audience.* In other words, decide whom the message should reach.

2 *Determine the response sought.* What would the marketer like the audience to do after they get the message?

3 *Choose the message.* Write the copy, or produce an appropriate image.

4 *Choose the channel.* Decide which newspaper, TV station, radio station or other medium is most appealing to the audience.

5 *Select the source's attributes.* Decide what it is about the product or company that needs to be communicated.

6 *Collect feedback.* For example, carry out market research to find out how successful the message was.

Communication is often expensive; full-page advertisements in Sunday colour supplements can cost upwards of £11,000 per insertion; a 30-second TV ad at peak time can cost £30,000 per station. It is therefore worth spending time and effort in ensuring that the message is comprehensible to the target audience, and is reaching the right people. Figure 2.2 shows how the communications mix operates.

In Figure 2.2, messages from the company about its products and itself are transmitted via the elements of the promotional mix to the consumers, employees, pressure groups and other publics. Because each of these groups is receiving the messages from more than one transmitter, the elements of the mix also feed into each other so that the messages do not conflict. The choice of method will depend upon the message, the receiver and the desired effect.

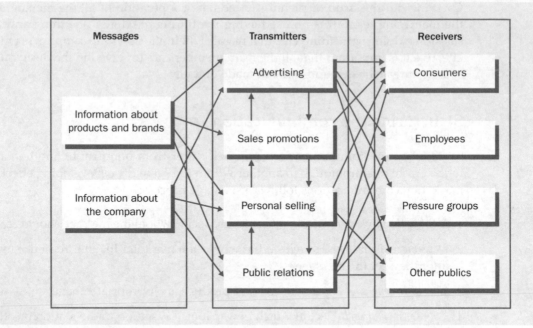

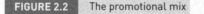

FIGURE 2.2   The promotional mix

Tactical considerations

The tactical possibilities in a marketing campaign are huge in number. Most of the tactics of marketing involve creativity on the part of practitioners, so it is virtually impossible to lay down any hard and fast rules about approaching different marketing problems. However, the following might prove to be useful guidelines:

- Marketers should always try to do something that the competition has not thought of yet.

- It is important to consult everybody who is involved in the day-to-day application of the plans. Salespeople in particular do not like to be told what to do by somebody back at head office.

- Most marketing activities do not produce instant results, but results should be monitored anyway.

- The messages given to the consumers, the middlemen, the suppliers and all the other publics should be consistent.

- Competitors are likely to make some kind of response, so marketers should try to anticipate what the response might be when formulating plans.

The SOSTT+4Ms structure for planning gives a useful checklist for ensuring that the elements of strategy and tactics are brought together effectively. Table 2.6 shows how the structure works.

TABLE 2.6	SOSTT+4Ms

Element	Explanation
Situation	Current position of the firm in terms of its resources, product range, and markets
Objectives	What the company hopes to achieve in both the long term and the short term
Strategy	Decisions about the correctness of the objectives and their overall fit
Tactics	How the strategic objectives will be achieved
Targets	Formalised objectives, target markets and segments of markets. Decisions about the appropriateness of these markets in the light of the firm's strategic objectives
Manpower	Both sexes, of course! Decisions about human resources; having the right people to do the job
Money	Correct budgeting and allocation of financial resources where they will do the most to achieve the overall objectives
Minutes	Timescales, deadlines and overall planning to ensure that everything happens at the right time
Measurement	Monitoring and evaluation of activities to ensure that they remain on course and work as they should

Cost effectiveness will always be an issue in promotional campaigns, and it is for this reason that there has been a growth in direct marketing worldwide (see Chapter 9). The accurate targeting of market segments made possible by computer technology has enabled marketers to refine the approach, and hence increase the response rate. Marketers now talk in terms of response rates from promotions, not in terms of contact numbers.

Integration of marketing communications

There is increasing interest in integration of marketing communications, and this is being extended to include all corporate communications (Nowak and Phelps 1994). The need for integration is shown in the following factors (Borremans 1998):

Changes in the consumer market:

- The information overload caused by the ever increasing number of commercial messages.

- Advertising in the mass media is increasingly irritating.

- Media fragmentation.

- Increasing numbers of 'me too' products, where differences between brands are minor.

- Complexity and change in FMCG (fast-moving consumer goods) markets, with increased distances between suppliers and consumers making it harder for publics to have an image of suppliers.

- Increasing media attention on the social behaviour of companies, putting goodwill at a premium.

Changes in the supplier market:

- Multiple acquisitions and changes in structure in and around corporations.

- Interest of management in short-term results.

- Increased recognition of the strategic importance of communication.

- Increased interest in good internal communications with employees.

Integration offers the possibility of reducing the ambiguity of messages emanating from the firm, and also of reducing costs by reducing duplication of effort. There are barriers to integration (Petrison and Wang 1996), and the factors below tend to mean that integration would actually detract from the effectiveness of communications:

- Database marketing allows customers to be targeted with individually tailored communications.

- Niche marketing and micromarketing. Suppliers can communicate with very small and specific audiences, using different messages for each group.

- Specific methods and working practices used for different communication tools will affect the message each transmits.

- Corporate diversification.

- Different international (and even national) cultures mean that a single message comprehensible to all is difficult to achieve.

- Existing structures within organisations mean that different departments may not be able or willing to 'sing from the same songsheet'. For example, salespeople may not agree with the public relations department's ideas on what customers should be told.

- Personal resistance to change, managers' fear of losing responsibilities and budgets. This is particularly true of firms that have adopted the brand manager system of management.

In practice, promotional mix elements often operate independently (Duncan and Caywood 1996), with specialist agencies for PR, advertising, exhibitions, corporate identity, branding, etc. all working in isolation. There are nine types or levels of integration, as shown in Table 2.7: note that these do not necessarily constitute a process, or represent stages of development, and indeed there may be considerable overlap between the types.

TABLE 2.7   Levels of integration

Level of Integration	Explanation
Awareness stage	Those responsible for communications realise that a fragmented approach is not the optimum one
Planning integration	The coordination of activities. There are two broad approaches: functional integration, which coordinates separate tools to create a single message where appropriate, and instrumental integration, which combines tools in such a way that they reinforce one another (Bruhn 1995)
Integration of content	Ensuring that there are no contradictions in the basic brand or corporate messages. At a higher level, integrating the themes of communication to make the basic messages the same
Formal integration	Using the same logo, corporate colours, graphic approach and house style for all communications
Integration between planning periods	Basic content remains the same from one campaign to the next. Either basic content remains the same, or the same executional approach is used in different projects

TABLE 2.7   Continued

Level of integration	Explanation
Intra-organisational integration	Integration of the activities of everyone involved in communication functions (which could mean everybody who works in the organisation)
Inter-organisational integration	Integration of all the outside agencies involved in the firm's communications activities
Geographical integration	Integration of campaigns in different countries. This is strongest in large multinationals that operate globally, e.g. the Coca-Cola Corporation (Hartley and Pickton 1997)
Integration of publics	All communications aimed at one segment of the market are integrated (horizontal integration) or all communications aimed at different segments are attuned (vertical integration)

Part of the reason for separating the functions is historical; traditionally, marketing communications were divided into **above the line** and **below the line**. Above the line means advertising; below the line means everything else. This came about because of the way advertising agencies are paid. In essence, agencies are paid commission by the media in which they place adverts (usually the rate is 15 per cent of the billing), and/or by fees paid by the client. Traditionally, any paid-for advertising attracted commission (hence above the line) and any other activities such as PR or sales promotion was paid for by fees (hence below the line). As time has gone by, these distinctions have become more blurred, especially with the advent of **advertorials** (advertisements which look like editorials) which are usually written by journalists, and with **ambient advertising** and other new media which do not attract commission.

Overall, the advantages of integrating communications almost certainly overcome the drawbacks, since the cost savings and the reduction of ambiguity are clearly important objectives for most marketers. There is, however, the danger of losing the capacity to tailor messages for individuals (as happens in personal selling) or for niches in the market, and there are certainly some major creative problems attached to integrating communications on a global scale.

INTERNATIONAL MARKETING COMMUNICATIONS STRATEGY

Single communications strategies rarely work for firms in the global arena. In fact, the few exceptions are so notable that they are used as examples time and again – Marlboro cigarettes, Coca-Cola, Levi jeans – and nearly all are American.

It is possible that the overwhelming influence of Hollywood in exporting American culture worldwide means that people in most countries are able to understand American cultural references (the Marlboro cowboy, for example) in a way that would not work for, say, the Brazilian gaucho or the Japanese samurai. Even then, local legal or cultural differences mean that the advertisements need to be adapted: in the years leading up to 2003, when all tobacco advertising was banned in the UK, the Marlboro cowboy could not be shown on billboards because there was a ban on showing 'attractive models' in tobacco advertising.

There is some common ground between countries, and there are identifiable international markets: the market for women's magazines has expanded in Europe as a result of deregulation, and magazines such as *Hello!* (originally *Hola!* in its native Spain) have managed to cross over successfully. This means that some print advertising within those magazines should also be able to make the transition.

The main reason for standardising communications is cost; it is clearly much cheaper to produce one advert and repeat it across borders than it is to produce separate adverts for each country. However, the savings are most apparent in producing TV adverts, where the costs of production can easily approach the costs of airtime. This is not the case with press advertising, so the thrust to internationalise is less apparent.

There are four basic strategies for international communications, as shown in Table 2.8 (Keegan 1984).

TABLE 2.8 Basic international strategies

Strategy	Explanation
Same product, same communication	Can be used where the need for the product and its use are the same as in its home market
Same product, different communication	Can be used where the need for the product differs in some way, but the basic method of use is the same, or when the cultural references differ. For example, oyster sauce is considered an exotic product in western Europe, but is a regular purchase item in Oriental countries
Different product, same communication	Sometimes the product formula has to change to meet local conditions, but the communication can remain the same. For example, the formulation of chocolate is different for hot countries due to the low melting point of cocoa butter, but this need not affect the advertising
Different product, different communications	Applies to markets with different needs and different product use, for example greetings cards and electrical appliances

Source: Based on Keegan (1984)

Most successful international campaigns are run on TV, which enables the advertiser to minimise or even omit words altogether. Standardising press communications is difficult owing to language differences. Some difficulties in this connection are more subtle – Arabic reads from right to left, for example, which can play havoc with before-and-after pictures.

The following tips for translating advertising copy have been identified (Majaro 1982):

- Avoid idioms, jargon or buzzwords.

- Leave space to expand foreign language text (Latin languages take 20 per cent more space than English, and Arabic may need up to 50 per cent more space).

- Check local legal requirements and codes of conduct.

- Ensure that the translators speak the everyday language of the country in question. The Spanish spoken in Spain and that in Latin America differ, as does UK English and American English, or French French and Belgian French (Walloon). For obvious reasons, people who are not native speakers of the language should never be used as translators.

- Brief the translators thoroughly so that they get a feel for the product, its benefits, the customer and competition. Do not just hand over the copy and expect it to be translated.

- Check the translation with customers and distributors in the local market. This also gives local users the opportunity to be involved and to make any criticisms of the promotional materials before they are published for use.

- Translate the materials back into English as a safety check. They may not come back exactly as the original version, but there should be a reasonable commonality.

There are many (probably apocryphal) stories about translations of brand names and slogans that have gone horribly wrong; Pepsi's 'Come Alive with Pepsi' translating as 'Come back from the grave with Pepsi', or the Vauxhall Nova translating as 'Doesn't go' in Spanish; any regular traveller will be aware of humorous (or obscene) brand names on foreign products (see Chapter 7).

Provided a universally recognisable icon is available, and it is possible to produce meaningful hooks in each language, it should be possible to produce good internationalised press advertising. Certainly factual information (for example, 'Open Sundays') should translate fairly easily, so sought communications are presumably more likely to transfer easily (see Chapter 12 for Internet advertising).

RESEARCHING THE EFFECTIVENESS OF COMMUNICATIONS

Having developed and implemented the strategic and tactical plans, the next stage is to gather feedback as to the effectiveness of the communication. Many of the tests of effectiveness focus on advertising since this is a high profile activity and often a very expensive one. Four elements appear to be important in the effectiveness of advertising: awareness, liking, interest and enjoyment. There is a high correlation between brand loyalty and brand awareness (Stapel 1990); likeability appears to be the single best predictor of sales effectiveness since likeability scales predict 97 per cent of sales successes (Biel 1990); interest clearly relates to likeability (Stapel 1991), and enjoyment appears to be a good indicator in advertising pre-tests (Brown 1991).

For many years, effectiveness was measured in terms of sales results, the premise being that the purpose of advertising is to generate sales. The problem with this view is that sales can result from many other activities (personal selling, increased efforts by distributors, increased prosperity and so forth), so that it is difficult to assess the importance of advertising in the outcomes. A more recent view has been that the role of advertising is to communicate – to change awareness and attitudes. This view crystallised as the **DAGMAR** model (Defining Advertising Goals, Measuring Advertising Results) (Colley 1961). DAGMAR implies that concrete and measurable communication objectives should be set for advertising, rather than sales turnover goals. Thus the outcomes that are measured are usually such things as awareness, brand recognition, recall of content, and so forth.

DAGMAR has been criticised on the grounds that it tends to lead planners to find out what can be measured easily, then to set that as a goal (Broadbent 1989). The simple objectives which can be measured do not tell the whole story of major-brand success. Advertising does other things which are hard to measure, such as encouraging brand loyalty or increasing word-of-mouth communication between consumers themselves.

Advertising effectiveness can be assessed by market research, by returned coupons and (sometimes) by increased sales. The last method is somewhat risky, however, since there may be many other factors which could have increased the sales of the product.

Table 2.9 shows some common techniques for evaluating advertising effectiveness.

TABLE 2.9	Advertising effectiveness

Technique	Description and explanation
Pre-tests	These are evaluations of the advertising before it is released. Pre-tests are commonly carried out using focus groups; research shows that this is the commonest method used by advertisers (Eagle *et al.* 1998)
Coupon returns and enquiries	The advertiser counts up the number of enquiries received during each phase of an advertising campaign. This allows the marketing manager to judge which media are working best, provided the coupons have an identifying code on them
Post-campaign tests (post-tests)	The particular testing method used will depend largely on the objectives of the campaign. Communications objectives (product awareness, attitude change, brand awareness) might be determined through surveys; sales objectives might be measured according to changes in sales which can be attributed to the campaign. This is difficult to do because of other factors (changes in economic conditions, for example) which might distort the findings
Recognition tests and recall tests	In recognition tests, consumers are shown the advertisement and asked if they recognise it. They are then asked how much of it they actually recall. In an **unaided recall** test the consumer is asked which adverts he or she remembers seeing recently; in an **aided recall** test the consumer is shown a group of ads (without being told which is the one the researcher is interested in) and is asked which ones he or she has seen recently

Any testing must be **valid** (must measure what it says it measures) and **reliable** (free of random error). A reliable test would provide consistent results every time it is used, and a valid test would enable the marketer to predict outcomes reasonably accurately. In order to ensure that this is the case, a set of principles called PACT (Positioning Advertising Copy Testing) have been established (Marketing News 1982). A good advertising testing system should:

- provide measurements that are relevant to the objectives of the advertising;
- require agreement about how the results will be used in advance of each specific test;
- provide multiple measurements because single measurements are generally inadequate to assess the advert's performance;
- be based on a model of human response to communication – the reception of a stimulus, the comprehension of the stimulus and the response to the stimulus;

- allow for consideration of whether the advertising stimulus should be exposed more than once;
- recognise that the more finished a piece of copy is the more soundly it can be evaluated. It should also require as a minimum that alternative executions be tested to the same degree of finish;
- provide controls to avoid the biasing effects of the exposure content;
- take into account basic considerations of sample definition;
- demonstrate reliability and validity empirically.

Advertisements can be tested on two dimensions: those related to the advertisement itself, and those related to its contents. Since these two issues are sometimes difficult for the consumer to separate there is no real certainty as to which is actually being tested.

Pre-testing and post-testing

Pre-testing the advertisement to assess whether it is likely to be effective has a mixed history. There has been considerable debate as to whether it is really possible to predict whether an advert will work or not, and there is of course no certainty about this even when sophisticated copy-testing methods are used. Testing almost certainly reduces the risk of producing an ineffective advert, and it is better to find this out before expensive space is booked in the media, and possibly before an inappropriate message is sent out.

    Post-testing is concerned with researching the effectiveness of the advert after it has appeared. Finding out whether the advertising has been effective in achieving the objectives laid down is much easier if clear objectives were set in the first place and if the advertising agency was given a clear brief.

Laboratory techniques

Testing can be carried out in the field, or in the laboratory; most pre-tests are carried out in laboratory conditions. Table 2.10 lists some of the available techniques.

TABLE 2.10   Laboratory techniques for testing advertising effectiveness

Technique	Explanation
Consumer juries	Groups of consumers are asked to judge whether they think the advertisement will work. This has the advantage that consumers (presumably) know what affects them most. The drawback is that they will sometimes 'play expert' and try to make recommendations about how to change the advertisement, or try to guess how it will be received by another group entirely. This will distort their responses
Focus groups	A moderator conducts a loosely structured interview with six to twelve respondents simultaneously. The respondents tend to discuss issues among themselves, so that a range of ideas is elicited. These data are **qualitative**; it is not usually possible or desirable to express them numerically, but the technique is an effective way to raise and focus on particular concerns
Portfolio tests	Respondents are shown test adverts (those the researcher wants to test) and control adverts (adverts whose effectiveness is already known) and asked to score them. The researcher can then compare the scores of the test adverts with the control adverts and see whether the test adverts will be as effective
Readability tests	The copy is analysed for readability without consumer interviewing. The foremost method is the Flesch formula (Flesch 1974). Readability is assessed by determining the average number of syllables per hundred words, the length of sentences, the human interest content and the familiarity of words. Results can be compared with predetermined norms for the target audience
Physiological measures	**Eye cameras** can be used to record the route an individual's eye takes when looking at an advert. This can be unreliable; lingering on one part of the advert might denote interest, or it might denote incomprehension. **Galvanic skin response** and **pupil dilation response** measure different aspects of interest; pupils dilate and the electrical resistance of the skin decreases when an object of interest appears. *Voice pitch analysis* measures how the respondent's voice pitch alters when exposed to the stimulus. Raised voice pitch denotes strong feeling, either positive or negative: the respondent can be asked about the direction of the feeling

Laboratory measures at first appear scientific and therefore objective; unfortunately this is often not the case. While the researcher might be able to maintain objectivity, it is unlikely that the subject (respondent) will and the knowledge of the artificiality of the situation is likely to cloud the respondent's judgement. Furthermore, the results of, for example, a galvanic skin response or pupil dilation response still need to be interpreted. Interest or excitement at seeing an advertisement does not necessarily stem from the communication itself, and almost certainly does not translate into the achievement of the communications objectives.

Field techniques

Typical field techniques include street surveys and self-completion question-naires. Each has the advantage of being quick, relatively cheap and relatively easy to interpret.

The main problems with these techniques are as follows:

- *Interviewer bias*. The interviewer (unwittingly or otherwise) leads the respondent to answer in a particular way.

- *Design bias*. The way the questions are worded elicits a particular response from the respondent.

- *Sample bias*. The wrong people are asked for their opinion, or an otherwise unrepresentative sample is taken.

These sources of bias are remarkably easy to generate. For example, a supposedly random sample of people might be sought by standing in a shopping mall on a Saturday morning and stopping everybody who comes past. This will not actu-ally be a random sample; some people will walk past without stopping, some people never shop in that particular mall, some people never shop on a Saturday morning. In each case those missing people might have given very different responses to a questionnaire on advertising.

Equally, a question such as, 'Have you seen this advertisement?' will provoke a yes response from many people who have not actually seen the advert. This may be because they do not want to appear stupid, or because they genuinely believe that they have seen it.

Field surveys can certainly be helpful, and they are still widely used; it is impor-tant to take care over the design and administration of the techniques, however.

CASE STUDY: THE POST OFFICE

In the ninteenth century, UK-wide postal services were established through the Royal Mail. Establishing a national system for posting (the first in the world) involved setting up offices all over the country to sell stamps, accept mail, handle parcels and so forth. As time went on, these post offices were seen as a convenient point at which government and people could interact – so more and more functions were added to the Post Office counter. People were able to pay taxes, apply for passports, apply for licences of all types from driving licences to dog licences. During wartime, the Post Office issued permits, ration books, identity cards and all the paperwork the government generates. During peacetime, the Post Office sold government bonds and savings certificates, paid out pensions and social security payments, and acted as an interface between government and individuals.

During the 1980s there was a drive to improve the efficiency of government departments by making them adhere to the same constraints as private industry. In other words, the Post Office was expected to show a profit. As part of the restructuring, Post Office Counters (the offices themselves) were made independent of the actual delivery service (which went through various incarnations before re-emerging as the Royal Mail). The Post Office therefore began to charge the various government departments it dealt with for handling their paperwork. This system worked well, until a cost-saving exercise at the Department for Work and Pensions in 2003 meant that pensions and social security payments would, in future, be paid direct into claimants' bank accounts. This made huge savings for the government, but meant that the Post Office lost around 40 per cent of its over-the-counter business.

Clearly this meant that the Post Office had to take drastic measures to recover its position. The organisation created a large project team of individuals from within the Post Office, working with outside consultants such as Sixty-One Integrated Communications, to create a new business, not as dependent on government contracts for its survival.

The Post Office aimed to build on its strength of being able to handle large quantities of diverse paperwork. Post Office Counters now offer foreign currency exchange, loans, insurance, non-government savings schemes such as equity bonds, telephone services and even offer deliveries of flowers. Some of the business is conducted online, but much of it is conducted face-to-face, over the counter. Because of the large number of people who need to call into their local post office for the purpose of posting letters and parcels or applying for licences, the opportunities to sell more products are many.

From a communications viewpoint, however, the new products created a problem. Since they covered such a wide range, the Post Office had a problem in communicating its brand. Was it a bank, an insurance office, a government department or a convenience store? Tying together all these different activities was difficult, but not impossible: the Post Office adopted the strap line, 'For the little things that make the big things happen'. The advertising campaign which followed used cartoon ants as its basis, implying that little things can achieve big things: the ants are shown carrying out everyday tasks and meeting the kinds of problems people deal with regularly (teenagers talking for hours on the 'phone, booking holidays, buying car insurance) and showing how the Post Office can help.

The Post Office carries the same theme through its TV advertising, press advertising and website, as well as billboards and in-store posters. The ants have become iconic in that people associate the ants with the brand, and relate to the humorous situations they find themselves in. Overall, the new business at the Post Office has more than compensated for the loss of the social security business; further services are in the pipeline, too.

Questions

1 How might the Post Office expand its business further?

2 What other promotional tools might help the Post Office to build its new brand image?

3 What problems exist in establishing the new products in consumers' minds?

4 What is the role of integrated communications in the process?

5 Why choose ants as the symbol of the new Post Office?

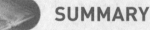

SUMMARY

It would be an oversimplification to assume that the promotional mix contains only the elements of advertising, public relation (PR), sales promotion and personal selling. There are a great many tools available to the marketer, and the borders between the various activities are being eroded to such an extent that the consensus view is that marketing communications should be integrated as far as possible and the remaining demarcation lines should be done away with altogether. This is probably also a simplistic view, but provided care is taken that brands are still allowed their own identity and cultural issues are accounted for when communications cross borders, integration will certainly reduce costs and increase impact.

Key points from this chapter are as follows:

- Not all marketing communications can be categorised as advertising, PR, sales promotion or personal selling.

- Creating a good communications mix is like cooking a meal: ingredients must be added at the right time, and in the right quantities.

- Most campaigns contain elements of both push and pull strategies.

- Objectives should be measurable, but an objective should not be rejected simply because it cannot be measured easily.

- Tactical planning should include elements that the firm's competitors have not thought of.

- Competitors will usually respond in some way.

- Messages can be consistent without being identical.

- If people like the advert, they are more likely to buy the product.

- Pre-testing is not perfect, but it does reduce the risk of issuing ineffective or inappropriate communications.

 ## CHAPTER QUESTIONS

1 What are the main advantages and disadvantages of integrated marketing communications strategies?

2 When might a marketer not carry out pre-testing on a communications campaign?

3 Why should marketers continually monitor the effect of their communications activities?

4 What are the critical factors in planning a communications exercise?

5 Why have the distinctions between above-the-line and below-the-line communications become blurred (or even irrelevant)?

 ## FURTHER READING

Mole, J. (1990) *Mind your Manners*. London: The Industrial Society. This gives some excellent insights into dealing with other cultures, and in particular gives some very readable and amusing examples of cultural conflicts which have led to disaster.

Smith, P. R. and Taylor, J. (2004) *Marketing Communications – An Integrated Approach*, 4th edn. London: Kogan Page. This has a good, practically orientated approach to the integration of communications.

REFERENCES

Biel, A. (1990) 'Love the ad. Buy the product?' *ADMAP*, **299** (September): 21–5.

Borremans, T. (1998) 'Integrated (marketing) communications in practice: survey among communication, public relations and advertising agencies in Belgium', *Proceedings of the 3rd Annual Conference of the Global Institute for Corporate and Marketing Communications*. Glasgow: Strathclyde Graduate Business School.

Broadbent, S. (1989) *The Advertising Budget*. Henley: Institute of Practitioners in Advertising/NTC Publications Ltd.

Brown, G. (1991) 'Modelling advertising awareness', *ADMAP*, April.

Bruhn, M. (1995) *Intergrierte Unternehmenskommunikation: Ansatzpunkte für eine Strategische und Operative Umsetzung Integreirter Kommunikationsarbeit*. Stuttgart: Schaffer–Poeschel.

Colley, R. H. (1961) *Defining Advertising Goals*. New York: Association of National Advertisers.

Duncan, T. and Caywood, C. (1996) 'The concept, process and evolution of integrated marketing communication', in Thorson, E. and Moore, J. (eds), *Integrated Communication. Synergy of Persuasive Voices*. Mahwah, NJ: Lawrence Erlbaum, pp. 13–34.

Eagle, L., Hyde, K. and Kitchen, P. (1998) 'Advertising effectiveness measurement: a review of industry research practices', *Proceedings of the 3rd Annual Conference of the Global Institute for Corporate and Marketing Communications*. Glasgow: Strathclyde Graduate Business School.

Evans, M. J. (1994) 'Domesday marketing?', *Journal of Marketing Management*, **10**(5).

Flesch, R. (1974) *The Art of Readable Writing*. New York: Harper & Row.

Hartley, B. and Pickton, D. (1997) 'Integrated marketing communications – a new language for a new era', *Proceedings of the 2nd International Conference on Marketing and Corporate Communications*, Antwerp, Belgium.

Internet World Stats (2005) www.internetworldstats.com

Institute of Public Relations (1984) *Public Relations Practice – Its Roles and Parameters*. London: Institute of Public Relations.

Keegan, W. (1984) *Multinational Marketing Management*, 3rd edn. Englewood Cliffs, NJ: Prentice-Hall.

Majaro, S. (1982) *International Marketing*. London: Allen & Unwin.

Marketing News (1982) '21 ad agencies endorse copy testing principles', *Marketing News*, 19 February.

Nowak, G. and Phelps, J. (1994) 'Conceptualising the integrated marketing communications phenomenon', *Journal of Current Issues and Research in Advertising*, **16**(1): 49–66.

Petrison, L. A. and Wang, P. (1996) 'Integrated marketing communication: an organisational perspective', in Thorson, E. and Moore, J. (eds), *Integrated Communication. Synergy of Persuasive Voices*. Mahwah, NJ: Lawrence Erlbaum, pp. 167–84.

Pickton, D. and Broderick, A. (2001) *Integrated Marketing Communications*. Harlow: Financial Times Prentice Hall.

Stapel, J. (1990) 'Monitoring advertising performance', *ADMAP*, July/August.

Stapel, J. (1991) 'Like the advertisement but does it interest me?', *ADMAP*, April.

3

Print media advertising

Objectives

After reading this chapter you should be able to:

- choose the right medium for a given campaign
- explain design issues in press advertising
- describe the differences between different print media in terms of advertising effectiveness
- explain the roles of the various regulatory bodies in controlling advertising
- explain the effects of different press distribution methods on advertising effectiveness
- describe some of the problems of internationalising press advertising

INTRODUCTION

This chapter is about advertising in newspapers, magazines, professional journals, directories and other print-based media. The printed page is still the most widely used advertising **medium** since it is relatively cheap, easy and convenient to use, and provides the customer or consumer with a permanent record of the advertisement for later reference.

PRESS ADVERTISING IN CONTEXT

Press advertising accounts for over £8 billion per year of advertisers' money in the UK alone (Advertising Association 2005), which is approximately 52 per cent of all advertising expenditure. TV advertising, by comparison, accounts for only 26 per cent of expenditure. The number of advertisers using the press is greater than those using TV; several million advertisers use print media, and there are over 12,000 publications in the UK alone. The biggest single share of this revenue goes to regional newspapers (£3.2 billion), with the national press, magazines and directories taking up the rest.

These figures are not necessarily constant for other countries. For example, newspaper readership in Denmark is 90 per cent of the population, with press advertising taking 82 per cent of the revenues. In Belgium, on the other hand, readership is only just over 50 per cent of the population, and print advertising only accounts for 44 per cent of national advertising revenues (Ostergaard 1997).

Press advertising has the following characteristics:

- Permanence – print stays there and can be reread or cut out for future reference. Even though newspapers tend to be thrown away fairly soon after purchase, magazines tend to be kept for long periods, and in particular can often be found in waiting rooms, hairdressing salons and even second-hand bookshops. Directories are often kept for years.

- Magazines, in particular, have a variety of subjects and approaches. This allows for strong segmentation and targeting, since advertisers can contact people with a specific interest in the product category.

- Print media can be read on trains, in buses or on aeroplanes, and frequently are; only rarely would someone carry a radio or TV on public transport. Therefore the medium tends to have the full attention of the reader.

- Results of the advertisements can often be assessed easily by coupon returns, particularly if the coupons are coded so that the periodical can be identified.

- Statistics are usually available on sales, circulation and readership (which are not necessarily the same thing), so media planning becomes easier.

Table 3.1 shows the advantages and disadvantages of press advertising.

TABLE 3.1 Advantages and disadvantages of press advertising

Advantages	Explanation
Cheapness	Small advertisements can be placed very cheaply, and even a fairly extensive campaign can be carried out on a relatively small budget
Ads can be inserted quickly	TV stations normally need considerable notice for accepting adverts – in Germany it can be over a year before an ad will appear, and in the UK the lead time is normally two months. Newspapers can often accept advertisements for publication next day
Response by coupon is possible	Order forms can be included in the press advert, unlike broadcast media. This makes mail order purchasing easy for the consumer, and also monitoring of the effectiveness of the individual magazine is easy for the advertiser
Targeting is easy	Because many magazines are aimed at specialist markets (for example, golfing magazines), the readers are actually interested in the advertisements as well as in the periodical. TV adverts, by contrast, are frequently 'zapped' with the remote control
The press can always accept more adverts	Most European countries have limitations on the amount of advertising allowed on TV, and in any case airtime is limited because space has to be left for programmes. The press need only add some extra pages – TV stations cannot add extra hours in the day
Products are often grouped together	Classified sections in the papers or specific trade sections in directories group advertisers together. This means that readers who are looking for a particular product will read the ads in those sections, so the ads can be smaller and therefore cheaper

Disadvantages	Explanation
Short life	Newspapers are particularly ephemeral; today's big news is wrapping fish and chips tomorrow
Poor print quality	Sometimes illustrations or photographs of the product do not look their best in newspapers, which are printed on cheap paper. Magazines generally fare better
Passive medium	The adverts do not reach out to the reader in the way that a TV ad or radio ad would
Static medium	Unlike TV advertising, there is no eye-catching movement in a press advertisement, although print technology is reaching the point where some movement is possible
Poorer literacy levels	In most of western Europe and the USA, literacy levels are falling, and many people are not in the habit of reading. This makes the press advert less accessible. On the other hand, 61.8 per cent of adults in the UK still read a national daily paper

Print advertising is, therefore, an important medium in most developed countries. Even within countries with low literacy levels, such as some developing countries, newspaper sales may still be high among the more educated and affluent members of society. This is particularly the case in those countries without extensive TV and radio coverage.

CREATIVE ISSUES IN PRINT ADVERTISING

Print advertising contains both **sought** and **unsought communications**. Sought communications are those which are actively looked for by potential customers during the information search phase of the purchasing activity. Unsought communications are those which the potential customer is not looking for but which may activate a need or become part of the internal search information at a later stage. **Display advertising** is usually unsought, whereas **classified advertising** is of the sought variety.

The distinction between sought and unsought communications is an important one in the planning process, particularly in terms of creativity. The unsought advert must be brief, have a high impact, and a clear message which would get across even if the reader simply flipped past the page. The **hook** in the advert might well be all that the reader takes away. Sought communications, on the other hand, must contain all the salient points that the reader needs to make a decision, including information about the firm's unique selling proposition (USP). Since the reader is actively seeking information, the advert can contain a large amount of **copy**. Note the differences between Figures 3.1 and 3.2. Figure 3.1 is an unsought communication, whereas Figure 3.2 is a typical sought communication.

| **FIGURE 3.1** | Example of an unsought communication |

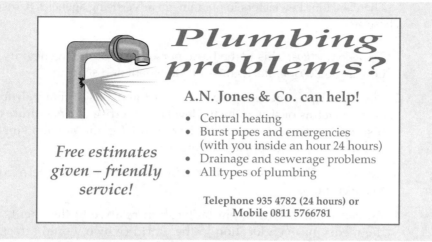

Plumbing problems?

A.N. Jones & Co. can help!

- Central heating
- Burst pipes and emergencies
  (with you inside an hour 24 hours)
- Drainage and sewerage problems
- All types of plumbing

Free estimates given – friendly service!

Telephone 935 4782 (24 hours) or
Mobile 0811 5766781

FIGURE 3.2   Example of a sought communication

The advert in Figure 3.1 has a clear image which most people would connect with coldness and winter (at least, those who live in temperate climates would) and the copy is kept to a minimum. It is extremely unlikely that anyone reading this advert would immediately rush out and buy Chocola; the intention is to plant the idea in the consumer's mind, positioning the product alongside other warming things (such as scarves and woolly hats) and to reinforce the product's image as a comforting drink for winter. This might mean that the reader would consider buying the product next time he or she is in the supermarket and sees the product on the shelves.

In Figure 3.2 the reader is being given plenty of information about the advertiser. The advertiser is able to say what they specialise in, to trigger the reader's interest, and is able to tell the reader that they provide a 'friendly service' and '24-hour emergency service'. These factors may well be what makes the reader choose A. N. Jones & Co., perhaps when looking for a plumber to repair a burst pipe at three in the morning. Since the plumber is guaranteeing to be with the customer inside an hour, it may not matter that the advert appears in the *Yellow Pages* next to forty other plumbers.

In the case of A. N. Jones & Co., the advert will probably have been created by the proprieter him/herself, and he or she will probably have tried a few different approaches before finding one that works. In the case of Chocola, the overall advertising spend is likely to be very high, it is likely that the press ads will need to tie in with the firm's other marketing communications, and the firm's overall commitment to the campaign is likely to be high. For these reasons the firm will almost certainly employ an advertising agency to deal with designing the advert and placing it in the appropriate media.

There are four key factors in planning in advertising agencies (Crosier *et al.* 2003). These are:

1 *The agency ethos.* This is the basic personality of the agency: its beliefs about how it should operate, its mission statement and so forth.

2 *The client type.* Agencies need to meet the needs of many different types of client, in terms of size, industry, level of advertising expenditure or even credit history. Credit history can be important for the agency since the agency assumes liability for paying the media.

3 *Agency size.* This can be considered in absolute terms or in terms of size relative to the client.

4 *Agency location.* This might be location relative to the client, or relative to the media, or even location in the world (which would affect the agency's legal position).

According to Crosier *et al.*, the actual planners can be categorised into five types:

1 *Voice of the Consumer.* The planners act as if they are representing the consumer, and ensure that consumers' needs are met in terms of communication accuracy and completeness.

2 *Strategic Pivot.* This role is likely to occur when the agency is the lead agency, working with other agencies or organisations.

3 *Creative Catalyst.* The agency sees its role as going beyond merely creating the advertising: the agency will seek to become involved in all the creative aspects of the product launch (packaging, design, personal selling, and so on)

4 *Client Confidant.* The agency operates as a trusted partner for the client, acting as a sounding-board for ideas.

5 *Super-planner.* The agency seeks to fulfil all four of the above roles.

The creative aspects of the advertisement usually involve two elements: the copy and the **graphics**. Usually in advertising agencies a copywriter and a graphic artist will form a team to work on the adverts, and they work from a brief given to them by the client.

Creative briefs cover all the key information the creative team needs, as follows:

- target audience and its perceptions, motivations and buying criteria;

- what the advert is supposed to communicate, particularly in terms of affect;

- choice of media;

- the objectives of the advertisement.

The creative brief is a contractual commitment between the advertising agency and the client, and as such is an important document. It therefore merits careful reading before signing.

Copywriters usually need to work with very few words, so much must be left unsaid. It has been said that a copywriter sells his soul for a potted message, and copywriters are among the most creative writers in the world. In order to condense the message, they frequently need to use parts of well-known quotations or literary references, puns, or other culturally based words and phrases to make a hook. This means that the advertisements rarely cross cultural boundaries; sometimes they are incomprehensible even to readers from different parts of the same country owing to regional dialects or local references.

This is less of a problem for the graphic artist, although images of local places or buildings would not necessarily be recognisable elsewhere. The difficulty for the graphic artist lies in creating an image which has the intended meaning for the majority of the target audience. What looks like a friendly smile to one person may be interpreted as a threatening grimace to another – and of course these problems multiply when crossing cultural borders.

Creating an eye-catching and effective advertisement means doing something unusual, which is risky. In recent years, advertisers have taken ever greater risks, and this is especially true in the not-for-profit marketing sector (West and Sargeant 2004). The creative teams in advertising agencies often believe that clients are unprepared to take risks, and there is evidence that women are less prepared to take risks than are men (El-Murad and West 2003).

If the campaign is a major one, the creative team will present **roughs** or **scamps** to the client for approval. Sometimes these are also pre-tested with potential consumers (see Chapter 2). The agency will also present a concept rationale, explaining how the advert will work and what the advantages of the approach are. Following client approval the advert can go into its final production stage before the campaign proper begins. In the UK, advertisers will often obtain the approval of the **Committee of Advertising Practice (CAP)** which is the watchdog organisation for British press advertising. The **Advertising Standards Authority (ASA)** is linked to the CAP and handles complaints from the public – if an advertisement causes offence, the ASA might ask the advertiser to withdraw it. The CAP is a voluntary organisation which has no statutory powers, so sometimes an advertiser might refuse to withdraw an advertisement which does not meet with CAP approval. In these circumstances the ASA can issue a media warning to its members, who include newspaper and magazine proprietors, which effectively bans the advertisement.

The sanctions do not have the backing of the law, but are real nonetheless; agencies that are persistent offenders risk losing their membership of the ASA, which would mean the loss of financial incentives and advantages.

Misleading advertisements can be forcibly withdrawn under the Control of Misleading Advertisements Regulations 1988, although this is rarely necessary since the ASA and CAP between them maintain effective control over offenders.

Obtaining approval from the CAP is advisable before starting an expensive campaign, as withdrawal could be expensive as well as embarrassing.

These arrangements do not necessarily apply outside the UK: most countries have legal restrictions on advertisers rather than voluntary codes of practice, and administration of the voluntary codes which do exist may have varying degrees of rigour. This can create problems in the international context, since an advertisement which is perfectly acceptable in one country may be entirely unacceptable in another.

MEDIA BUYING

Choosing the right periodical to advertise in is both a qualitative and a quantitative exercise. Audience size is measured in two ways: **circulation** and **readership**. Circulation is the number of people who buy the periodical, but since many periodicals are passed on to other readers, the readership figure may give a more accurate picture of the number of people who are likely to see the advert. Sometimes readership can be seven or eight times the circulation figure.

Circulation figures are monitored in the UK by the **Audit Bureau of Circulations (ABC)** which publishes audited circulation figures for its member periodicals. These figures are as accurate as possible and can therefore be trusted and used for comparisons. Unfortunately, it is the readership figure that is the more important. A women's magazine such as *Heat or Hello!* might have a readership many times that of its circulation because the magazines are left in hairdressing salons and are read by possibly several hundred women before being discarded. The same is true of many hundreds of titles.

To overcome this problem, most periodicals conduct their own readership research and send it out to any potential media buyer who asks for a **rate card**. The rate card is a price list for advertising spots in the periodical, and applies to both display advertisements and **linage** advertisements. The readership research includes not only the number of readers but also, usually, a demographic profile. This is useful in cases such as golfing magazines, whose typical readership is mainly from the ABC1 socio-economic groups and therefore may be prime candidates for non-golfing products such as prestige cars, investment plans or upmarket hotels. The problem with using readership figures for comparison is that the advertising departments of the periodicals might be tempted to 'massage' the figures to make the magazine look more desirable. ABC, on the other hand, is independent, and therefore is seen to be honest.

The standard way of comparing periodicals is to use the **cost per thousand (CPT)** ratio. For example, one newspaper might charge £15,000 for a full-page advert whereas a rival newspaper might charge £20,000. At first sight the first paper is much cheaper. If, however, the readership of the first paper is 1.5 million, the cost per thousand would be £10. If the readership of the second paper is 4 million, the cost per thousand would be only £5 and advertising in it would therefore be better value.

Cost per thousand is not the only criterion for comparison, and in some ways is not the most important. Apart from knowing the number of people who read the publication, the media buyer needs to know what kind of people the readers are. Again, periodicals often conduct reader surveys or commission research to find this out, and will make the results available to media buyers. National newspapers target particular demographic groups and people with specific political leanings, and magazines aim for special interest groups or groups segmented by lifestyle, sex or age. Directories are distributed within particular industries or special interest groups such as those who share a hobby. The classic exception is the *Yellow Pages*, which circulates to every telephone subscriber and is a worldwide institution.

Table 3.2 lists the different types of periodical.

TABLE 3.2	Categories of periodical
Type of periodical	**Description**
National newspapers	Newspapers which are published throughout the country. These don't always exist in some large countries, although there may be regional newspapers which have national distribution (e.g. the *New York Herald Tribune* in the USA, or the *Frankfurter Allgemeine* in Germany). National newspapers often segment their markets by lifestyle or political affiliation
Regional and local newspapers	Segmented geographically. Very useful for businesses which are also local in nature; usually much cheaper to advertise in than national dailies
Freesheets	Newspapers published weekly and given away by door-to-door delivery. They have the advantage that they have a known circulation, but the disadvantage that they are not always read, unlike paid-for titles
Specialist magazines	Magazines linked to particular hobbies or interests. For example, there are magazines for anglers, golfers, computer game players, amateur astronomers and so forth. They are an excellent vehicle for targeting specific markets
Consumer magazines	General magazines aimed at a wide audience. Most women's magazines fall into this category, as do news review magazines such as *Time* and *Newsweek*, and the ubiquitous *Reader's Digest*
Technical journals	Magazines such as *Hairdressers' Journal* are aimed at particular jobs or professions and carry technical articles. These offer very accurate targeting in the business-to-business sector

TABLE 3.2   Continued

Type of periodical	Description
Professional journals	These are similar to technical journals, but aimed at professionals such as accountants or lawyers. The *Lancet* falls into this category. Most are published by professional institutions or trade unions
Directories and yearbooks	The best-known of these is the *Yellow Pages*, but many are published for professionals in particular occupations, or for businesses in particular trades. They have the major advantage of permanence and are the ideal place for sought communications

In the UK, periodicals are listed in **British Rate and Data (BRAD)**, which is available from most public libraries. The directory contains ABC circulation details of each publication, some guidance on cost of advertising, and usually some information provided by the periodical about its target audience, editorial policy and so forth.

It is frequently worth paying a higher CPT rate to gain access to a prime target audience. Some trade or professional journals still attract advertising at rates of £200 per thousand readers simply because their readership is high profile and influential.

Finally, most advertising sales departments in periodicals are proactive: they actively seek out new advertisers. This means that placing an advert in one periodical is likely to lead to a flood of telephone calls from other periodicals in the same market, all trying to sell space. This can actually be beneficial; it can mean being able to negotiate favourable terms with the periodicals concerned.

DISTRIBUTION METHODS

In the UK, there are three main methods of distributing periodicals.

1 *Sold through newsagents and shops*. These are predominantly for paid-for publications.

2 *Delivery to the home*. This may be from newsagents (for paid publications) or direct from the publisher (in the case of freesheets and some product-linked magazines).

3 *Subscriptions*. Again, the magazine or journal is mailed direct from the publisher, but this time it is paid for.

In general, paid-for publications are more likely to be read thoroughly than are freesheets. First, the buyer has made a commitment (however small) and has exercised choice in buying a paid-for publication, implying an interest in the content. Second, freesheets typically have much higher ad-to-copy ratios, usually

80/20 rather than the more common 60/40 of a newspaper or 40/60 of a magazine. This means that the freesheet is less interesting to read and also there is more advertising clutter. Freesheets do guarantee circulation, however, and this is verified by the **Verified Free Distribution (VFD)** system, which is an independent research organisation that checks the circulation of freesheets.

It is probably worth noting that purchasers of newspapers are unlikely to read the whole publication. Typically, a newspaper buyer would read less than 20 per cent of the editorial content, and even less of the advertising content.

Home delivery opens up the possibility of leaflet distribution with the papers, or placing **inserts** inside the periodicals. These have the following advantages over advertisements printed in the periodical itself:

- They can be targeted geographically with great precision – down to individual streets if necessary.

- They tend to be more noticeable than adverts in the periodical.

- They can be printed to a higher standards than the newspaper can.

- They are often cheaper than advertising, if the area to be covered is small.

Most national-circulation magazines are prepared to segment inserts geographically; in other words they will ensure that the insert goes into magazines destined for a particular geographical area. This is not as accurate as home delivery, however, since a magazine might be bought by a motorist or train passenger on the way to a different part of the country.

The main disadvantage of inserts is that many people find them irritating and throw them away without reading them: sometimes people shake the magazine as they pick it up from the newsagent's shelf in order to let the inserts fall out.

Although it is impossible to obtain the names and addresses of customers the individual newsagents deliver to, it is sometimes possible to obtain a profile of subscribers to magazines. Many magazines are prepared to supply statistical breakdowns of their subscriber lists, and many are prepared to conduct mailshots of their subscribers on behalf of other firms, or even sell the list of names and addresses. The cost of this varies according to the prestige value of the list; a list of investment bankers is probably going to cost a great deal more than a list of lorry drivers.

MONITORING RESULTS

Tracking studies usually consist of questionnaire-type surveys, with the public using either prompted recall or unprompted recall of the advertising. The results are shown in a table such as the example in Table 3.3.

TABLE 3.3   Example of a tracking table

Attribute	Our Brand A	Brand B	Brand C
Unaided recall	34.7	24.0	26.5
Value for money	27.8	32.4	14.8
For people like me	18.5	22.3	19.6
For people I admire	25.7	17.4	26.5
I sometimes purchase	23.5	28.2	21.8
I like the adverts	26.8	27.4	23.5

There will often be a great many more dimensions on which the brand and the advertisement are tested. The numbers are the ratings (aggregate scores out of 50) given by a group of typical consumers from the target audience; there will be other tables for other groups so that the advertiser can see which audiences like the product best.

The tables are not necessarily easy to read, but they can be looked at in two ways: advertisers can look at the overall scores for their own brand and compare them with scores taken before the advertising campaign started (which will tell them what effect the campaign has had), or they can look across the table to see how the brand scores against the others on each attribute.

Tracking allows advertisers to **benchmark** the campaign. Benchmarking involves trying to meet the best scores on each attribute regardless of which brand; marketers who can do this become the 'best of the best'. For example, in Table 3.3, Brand B scores highest on likeability of the adverts and on value for money. Brand C scores highest on the aspirational attribute, 'for people I admire'. These can be used as targets to aim for in future campaigns.

The danger with these tables is that the scores may be reflecting halo effect. In our example, the consumers in the target group appear to be more likely to buy Brand B regularly, and they also see the brand as value for money, as being for people like them, and they like the adverts. There may be some difficulty in sorting out cause and effect from this type of study; if this is the customer's usual brand, he or she might be loyally saying that the brand's advertising is good. Conversely, it may be the good advertising that leads to brand purchase. To sort these things out the marketer may need to undertake some qualitative research as well (see Chapter 2).

Unaided brand recall scores high for Brand A, but this may be because the firm has just run a campaign, whereas the others may not have run theirs for some time. This means that the marketers need to look at the overall spend for each brand, and track the competitors' campaigns as well if they are to make meaningful comparisons. In the UK, **Media Expenditure Analysis Ltd (MEAL)** publishes figures on the media spend for various firms and brands.

Perhaps at this point it is worthwhile looking at some of the arguments about advertising in general and the way it works (or is supposed to work). The view in the past has been that advertising seeks to persuade consumers to buy products. Although this may be true, the evidence is that it doesn't work in this way; few consumers are persuaded – after all, they usually skip straight past advertisements, and in any case their own direct experience of their favourite product is likely to be far more powerful than a newspaper advert (Ehrenberg *et al.* 1997). Traditionally, advertising has been viewed as a strong force for persuasion, and consequently managers have tended to seek to justify advertising budgets on the basis that the advertising will bring in more business. An alternative view is that advertising is, in fact, a weak force which works mainly by reminding consumers about the product, and perhaps ensuring that the product remains in the consumer's mind when the actual purchase takes place, which could be months or even years after the advertisement was originally run. The view of some managers that advertising budgets can be measured against sales results within a single financial year is probably therefore not realistic in most cases.

In most cases advertising is aimed at increasing brand share within a given product category, except in the rare cases when advertising is used as part of a new product launch (Bloom 1989). There is considerable evidence, for example, showing that bans on tobacco advertising do not affect the overall market for tobacco, but do affect brand share (and, incidentally, help tobacco companies' profits by removing advertising costs from the equation). These studies have been carried out in Australia, Korea, the USA, UK and OECD countries (Johnson 1986; Wilcox and Vaquero 1992; Stewart 1993; Wilcox *et al.* 1994).

Not every firm advertises. In the UK, the retail chains BHS and Mothercare rarely advertise, and Body Shop never does so. Each relies on other means of communication, mainly public relations exercises and sponsorship, yet each manages to maintain a substantial market share.

INTERNATIONAL PRESS ADVERTISING

The press is well developed in most countries, and newspapers are often more widely available in Third World countries than is television or even radio. As with any other marketing communications, taking the message across national borders implies a great deal more than merely translating advertising slogans into a different language. For example, most European languages read from left to right, but Arabic reads from right to left. This can cause a problem if the advertisement uses before-and-after pictures, since the reader is likely to reverse the order of the pictures.

Few advertising slogans translate readily, in any case. This is because most of them use idioms and half-statements that become meaningless outside their cultural context. For this reason it is usually better to hire native speakers to translate advertisements.

Some periodicals have identified global market segments and have successfully crossed borders. For example, the women's magazines *Cosmopolitan* and *Hello!* are sold in many countries around the world. In each case the magazine has needed to be adapted in some ways; for cultural reasons the target market for the Indian edition of *Cosmopolitan* is clearly not identical with, for example, its American market. The Indian edition of *Cosmopolitan* carries advertisements for washing machines and children's toys, and has articles on homemaking and recipes. Also, it appears to have a substantial male readership: many of the letters in its letter columns are from men, apparently under the impression that it is a pin-up magazine. Since relatively few career women exist in India, and nearly all of them seem to live in Bombay, the magazine needs to appeal to a wider audience (perhaps comprising those who wish they were career women) if it is to survive.

It is therefore not advisable to make assumptions about the content and targeting of magazines, even when dealing with overseas editions of familiar titles.

Apart from cultural problems, there is the difficulty of buying space in media in countries where the circulation figures for periodicals are not published or are collected by unreliable means. Circulation figures for directories may not be accurate, and in many large countries there are few, if any, newspapers with national coverage (the USA being a prime example). This can mean dealing with several different agencies in order to cover the whole country.

Having said all that, press advertising will often reach places and people that almost no other medium can; remote areas where television does not reach and billboards are few and far between will still have the daily newspapers delivered (sometimes days late) and magazine subscribers are often found in the most unlikely locations. Press advertising can sometimes be almost the only way to reach such individuals.

CASE STUDY: FOOTJOY

Outside the world of golf, Footjoy is virtually an unknown brand. The company was founded in 1857 as a general shoe manufacturing firm, but quickly began to specialise in golfing shoes. By 1927, the Footjoy range of golfing shoes was well established, and widely regarded as the market leader. In 1970, the firm also began making gloves, and eventually branched out even further and began marketing socks to golfers.

Footjoy therefore produces a very narrow range of products aimed at a specialist, niche market. The company has now become part of the Acushnet group, which includes Titleist golf balls, clubs and accessories. Golf is traditionally a game for the better-off individual: club membership fees can be steep, and the equipment needed to play is by no means cheap either. On the other hand, golf is a minority sport: advertising in a mass medium such as television would waste resources, and for a relatively small company this would not be realistic. Footjoy therefore uses press advertising, in particular advertising in golfing magazines and journals.

Golfing magazines are an interesting area of print advertising, for two main reasons: first, they reach an audience which is often elusive: better-off individuals, usually professionals, with high disposable incomes. Second, their readership is typically around ten times the circulation figure, because the magazines are left lying around in golf club reception and meeting areas. Often the magazines will remain 'in circulation' in this way for months.

For example, *Golf Monthly* has a circulation of 77,000, a readership of 694,000, and reaches an audience with an average income of £25,000 a year (about 15 per cent higher than the UK national average income). In a survey conducted in 2004, 60 per cent of these readers said that they had bought something as a result of seeing it advertised in *Golf Monthly* – an extremely impressive figure since many people might not have remembered seeing the product in the magazine before seeing it in the pro shop.

Footjoy ran a series of advertisements in the golf press during 2005, with the theme, 'What would you do if you walked into your local pro shop and your favourite PGA Tour players were there?' Using golfing stars such as Ernie Els and Freddie Jacobsen, the adverts invited readers to consider how they would feel if these top players were their club pros – and, more importantly, how they would respond to the advice to 'buy Footjoy'.

Of course, everyone knows that professional golfers endorse products in exchange for money, but the mental associations are there, and the adverts are certainly eye-catching. In each case, the professional is shown in a pro shop, putting the shoes on to a display shelf: the reader is invited to imagine what it would be like to have a world-class golfer as the club professional, which of course is an appealing thought for any serious golfer.

Footjoy shoes and gloves are far from cheap – the company has no intention of competing on price. The aim is for the shoes and gloves to be the most comfortable and effective available – coupled with being stylish enough to suit the relatively wealthy audience who buy them. The appeal of the advertisements was enormous: added to Footjoy's already impressive reputation, the press advertising drove sales to new highs.

Ultimately, people who have plenty of money are difficult to sell to (after all, most of them did not get rich by spending money), so Footjoy's press campaign was even more impressive in that it helped to promote the product to people who have high sales resistance.

Questions

1 Why might the company have used golf stars in their promotion?

2 What other media might Footjoy consider?

3 Why show the star golfers as shopkeepers rather than show them wearing the shoes in a tournament?

4 Why specialise in such a narrow market?

5 How might Footjoy build on the campaign?

CHAPTER SUMMARY

Press advertising is sometimes regarded as mundane, and indeed the press lacks the glamour of broadcast media, yet it is still the most popular medium and attracts (overall) the biggest share of the media spend in most countries and for most firms. It therefore deserves to be treated with the same care as TV advertising, and as a powerful communications tool it has much to offer.

Print media are particularly important for unsought communications; directories and classified sections of newspapers and magazines are often consulted in the search phase of the decision-making process.

The key points from this chapter are:

- Press advertising takes the lion's share of media spend.

- Print advertising has a permanence lacking in other communications media.

- Press advertising is easily targeted psychographically (i.e. according to attitudes and aspirations), demographically and geographically.

- The results of print advertising are often easier to assess than those of other communications media.

- Press advertising is often more flexible in terms of ease of insertion of advertisements.

- Sought communications can and should be much more informative than unsought ones; sought communications work on cognition, unsought on affect.

- Creative briefs are important legal documents, and should be drawn up with care.

- Periodicals will often supply useful information about their readership, but the information should be approached with caution.

- Circulation is not the only criterion for choosing a medium, nor is cost per thousand; the readership profile is at least as important.

- Paid-for publications are more likely to be read than are freesheets.

- Benchmarking may help the advertiser to become the 'best of the best'.

CHAPTER QUESTIONS

1 Why is the creative brief so important?

2 How might print advertising be used to back up other media?

3 Why is the approach used for unsought communications different from that for sought communications?

4 What methods exist for tracking the effectiveness of press advertising?

5 What criteria might be used when choosing a print medium to advertise a prestige hi-fi system?

FURTHER READING

Broadbent, S. (1997) *Accountable Advertising*. Henley-on-Thames: ADMAP Publications. This gives a comprehensive rundown of the various methods used to ensure that advertising is cost effective.

Ehrenberg, A., Barnard, N. and Scriven, J. (1997) *Justifying our Advertising Budgets*. London: South Bank University. The series of reports expands on the argument that advertising is not the strong force that it is often taken for; rather, it is a weak force that seeks to develop markets over a long period. These reports are thought-provoking, giving a different perspective on the traditional view of advertising, and therefore on justifying budgets.

Ogilvy, D. (1983) *Ogilvy on Advertising*. London: Pan. This is still the classic text on advertising. David Ogilvy was a partner in one of the most prestigious advertising agencies in the world, and his text offers practitioners and academics a fascinating insight into the nature and practice of advertising.

REFERENCES

Advertising Association (2005) *Marketing Pocket Book*. Henley: Advertising Association and NTC.

Bloom, D. (1989) 'Do we need to worry about long-term effects?' *ADMAP*, October.

Crosier, K., Grant, I. and Gilmore, C. (2003) 'Account planning in Scottish advertising agencies: a discipline in transition', *Journal of Marketing Communications*, **9**: 1–15.

Ehrenberg, A., Barnard, N. and Scriven, J. (1997) *Justifying our Advertising Budgets*. London: South Bank University.

El-Murad, J. and West, D.C. (2003) 'Risk and creativity in advertising', *Journal of Marketing* **19**: 657–73.

Johnson, L. (1986) 'Advertising expenditure and aggregate demand for cigarettes in Australia', *International Journal of Advertising*, 5.

Ostergaard, B. E. (ed.) (1997) *The Media in Western Europe*. London: Sage/Euromedia Research Group.

Stewart, M. (1993) 'The effect on tobacco consumption of advertising bans in OECD countries', *International Journal of Advertising*, **12**(2).

West, D. C. and Sargeant, A. (2004) 'Taking risks with advertising: the not-for-profit sector', *Journal of Marketing Management*, **20**(9/10): 1027–45.

Wilcox, G. and Vaquero, B. (1992) 'Cigarette advertising and consumption in the United States, 1961–1990', *International Journal of Advertising*, **11**: 269.

Wilcox, G., Tharp, M. and Yang, K-T. (1994) 'Cigarette advertising and consumption in South Korea, 1988–1992', *International Journal of Advertising*, **13**: 333.

4

Active media: TV, radio and cinema

Objectives

After reading this chapter you should be able to:

- explain the advantages and disadvantages of advertising on television and radio
- describe the basic principles of dealing with TV and radio commercial production
- understand the issues surrounding the planning of a TV campaign
- explain the pricing structure of TV advertising in the UK
- explain the role of regulatory bodies
- describe the features of cinema advertising which make it a highly effective medium

INTRODUCTION

Radio, TV and cinema are among the most attention-grabbing of advertising media because they are active – these are media that actually do something, rather than sit passively on paper.

Radio and TV advertising are in some ways the most obvious and obtrusive media. Television ownership in western Europe is close to 100 per cent, with many homes owning several sets. TV viewing has almost replaced conversation as the most common entertainment medium, and millions of people listen to radio in their cars, in bed in the morning, and while working or doing house-work. Radio and TV are part of people's lives in a way that no billboard or press medium can equal. On the other hand, as with any other medium, broadcasting has its drawbacks. The medium is impermanent; the TV viewer often leaves the room while the adverts are on; and the radio listener is often not really listening to the set, but is concentrating on something else.

Cinema, like TV, offers the chance to show the product in use and to engage both sight and hearing; cinema advertising offers the further advantage of having a captive audience.

TV ADVERTISING

Television advertising remains one of the most powerful mass communication media in existence. Television ownership is widespread; 98 per cent of British homes have at least one set, and most have more than one. TV ownership figures for western Europe are shown in Table 4.1.

People watch TV while eating, while doing housework and while relaxing. In many homes the set is rarely switched off except overnight. It is significant that the biggest selling consumer magazines in most countries are the TV listing guides.

Television advertising has the advantages shown in Table 4.2 (Jefkins 1994).

TABLE 4.1	TV ownership in western Europe

Country	Percentage of homes owning a TV
Austria	96
Belgium	97
Denmark	98
France	97
Germany	97
Greece	99
Ireland	97
Italy	82
The Netherlands	98
Portugal	86
Spain	99

Source: Reprinted by permission of Sage Publications Ltd from Ostergaard, B.E. (ed.) (1974) *The Media in Western Europe* © The Euromedia Research Group 1992, 1997.

TABLE 4.2	Advantages of TV advertising

Advantage	Explanation
Realism	It is possible to show the product in use in a realistic scenario. This helps position the product; the audience can also see the type of people who are using the product (perhaps placing their social class by their accents) in a way that is difficult or impossible in print ads
Receptive audiences	TV adverts are often seen as entertainment; many are produced to very high standards and are interesting in their own right. The Stella Artois advertisements which have been running in the UK for some years now have clear story lines with amusing twists: despite the fact that the advertisements are scripted entirely in French, the themes are clear. Interestingly, Stella Artois is produced in a Flemish-speaking area of Belgium
Repetition	Adverts can be repeated until sufficient of the target audience has seen it. Agencies monitor this using **Broadcast Audience Research Bureau (BARB)** ratings to identify how many people watched the show and might reasonably be supposed to have seen the advert

TABLE 4.2   Continued

Advantage	Explanation
Appeal to retailers	Most retailers have a strong belief in the power of TV advertising and are more likely to give products prominence on the shelves if a campaign is planned. This in itself will increase sales; it may be difficult to ascertain the reasons for the increase because of this
Zoning and networking	In the UK and most other countries it is possible to localise advertising to the immediate TV region, or to 'go national' with ads which are broadcast throughout the network
Links with other media	Further information (or coupons to return) can be printed in TV guides. This combines the strengths of press advertising with the power of television.

Of course, television also has disadvantages, as set out in Table 4.3.

TABLE 4.3   Disadvantages of television

Disadvantage	Explanation
Lack of selectivity	TV tends to reach mass audiences; it is harder to segment demographically than press advertising, and geographically than billboards
Impermanent medium	It is difficult for interested prospective customers to take note of where products are available, or indeed of any detailed information in the adverts
Zapping and zipping	Remote controls allow audiences to 'zap' commercials by switching channels, or 'zip' past advertisements that have been recorded on a VCR. Zapping has been called 'the greatest threat to capitalism since Karl Marx' (Kneale 1988)
Clutter	In some countries, TV advertising rates are so low that frequent, and lengthy, advertising spots are sold; the USA and Italy are examples of this. Viewers become bored with the sheer volume of advertising
Audience fade-out	Audiences often leave the room while the adverts are on, so although the ratings for the show might be high, the adverts may not actually have been seen.

TABLE 4.3	Continued
Cost	TV advertising can be very expensive; although it reaches a large audience, and therefore the CPT (cost per thousand) may be favourable, the audience may not be composed of the right target segment. The entry threshold is high; a 30-second ad at peak time can cost £10,000 per region
Long lead times	Booking airtime can be a lengthy process (two months in the UK, over a year in Germany). This means that it is difficult to place adverts at short notice, for example emergency recalls of defective products. Also, production times for commercials can be long
Restrictions on content	In the UK, the Independent Television Commission tends to take a conservative view on what is acceptable in TV commercials as opposed to press advertisements. Sexual innuendo, nudity and swearing are all taboo (despite their prevalence in the programming) and some categories of product cannot be advertised at all (tobacco and condoms being two examples). Most countries have similar restrictions: in France retail stores cannot be advertised on TV, in Germany toys cannot be advertised during children's programmes
Erosion of audiences	As the number of available channels has increased (from two in the UK during the 1960s to around fifty now, plus the availability of DVDs) the audiences have become spread more thinly. Also, high quality programmes are spread across more channels so that the average quality of programming has fallen. This has led to a reduction in the time spent watching TV and an increase in other activities. This trend may be peaking – recently some TV companies have gone bankrupt, indicating that there is a limit to the number of channels that the audiences are prepared to support

Because television advertising is largely an unsought medium (viewers do not usually switch on in the hope of seeing a favourite advert), it works best for activating needs or providing information for the internal search (see Chapter 1). In most cases advertisers are aiming to build the image of their product or firm, and to a large extent these aims can be met by television (McKechnie and Leather 1998).

There is a clear relationship between liking the advert and subsequent sales, but it is not necessarily a positive relationship. Liking the advert seems to be related to whether the product is meaningful and relevant to the consumer at the time (Biel 1990); there seems to be some evidence that food and beverage adverts are more likely to be liked than are non-food adverts (Biel and Bridgewater 1990). Liking is usually linked to a positive view of the product, and this is likely to lead to an increase in sales (Biel 1990; Stapel 1991). However, the situation may be reversed when dealing with many financial services products.

Wells (1980) postulated that products could be placed on an approach–avoidance continuum, with products that are inherently attractive (such as food, clothes and cars) at the approach end of the scale and products which elicit unpleasant thoughts (such as pensions and life insurance) at the avoidance end of the scale. This is because such products are only bought in order to avoid bad outcomes, and most people prefer not to think about ageing and death (Mintel 1993). Because the adverts must necessarily deal with unpleasant matters, the more unpleasant the message is the more likely it is to result in a purchase (McKechnie and Leather 1998). It may be difficult to untangle all the factors involved, since an unpleasant advert is likely to be ignored, and the viewer is therefore less motivated to process the information cognitively. The elaboration likelihood model (see Chapter 1) implies that such viewers would only process the information peripherally, and that therefore adverts for financial services work best as image-builders (Petty and Cacioppo 1983). This may be true of TV advertising generally, since relatively few of the audience will be involved with the given product category just at the time the advert goes out, and will therefore not give the advert their close attention.

Interestingly, there is some US evidence that commercials which are zapped are more likely to have a positive effect on brand purchase than those which are not zapped. This is because the viewer has to watch the advert and process the content to know that it is a candidate for zapping (Zufryden *et al*. 1993).

This area of advertising effectiveness is difficult to research because showing the respondents the advert in a laboratory situation predisposes them to watch the advert carefully ('we will be asking questions later' is a well-known way of making someone pay attention). The situation is therefore not realistic compared with the usual viewing environment where there are many distractions and tempting diversions to draw the viewer's attention away from the screen.

Research at the London Business School shows that people do not necessarily watch the advertisements even if they are still in the room when the advertisement airs (Ritson 2003). The researchers identified a total of six behaviours which occur while the advertisement is on-screen; these are shown in Table 4.4.

TABLE 4.4	Behaviours in commercial breaks

Behaviour	Explanation
Social interaction	People often talk about their day, discuss household problems or gossip while the commercial break runs
Reading	Many people watch TV with a book or magazine at hand, to read during the breaks. Sometimes the reading will be a TV guide
Tasking	The commercial break often affords an opportunity to load the dishwasher, clean the house, do the ironing, pay bills or make telephone calls

TABLE 4.4	Continued
Flicking	Jumping from one channel to another appeared to be mainly a male activity. Flicking falls into two categories: almost random surfing across a number of other channels while waiting for the programme to restart, or alternatively going to a 'visit channel' such as a news channel for a specific length of time before returning to the programme
Watching an advertisement	In many cases, advertisements were actually watched, and often commented on by the family members
Advertising interaction	The final behaviour involved not only watching the advertisement, but commenting on it, singing along with the jingles and even playing a game in which family members scored 'points' by being the first to recognise the brand

Of all these behaviours, the last two are obviously the ones most desired by advertisers – in particular the last one, since the viewers are interacting with the advertisement and are certainly going to remember what they have seen.

Off-the-screen commercials

The exception to much of what has just been said, and indeed a type of advertising that breaks all the rules, is the off-the-screen commercial. These adverts are the entire communication package for the advertiser: viewers are invited to call a hotline, with their credit card details, to buy the product directly. Products sold in this way range from garden equipment to music collections, and in some countries (for example, Spain) seem to comprise the major part of the TV advertising.

Off-the-screen selling has the following advantages for the advertiser:

- It shortens the channels of distribution, which may reduce costs.

- Like other mail order systems, the advertiser receives the money before the goods are despatched, which helps with cash flow.

- The effects are virtually instantaneous (viewers call while the ad is on the screen), so it is easy to schedule demand. Much of the handling of calls can be dealt with by computer systems.

- TV gives the advertiser the capacity to use sight, sound and movement to demonstrate the product in a way that often would not be possible even in a retail shop.

Off-the-screen selling means that the advertisement itself has to be crammed with information; it is, after all, the only communication the consumer will see before buying the product. Often the adverts will have written words on screen, spoken words, background music (particularly with record compilations), and filmed activities demonstrating the product or showing typical users of the product. The ads themselves can be expensive to produce, but the main cost is buying sufficient airtime to ensure a good response.

A US variation on this is the **infomercial**. This is typically a half-hour programme consisting of entertainment and news about a specific product; for example, an angling programme which demonstrates a new type of fishing lure. Infomercials are illegal on free-to-air television in the UK, but make up around one-quarter of the programming time for cable stations in the USA (Steenhuysen 1994). The advantage of the infomercial is that it gives enough time to inform and persuade potential customers of the product's benefits; from the cable company's viewpoint, it fills up airtime which would otherwise have to be filled with paid-for programming.

Government controls on television

Many governments worldwide have been fearful of the insidious nature of television, and have sought to ensure some measure of control over the medium. Originally TV in the UK was not commercial. The first broadcasts took place in 1936 from the BBC's station at Alexandra Palace in London; this was the world's first public television service, and was funded from licence fees rather than advertising. When commercial TV started in 1955, only one commercial station was allowed in each geographical area of the country and strict rules about ownership were imposed. Despite this, Sir Lew Grade (the founder of Granada Television) called commercial TV 'a licence to print money'.

The government's intention was to avoid the cut-throat competition and ratings wars that were becoming evident in American commercial TV. The view was that such battles reduced the quality of programming because of a scramble to attract mass audiences with cheaply produced game shows and sensational soap operas. At the time, American TV shows were sponsored by advertisers; this meant that the network had very little control over content, and the sponsors used the shows to 'plug' their own products relentlessly.

In the UK, TV companies must periodically re-apply for their licences to broadcast. The licensing authority (the Independent Television Commission) takes account of the station's programming policy and the quality of its home-produced programmes as well as its bought-in programming. In fact, UK viewers have come to expect high quality programming, including documentaries and a wide range of drama, from Shakespeare to soaps.

In Canada, the Massey Report suggested that Canada should not have commercial TV until the Canadian Broadcasting Corporation had established national coverage of non-commercial programming; this view was undermined by the ease with which 60 per cent of Canadians could tune into US TV stations just across the border (Leiss *et al.* 1990). Even in the USA, the Federal Communications Commission established a moratorium on new TV stations between 1948 and 1952 in order to impose some order on the chaos resulting from unlimited establishment of TV stations. In order to provide an alternative to commercial TV, the US government funds public service television. Unfortunately, much of the programming is regarded as boring or even as propaganda.

In much of western Europe, commercial TV has only become deregulated since the 1980s as a result of satellite broadcasting, which, being extraterrestrial, proved difficult to control or regulate. Deregulation in Italy and France led to a proliferation of stations; in Italy these eventually became consolidated into major networks controlled by the companies responsible for selling advertising space. For example, Silvio Berlusconi established a network which encompassed 60 per cent of Italian stations by the simple expedient of providing small independent stations with taped programmes with the advertisements already included. In effect, governments throughout the world have recognised that it is no longer feasible to exercise strict controls over television since so much TV is broadcast from outside the atmosphere.

The meteoric rise in cable access and the increasing sophistication of the Internet mean that TV is now independent of radio waves. The next generation of TV, digital television, will be in use throughout the UK by 2010. Digital TV offers the capability of interactivity as well as much higher picture quality and more channels. The proliferation of channels will not necessarily mean more programmes, however: current thinking is that it will allow viewers to choose what time they elect to watch a particular programme, meaning that the programme is actually 'broadcast' simultaneously on several channels at once.

Free-to-air TV versus satellite and cable

Free-to-air (network) TV is the conventional form of television transmitted via radio waves through the air. Much of it is controlled by legal restrictions, and this led to the advent of cable systems in the USA in order to overcome government regulations about censorship and airtime. Satellite systems broadcast from space direct to dish aerials on the consumer's roof. Satellites have most of the advantages of cable and are cheaper to launch than ground transmitters are to build; they have enabled large countries like India to establish a nationwide TV network quickly and cheaply. Both satellite and cable have the capacity to carry large numbers of channels in a way that, for technical reasons, free-to-air transmitters are unable to achieve.

The advent of cable and satellite has meant a proliferation of TV channels, and a consequent increase in consumer choice. This has, in turn, meant a fall in the number of people watching a given programme at any one time, but also has opened up access to TV advertising for many small firms (or firms with small budgets) since cable rates are usually much lower than network rates. Also, cable stations target specific audiences much better than network stations: MTV very accurately targets the world's youth audience; Discovery targets people who enjoy learning; Nickelodeon targets children. For precise targeting, cable and satellite probably represent better options than free-to-air TV. For technical reasons, cable usually offers better picture quality than free-to-air TV owing to very much reduced noise and interference; for some products this may be an important factor.

Digital television offers even greater broadcast quality, and has the further advantage of offering greater bandwidth so that even more channels can be transmitted. Because of the greater information-carrying capacity of a digital link, future possibilities include interactive TV (customised programming) and links to personal computers. The advent of digital TV does create some problems for advertisers. First, the evidence from satellite and cable networks is that advertising is a small part of the station's revenue compared with subscription income (in the case of the UK's Sky channel, only 11 per cent of the revenue comes from advertising), so that the influence of advertisers is greatly weakened compared with free-to-air networks. Second, traditional audience measurement techniques become unmanageable in an environment where viewers can receive over one hundred channels (Crawford 1997).

One development of interest is the establishment of home shopping channels (presumably for people who like shopping). The QVC channel shows only commercials, yet it attracts a sizeable audience and makes substantial sales, and since QVC is a cable channel some viewers have to pay a subscription to receive it. For some people it would appear that the commercials are more interesting than the programmes, to the extent that they are prepared to pay for the privilege of being sold to.

Because of the need to make advertisements appealing to the viewer, the boundaries between advertising and entertainment have become blurred in the traditional context of TV programming, but QVC has taken this a stage further by making the advertisements the sole entertainment, with no programming to interrupt them. Window-shopping (which is sometimes thought to be a manifestation of the hunter–gatherer instinct) has been brought to the home.

As yet, little research has been conducted into the apparent contradiction between zapping advertisements and deliberately tuning into a shopping channel. Possibly the shopping channel has a similar appeal to a street market or an auction: the viewer hopes that a bargain will appear any minute. The typical shopping channel operates on the assumption that it is providing a sought communication, and apparently the subscribers accept this view.

Producing TV advertisements

Producing TV advertisements is a creative process. Since it entails so many different elements, the process will involve a number of creative people and also a number of distinct stages. Having said that, there are no hard and fast rules and the process will vary greatly from client to client and product to product – and especially from audience to audience.

The first step in the creative process is to plan the production of the advert with all those who are to be involved. This would normally take place at the advertising agency and include the creative director, writers, an art director and possibly a business manager. The meeting is briefed on the overall aims of the advert, and each person present is asked for ideas within his or her speciality. Once a clear idea is fixed on, the process follows that set out in Table 4.5.

| TABLE 4.5 | Producing a TV advert |

Stage	Explanation
Scriptwriting	The writer is asked to produce a script in which the pictures and soundtrack are specified in detail. A 30-second voice-over probably contains 50–60 words
Storyboard	The artist illustrates a key frame from each scene in the script. The frames are assembled in order, with the spoken script printed underneath each frame. This is called a presentation storyboard
Client presentation	The finished script and storyboard are shown to the client for approval. Sometimes copies are handed out to the interested parties. More sophisticated presentations involving slides or computer animations are sometimes used
Audience testing	The advert may be concept-tested with consumers before shooting begins (see Chapter 2)
Pre-production	Meetings are held with those responsible for the shooting to determine overall costs and timescales. The producer is the agency's business manager who acts as the interface between the creative artists and the 'real world' of legal and financial restrictions. Legal clearance with regulatory bodies is often sought at this stage, as is client approval of budgets and timescales
Pre-bid sessions	Following approval of the storyboard by creative, legal, client and agency interests, bids are invited from production companies
Selection of production company	The production company will be selected according to the size of its bid and the quality of its work. Although the bid must be within the budget, quality of production should be the overriding consideration; the cost of the airtime is almost always going to be greater than the cost of production, and it is clearly not worth spending a lot of money to air a poorly made commercial
Shooting	Adverts are often directed by well-known directors using famous actors and actresses; other times they are produced on a low budget with unknowns

Although scripts are not written to a formula, there are five rules which many scriptwriters follow:

1 Make it *clear*.

2 Make it *complete*.

3 Make it *important*.

4 Make it *personal*.

5 Make it *demanding*.

From the client's viewpoint, the main criterion for ensuring a successful advertisement is to give a clear and detailed brief. It is in the interests of all concerned that the campaign should be a success: artists, scriptwriters, actors, directors and the agency would all much prefer to be associated with a successful, high impact campaign than with a flop. It is therefore essential that everybody involved understands what the advert is intended to achieve and who it is aimed at.

Some creative aspects of advertising production have been researched. For example, fast-paced advertisements have a positive effect on involuntary attention (in other words they are more eye-catching), but unfortunately they tend to focus people's attention on the style of the advertisement rather than on the brand being advertised (Bolls *et al.* 2003).

Buying airtime

The method of buying airtime varies from country to country. In the UK, free-to-air stations operate a standardised rate card which lays down the spot rates for airtime. All airtime is pre-emptible, which means that it is sold to the highest bidder. Although it is possible to book a peak-time slot for as little as £1,000, it is extremely likely that another advertiser will bid more for the spot so that the first advertiser is then excluded. Since airtime is limited (an average of only six minutes per hour), popular spots such as the middle break in the late evening news will always be oversubscribed.

In the USA, much more generous ratios of advertising time to programme time are allowed, with up to sixteen minutes per hour being allowed in prime time. Rates are decided on the basis of the popularity of the programmes (the **Nielsen ratings**), so that a popular show will not only attract more advertisers, but a higher spot rate as well. This can cause problems for high quality programmes which nevertheless do not attract mass audiences; in some cases, programme producers have been able to demonstrate that their programmes attract a particularly desirable audience (for example a better-educated or wealthier group than average). This can save a programme which would otherwise fall victim to low ratings.

In Germany, airtime is bought by advanced bid and allocation, usually a year in advance; this means considerable delays, and since current advertisers are usually given priority in the allocation it is difficult for new firms to break into television. Cable TV has made considerable inroads into German advertising revenues as a result of this.

Premier rates on UK TV vary from £1,760 per 30 seconds (on S4C – Welsh Channel Four), up to £33,600 per 30 seconds on Meridian. Standard rates run from £30 up to £21,000. Time slots are sold in 10, 20, 30, 40, 50 and 60 second sizes. Volume discounts are available, and these vary according to the region. Full campaign details must be submitted eight weeks before the broadcast month, so that for May, broadcast details must be submitted by the end of February. As with other media, agencies are given a 15 per cent discount, which is in effect their fee.

Variations on the standard 30-second slot include top-and-tailing (running an advert at the beginning of a commercial break, then running a brief reminder at the end), or running very brief images between the other advertisements in the break. These non-standard packages attract a 10 per cent premium over the basic cost of the airtime.

TV advertising and culture

Although TV advertising must reflect the culture in which it has its roots, it also has the capacity to mould the culture on which it impinges. Television is a powerful medium, engaging the attention of the viewer as no other medium can, and the advertisements are designed to have maximum impact, so it is not surprising that TV advertising slogans, jingles and themes pass into daily life. As a basis for jokes, as themes for fancy-dress parties or as topics for discussion, TV adverts have few rivals.

Research shows that many people take pleasure in thinking about things they have seen or heard in TV adverts (Yoon 1995); the same research reports that many consumers believe that TV advertising distorts society's values.

Children are often particularly susceptible to TV advertising. Research by Oates et al. (2003) has shown that children aged under 6 years do not understand that TV advertising is intended to persuade people, and that even some 10-year-olds are unable to articulate any understanding of this.

RADIO ADVERTISING

Radio is the Cinderella of advertising, often ignored in favour of the higher profile of TV advertising. In the UK, commercial radio is a relative newcomer. During the 1930s, 1940s and 1950s the only commercial radio available was transmitted from Luxembourg; reception was so poor that radio engineers still refer to fading signals as Luxembourg effect. In the 1960s, pirate radio stations began broadcasting pop music from ships anchored outside the three-mile limit (thus avoiding restrictions on commercial broadcasting), but this was ended in 1967 by legislation forbidding advertisers to use the stations. Commercial radio was reinstituted in the 1970s, and currently there are almost three hundred commercial stations broadcasting in the UK. Most of these are local stations serving communities or ethnic groups within major cities. Relatively few have national coverage.

Independent local radio usually transmits in **FM (frequency modulated)** format. This format gives very good sound quality, but short range. National stations use **AM (amplitude modulated)** format which gives longer range at the cost of poorer sound quality. Audience numbers vary significantly; a local radio station in a rural area might be able to reach only a small number of people compared with a station in a city, but on the other hand will have fewer competing stations within receiving range. **Radio Joint Advertising Research (RAJAR)** is jointly owned by the BBC and the independent radio stations, and provides independently audited figures on audience sizes, allowing comparison between stations. RAJAR surveys approximately 130,000 adults (aged over 15) and 20,000 children (aged between 4 and 14) each year.

Part of the reason for the neglect of radio as an advertising medium in the UK is historical; commercial TV pre-dates commercial radio, so the TV stations already had well-established links with advertisers, whereas radio has had to carve out a separate niche. This is the reverse of the situation in most countries, where commercial radio preceded commercial TV.

The advantages of radio advertising are set out in Table 4.6.

TABLE 4.6	Advantages of radio advertising
Advantage	**Explanation**
Radios are cheap and portable	Most people own a radio, and most households own several; they are often taken on trips to the beach or taken to work
No need to be literate to enjoy radio	The spoken word is understood by everyone who is native to the country. This is a useful characteristic in many markets
Live medium	Like TV, radio is active, so it can grab the attention better than press advertising
Does not require the listener's sole attention	Radio is often listened to while driving, working, doing housework or engaging in leisure pursuits
Hard to zap ads	Unlike TV, radios are not usually fitted with remote controls so the listener usually hears the advertisements

TABLE 4.6	Continued
Can be localised	FM stations are short range and adverts can therefore be tailored to a local audience
Can be aimed at different people at different times of day	Workers listen for time-checks around breakfast time; drivers listen while driving to and from home, housewives and factory workers listen during the day. This ability to target accurately has been called **narrowcasting**
Cheapness and flexibility	Radio has much of the immediacy of TV but at a fraction of the cost; in particular, production costs of radio adverts are tiny by comparison with television commercials
Intimacy of the medium	People usually listen to the radio in a relaxed and private situation – while in bed, while driving, in the bathroom or while doing housework. This makes radio a more friendly medium than, say, billboards or even TV

According to one UK radio station:

- 44 per cent of radio listeners wake up to a radio alarm;
- 27 per cent of people listen to radio in the bathroom, and 43 per cent of the 15–24 age group do so;
- 72 per cent of adult listeners listen in the kitchen;
- 44 per cent of car drivers listen to the radio while driving;
- 44 per cent of employees listen to the radio in the workplace;
- 53 per cent of adults aged 15–24 listen to their radios in the garden.

As with any other medium, there are disadvantages, as shown in Table 4.7.

Radio advertising tends to have a more important role in countries outside the UK, especially those countries where TV does not have national coverage, or in large countries where TV reception can often be poor. Within the UK, radio is often used as reminder advertising to back up TV campaigns.

TABLE 4.7 Disadvantages of radio

Disadvantage	Explanation
Audio medium only	This means it is impossible to show the product, and in particular makes it almost impossible to model it
Relies heavily on audience imagination	This makes it difficult to position the product, since the audience's perceptions play a bigger role, and the advertiser has less control over events. The joint message construct between sender and receiver is heavily biased in favour of the receiver
Transient medium	Adverts are impermanent, so details such as price, addresses of stockists etc. cannot easily be retained by the listener
Inattention of listeners	Radio is often merely a background noise used to make boring tasks more tolerable – the listener is not listening very closely
Low number of listeners	The number of listeners is usually small compared with the number of people within the broadcasting range of the station
Difficult to measure	Unlike press adverts, where coupon returns might be used, or other communications media such as exhibitions or sales calls, it is hard to know who has heard the advertisements and how it has affected them. Much of the effect is below the conscious level

Planning radio advertising

As with other forms of advertising, all planning begins with deciding what is to be achieved. Realistic objectives for radio will be concerned with image building and raising awareness; it is extremely difficult to run direct-response advertising on radio, and in fact this is virtually never attempted. Radio stations, like press media, produce rate cards which give a breakdown of their audience demography and audience figures for different times of day. These figures are usually independently audited by RAJAR and occasionally include comparisons with other radio stations in the area – naturally, only those that are favourable to the station concerned are likely to be included.

Comparison of rate cards should indicate which station is reaching the right target audience, and this should be the main criterion for deciding which station to go with. Spot rates vary greatly between stations, according to the audience figures and location; as with press advertising, it is unwise to rely solely on CPT (cost per thousand) calculations. Also, spot rates vary within stations according to the time of day and type of listener. For example, the drivetime slot between 5 pm and 7 pm is often a premium spot because many motorists listen to the radio on their way home from work. These are people with jobs that pay well enough for them to be driving a car, so they are likely to be a prime audience for many products, in particular anything to do with motoring needs. Fixing charges are applied for particular spots (for example, immediately after the news bulletins), and discounts are available for volume if the advertiser is placing enough advertising with the station.

Problems arise if the advertiser wants to 'go national'. This is because the market is fragmented, with many small independent stations, and although some agencies can arrange multiple bookings of airtime, they work only for certain stations. BRAD has details of these agencies.

Producing radio advertisements

Having selected the radio stations, target audience and time of transmission, the creative aspects of producing the advertisement come into play. This is much simpler than producing TV advertising because there is only sound to consider; in essence this means the spoken word, music and sound effects. All radio stations offer production facilities and will supply music, actors and sound effects (at a price) if required. Radio offers the opportunity for businesspeople to appear in their own adverts; this seems to work well on radio, whereas it is often a disaster on TV where the individual's lack of acting training is much more apparent. Such an appearance by the real owner has an immediate personal impact on the listener, and makes the advert much more intimate – an important consideration when the listener is in a home environment.

Scripting radio adverts is much like scripting TV adverts, except that everything must be conveyed in the script. Sound effects become important as triggers for the listener's perception: the sound of a champagne cork popping signifies celebration to most people, the sound of waves on a beach and children playing signifies holidays, and so forth. These triggers are culturally based; devout Muslims are unlikely to associate alcohol with celebrations, and many Australians have rarely visited the seaside. Because radio requires a certain amount of imagination on the part of the listener, the advertisement may actually be more effective because it is more interactive (Ritson and Elliott 1995).

The role of music in adverts is to attract the listener's attention and to help with the perceptual mapping of the product into an appropriate position. Pop music provides linking value – it helps the listener make sense of the world (Cova 1997), and therefore it has been argued that pop music is most effective in adverts when it is used to promote other products which also have linking value (Shankar 1998). Clothing ads can usefully use pop music because the clothes themselves are a linking product, being a statement about the wearer. Although this is as true for TV adverts as it is for radio adverts, on radio the music has a stronger role. For firms on low budgets, computer software is now available for composing simple background music which is non-copyright and therefore royalty free.

The use of words in advertisements is particularly important on the radio. Making a slogan which sticks in the mind can be the product of several devices, as shown in Table 4.8.

TABLE 4.8 Making slogans stick

Device	Explanation
Rhythm	'A Mars a day helps you work, rest and play' is a catchy rhythm known to most British people. The rhythm is complex but regular, and it echoes the older saying, 'An apple a day keeps the doctor away'. The slogan has stuck in people's minds even though it has not been used by Mars for some years now
Foregrounding	Bringing the slogan to the forefront of the mind is achieved either by parallelism (an unexpected regularity, as in the Mars slogan above) or by deviation (an unexpected irregularity)
Alliteration	Using the same sound repeatedly often creates a resonance; this does not necessarily mean using the same spelling. For example, 'nb' as in 'Canberra' sounds like 'm'
Assonance	The repetition of vowel sounds, as in the slogan 'Gillette – the best a man can get'. The assonance of 'Gillette' and 'get' makes the slogan more memorable. This also applies to brand names such as Coca-Cola
Rhyme	Rhyme works better in some languages than in others. Italian, Welsh and Spanish have a lot of words with the same endings and also have a natural rhythm due to the position of stresses in the words. German and Greek are less rhythmic
Intonation	Stressing different syllables from those expected in ordinary speech can add to the deviation effect
Puns	**Homophones** are words which sound similar but have different meanings. Carefully used, these can have a high impact; foreign languages are a rich source of possibilities here. Homophones often work better in print than on radio, however

In practice, copywriting is more art than science. Scriptwriters more usually come up with a catchy slogan and then rationalise it afterwards rather than carefully calculating all the possibilities first.

Questions are powerful. Asking a question causes the audience to think in an attempt to find the answer. Also, questions can often contain assumptions which are taken for granted because the listener is distracted by the question itself. For example, 'How can you remove those stale smells from clothing?' assumes that the clothing in question smells stale, and the listener can easily accept this assumption while trying to think of how to remove the smells.

Most questions used in advertising are rhetorical: they assume that there is only one answer. This type of question can easily mould opinion. For example, 'Would you like to save money on car insurance?' has only one answer; the listener can easily assume that what follows (an advert for an insurance broker) will solve the problem by saving money.

Government regulation of radio

As with TV, radio is regulated by the government. The original UK regulator, the Independent Broadcasting Authority (IBA), was replaced by the Radio Authority in 1991, and this body now exercises control over what may and may not be broadcast. The main provisions of the code of conduct are shown in Table 4.9.

TABLE 4.9   Main provisions of the Radio Authority code of practice

Provision	Example
Prohibition of some products entirely	Cigarettes, pornography, escort agencies
Endorsement by presenters	Station presenters may not recommend advertisers' goods, so advertisers cannot employ them to do voice-overs
Adverts must not offend against taste or decency	No racist or sexist language is allowed (even as a joke), or obscene language
Adverts must not use knocking copy	Advertisers are not allowed to make derogatory references to competitors' products (this tends to be counterproductive anyway)
Adverts must not use sound effects which might endanger drivers	Sounds of police sirens or tyres squealing might well distract or confuse drivers
Adverts must not mislead the audience	Although a certain amount of advertising puff is expected, adverts must be truthful; this especially applies to medicines, financial services and environmental claims

The radio station will help with complying with the code of practice; it is not usually necessary to submit scripts to the Radio Authority for approval. As with TV advertising regulation, the systems in other countries may be very different from the UK systems.

Because radio adverts are quick to produce, and the airtime is usually available, radio advertising can be used for emergency advertising or for advertising that is timely; for example, adverts for weather-related products can quickly be produced and aired. An advertising campaign can also be adapted quickly in the face of changed circumstances (for example, competitive activities).

CINEMA ADVERTISING

For many years, the cinema was the main visual advertising medium. The advent of television meant that cinema attendances declined rapidly since people were more easily entertained in their homes. Over the past ten years, however, this trend has reversed, with the arrival of multiscreen cinemas and blockbuster movies which have impact on the big screen. The disappearance of 'fleapit' cinemas and their replacement by plush, comfortable multiscreen centres has meant a resurgence in attendances, and consequently a resurgence in interest in advertising in the cinema.

From the advertiser's viewpoint, cinema has all the advantages of television plus one other: it is impossible to zip, zap or leave the room while the advert is on. This means that it offers an unrivalled opportunity to have an attentive audience. Cinema attendances have risen sharply in recent years – government statistics for the UK show that admissions have risen from 34 million in 1988, to 50 million in 1994, 56 million in 1999 and 55 million in 2001 (www.ukonline.gov.uk). The industry expects this figure to rise as improvements in production techniques occur and as the wealth of the general population increases. A further factor is the relatively poor quality of TV programming: as advertising revenues and creative talent become spread across more channels, the quality of TV is almost certain to suffer, providing opportunities for the high quality productions on offer in cinemas.

Typical cinema audiences are young people in their teens and early twenties; 36 per cent of cinema visitors are aged 15–24, although they represent only 15 per cent of the UK population (Pearl and Dean 2005). This audience is also strongly ABC1 in socio-economic profile. In some developing countries, notably India, cinema is enjoyed regularly by the majority of the population, since television ownership is considerably less widespread than in the wealthier European, American and Pacific Rim countries.

The medium is extremely flexible – cheap packages are available for small local firms, using standard film clips or still slides with a voice-over, or large national firms can run their TV commercials on the big screen. In most countries, cinema advertising is less regulated than TV advertising; in France it is legal to advertise retail shops in the cinema whereas this is illegal on TV; and condoms cannot be advertised on UK TV but are legally advertised in the cinema. In the UK, any cinema advertisement of 30 seconds or more has to be passed by the British Board of Film Censors, which rates its suitability for young audiences and children, and there is a voluntary code administered by the Cinema Advertising Association in place which prevents cinemas from showing adverts for alcohol to very young audiences.

Cinema advertising is often more creative than TV advertising because the audiences are much more receptive and will be paying attention. For many firms, the cinema offers the only outlet for a filmed advertisement (owing to TV bans) and therefore it is worth spending a lot of money and effort on producing the adverts. In addition, the audience is predominantly intelligent and well-off, with an appreciation of visual entertainments, and they are therefore actively looking for a creative, entertaining advert.

Cinema is probably well underused in favour of television. It accounts for only 0.5 per cent of advertising expenditure in the UK (Advertising Association 1998), and yet it offers a relatively cheap way of reaching a key target audience.

CASE STUDY: PEARL AND DEAN

Any UK cinema-goer is familiar with the advertising company Pearl and Dean. The jingle which introduces the advertisement break is as much a part of the experience as the main movie, and the company has almost 40 per cent of the UK market for big-screen advertising.

Pearl and Dean was founded by two brothers, Ernie and Charles Pearl, and their friend Bob Dean in 1952. In 1969 the founders sold the company to British Lion, and after several changes of ownership the firm was sold in 1998 to SMG. Pearl and Dean (P&D) has always prided itself on providing a full service which, given the specialised nature of cinema advertising, is an important consideration. At the outset, P&D works with the advertising agency or the client to plan the campaign, which can include foyer advertising as well as on-screen advertising: P&D will even arrange promotional activities such as handing out free samples of products. When the advertisement itself is produced (in many cases it is simply the firm's TV advert, possibly with some adaptations), P&D will take it through the somewhat complex permissions process. Because all advertising shown in cinemas needs approval from both the Cinema Advertising Association and the British Board of Film Censors, there would be delays if the process is not handled by experts. In most cases, companies use videotape for their TV advertising, so P&D also provides a transfer and copying service to create the hundreds of copies needed on 35 mm film for distribution to the cinemas.

An integrated campaign organised by P&D can be extremely effective in reaching the young, affluent cinema audiences. For example, when hair cosmetics company Wella wanted to generate trials of its new Shock Waves products, it used P&D as a way of reaching the youth market. The campaign was run over the opening weekend of the new *Star Wars* movie and included foyer displays, an on-screen movie and free samples handed out in goody bags as the audience left the cinema. Attendance figures for the movie were calculated so that the company could provide the right number of samples (in this case 130,000), and P&D recruited and trained the people who handed out the bags. Each bag contained a money-off coupon so that Wella could track the responses.

Wella wanted to position Shock Waves as the cool product for teenagers, so it aimed to establish a presence in venues where there would be large numbers of teenagers. The opening of *Star Wars* was perfect for this. The redemption rate for the money-off coupons was exceptionally high, showing that the audience had liked the sample enough to buy more.

Companies who have used P&D include J. Sainsbury, which wanted to target families who were doing something together, Boddington's, the brewery, which wanted to run a humorous campaign aimed at a young audience, and Daewoo, the car manufacturer, which wanted to approach the over-25s with a promotion for the Matiz model. In each case, P&D was able to advise on which movies were likely to attract the target audience required, and to help with creative promotions (for example, in the Daewoo campaign P&D had promotional staff dressed as traffic wardens putting promotional material and free cinema tickets on the windscreens of cars in cinema car parks).

Cinema advertising has an enviable ability to reach specific target audiences: specific films attract specific audiences, and P&D is extremely well placed to advise companies on how to reach those audiences. With little competition, P&D looks set to succeed for many years to come.

QUESTIONS

1 How might a company seeking to target an older audience (for example, affluent 'greys' in their 50s and 60s) be able to use P&D?

2 Why do companies seeking a young audience use cinema advertising?

3 Why does P&D offer such a comprehensive service?

4 What advantages are there to advertisers in using cinema rather than TV?

5 What disadvantages are there in using cinema advertising?

SUMMARY

TV is undoubtedly the highest profile medium. It is the first medium most people think of when discussing advertising, and it is the one that attracts the most expenditure in terms both of buying airtime and of spending money on producing adverts. The main drawbacks are the cost and the ease with which viewers can avoid the adverts.

Radio has been described as 'a communication between two friends' (Manning 1982). It has an intimacy unrivalled by any other medium, since it is listened to in bed, in the car, in the home and at work. Because of this, radio is the closest medium to word-of-mouth, which is known to be one of the most powerful communications media.

Because radio requires some imagination on the part of the listener, it may be more involving than other media. The disadvantages of radio are that it is often used as a background (and therefore not fully listened to) and it cannot actually show the product. This may be part of the reason why radio is underused, in the UK at least.

Finally, cinema advertising is probably the most involving medium of all the forms of unsought advertising because the audience is unable to avoid the advertisement and is also likely to be appreciative of it and receptive to it.

Key points from the chapter are as follows:

- TV and radio are a part of people's lives in ways that no other media can match.

- TV has the capacity to model products in a realistic way.

- TV appeals to retailers more than any other medium.

- Most countries have strict government control on TV advertising content.

- Zapping and zipping undermines the effectiveness of TV advertising.

- TV advertising is expensive to produce and to air; its CPT (cost per thousand) often compares unfavourably with that of other media.

- Liking the advert usually leads to liking the product – but there may be exceptions to this general rule.

- Off-the-screen selling is often more effective than off-the-page mail order selling.

- The most important element in dealing with agencies and advert producers is giving a clear brief.

- Radio is an intimate, friendly medium.

- Radio is predominantly local, and therefore offers clear geographical segmentation, but also offers clear demographic segmentation in terms of types of audience per station or per time of day.

- Radio ads are quick and cheap to produce and air.

- Cinema audiences are young, relatively well-off, and watch the advertisements.

CHAPTER QUESTIONS

1 Why is radio similar to word-of-mouth communication?

2 Why do viewers zap (or zip) TV advertisements? What might be done to prevent this?

3 If the CPT for TV is unfavourable compared with a press advert, why should anyone use TV?

4 Explain the purpose of using off-the-screen selling.

5 How might radio adverts be used to support other media?

6 What categories of product might best be advertised in the cinema?

7 In terms of communications theories, why are cinema advertisements likely to be more effective than TV advertisements?

FURTHER READING

Conrad, J. J. (1983) *The TV Commercial – How It is Made*. New York: Rheinhold. For a TV commercial producer's view, this book has a lively (though overtly American) account of the nuts and bolts of making TV commercials. The text is liberally sprinkled with anecdotes, and although some of the technical aspects have now been superseded by new technology, it still provides a practical insight into the trials and problems of TV production.

Maitland, I. (1996) *How to Plan Radio Advertising*. London: Cassell. This book gives a comprehensive practitioner's guide to radio advertising.

Myers, G. (1994) *Words in Ads*. London: Edward Arnold. This is a fascinating guide to the linguistic aspects of advertising. The author is an expert on linguistics and the English language, and the book is written in an amusing and accessible way, with plenty of real-life examples.

REFERENCES

Advertising Association (1998) *Advertising Association Yearbook*. Henley: Advertising Association.

Biel, A. L. (1990) 'Love the ad. Buy the product?' *ADMAP*, **299**(September): 21–5.

Biel, A. L. and Bridgewater, C. A. (1990) 'Attributes of likeable television commercials', *Journal of Advertising Research*, **30**(3): 38–44.

Bolls, P. D., Meuhling, D. D. and Yoon, K. (2003) 'The effects of television commercial placing on viewers' attention and memory', *Journal of Marketing Communications*, **9**(1) 17–28.

Cova, B. (1997) 'Community and consumption; towards a definition of the linking value of products and services', *European Journal of Marketing*, **31**(3/4): 297–316.

Crawford, A-M. (1997) 'Digital revolution', *Marketing*, 3 July.

Jefkins, F. (1994) *Advertising*. London: M&E Handbooks.

Kneale, D. (1988) 'Zapping of TV ads appears pervasive', *Wall Street Journal*, 25 April.

Leiss, W., Kline, S. and Jhally, S. (1990) *Social Communication in Advertising: Persons, Products and Images of Well-being*. London: Routledge.

Manning, B. (1982) 'Friendly persuasion', *Advertising Age*, 13 September.

McKechnie, S. and Leather, P. (1998) 'Likeability as a measure of advertising effectiveness: the case of financial services', *Journal of Marketing Communications*, **4**: 63–85.

Mintel (1993) 'Advertising financial services', *Personal Financial Intelligence*, **1**: 1–48.

Oates, C., Blades, M., Barrie, G. and Don, J. (2003) 'Children's understanding of television advertising: a qualitative approach', *Journal of Marketing Communications*, **9**(2): 59–71.

Ostergaard, B. E. (ed.) (1997) *The Media in Western Europe*. London: Sage/Euromedia Research Group.

Pearl and Dean (2005) www.pearlanddean.com/marketdata/audience.html

Petty, R. E. and Cacioppo, J. T. (1983) 'Central and peripheral routes to persuasion: application to advertising', in Percy, L. and Woodside, A. G. (eds), *Advertising and Consumer Psychology*. Lexington, MA: Lexington Books.

Ritson, M. (2003) Assessing the value of advertising. London Business School.

Ritson, M. and Elliott, R. (1995) 'A model of advertising literacy: the praxology and cocreation of meaning', *Proceedings of the European Marketing Association Conference*. Paris: ESSEC.

Shankar, A. (1998) 'Adding value to the ads? On the increasing use of pop music in advertising', *Proceedings of the Academy of Marketing Conference, Sheffield*.

Stapel, J. (1991) 'Like the advertisement but does it interest me?', *ADMAP*, April.

Steenhuysen, J. (1994) 'Adland's new billion-dollar baby', *Advertising Age*, 11 April.

Wells, W. D. (1980) 'Liking and sales effectiveness: a hypothesis', *Topline*, **2**(1).

Yoon, K. (1995) 'Attitudes towards advertising held by the boomers and the busters: some facts and myths', *Journal of Marketing Communications*, **1**(1).

Zufryden, F. S., Pedrick, J. H. and Sankaralingam, A. (1993) 'Zapping and its impact on brand purchase behaviour', *Journal of Advertising Research*, **33**: 58–66.

5 Outdoor advertising

Objectives

After reading this chapter you should be able to:

- explain the advantages and disadvantages of outdoor media
- describe ways of designing billboards so as to attract maximum attention
- explain how outdoor advertising can tie in with other media
- compare the different forms of outdoor advertising
- describe some of the legal restrictions on advertising that both help and hinder outdoor advertising
- explain how ambient advertising makes its impact, and describe some of the techniques used

INTRODUCTION

Outdoor displays are the oldest form of advertising; such signs have been found in the ruins of Pompeii and in medieval towns throughout Europe. The term 'outdoor advertising' covers a number of different types of advertising: billboards, posters, advertising on street furniture such as litter bins and bus shelters, posters on the sides of buses and taxis, posters inside buses and trains, and even airships, blimps and hot-air balloons.

A relatively recent development in outdoor advertising is ambient advertising, in which the medium becomes the message. Ambient adverts become part of the environment, creating an impact much greater than that of a simple poster or billboard.

BILLBOARDS

Billboards are probably the most ubiquitous and obtrusive of outdoor advertising media. Most vacant sites in cities have billboards in front of them, and they appear on the sides of buildings, by the sides of main roads, and even mounted on trailers and towed through the streets. Billboards have the following advantages.

- *Low cost*. A billboard poster is relatively cheap to design and print, and site rentals are low compared with other media.

- *Can be localised for geographical segmentation*. Either a group of sites can be booked within a specific target area, or one site can be booked to promote a local retail outlet, for example.

- *Can be used seasonally for short periods*. The posters can be changed readily, and the products advertised can be adjusted according to the season.

- *The posters can be easily changed to suit changing circumstances*. For example, during a general election the posters are changed regularly to reflect the changing issues or to make use of a political opportunity.

One of the major advantages of billboards is their usefulness in teaser campaigns. A teaser campaign is one in which an initial advertisement is shown which in itself means nothing. Later on, a further advertisement reveals the 'punch line' of the first advertisement. For example, Elf Aquitaine, the French petroleum company, ran a series of billboard adverts which said 'Now, for Britain itself . . .'. This advert was intriguing because the meaning was obscure, raising a question as to exactly *what* was for Britain itself. The **denouement** came after a few weeks, when the billboard sites were pasted over with 'Now, for Britain it's Elf'. The initial interest was satisfied by the answer, and the pun in the advert helped the company's name to stick in consumers' minds.

Billboard advertising is widely used during political campaigns because the posters can be changed quickly as different political issues come to the forefront of the debate. Often the billboard campaigns are controversial enough to become news in themselves, thus increasing the impact (see Chapter 6). For this reason, billboards are useful in reinforcing PR campaigns and in corporate advertising.

In recent years, billboards have been widely used to promote websites. One of the paradoxes of the Internet has been that generating hits on the website has relied heavily on the use of traditional media, and since web addresses need to be entered accurately if the site is to be accessed, permanent print media rather than broadcast media are the favoured vehicles. Billboards have the advantage of high visibility and permanence, so that a commuter would be able to note down an interesting web address, or would be sensitised to a print advert in a magazine or newspaper.

Billboard advertising can be more useful in generating controversy than other media because of its public nature. In most countries, posters do not need prior approval from regulatory bodies, so it is possible to produce highly controversial campaigns such as the Europe-wide and much-studied Benetton advertising campaigns. The shock value of such posters creates much more publicity than can be accounted for by the relatively low cost of the billboard campaign.

The lack of regulation of billboard advertising means that it is a medium which can be used where other, more regulated media cannot. Alcohol advertisers make extensive use of billboards, and in some countries (notably Ireland), posters advertising alcohol appear on almost half the billboards.

Advertising folklore has it that two-thirds of consumer decision making takes place immediately before the purchase, at the point of sale (Brierley 1995). Billboards are often used as a last reminder before purchasing, which is why they are widely used for advertising frequently purchased items such as soft drinks and snacks. Also, because billboards are large they can accommodate life-size pictures of large products such as cars.

Billboards have disadvantages too, of course, as set out in Table 5.1.

Because of these limitations, billboards are often found to work best as reminders of campaigns run in other media. As a support medium, billboards can be very effective; they can be used as reminders of TV campaigns or press advertising, and therefore they have a strong role in an integrated communications strategy. Since billboards are by their nature an unsought medium, they are probably best used for activating needs rather than giving detailed product information. The exception to this is inside transport advertising, which is covered later in this chapter.

Tactical issues

Billboards come in a variety of sizes, from small **double crown** bills (30 × 20 inches) to 48-sheet or even 96-sheet panels. The sheet size is measured in double crown, so a 48-sheet billboard is 48 times the size of a double crown and measures 10 feet by

TABLE 5.1	Disadvantages of billboard advertising

Disadvantage	Explanation
Limited capacity	Since billboards are usually read literally in passing, the copy must be very brief, and the message has to be conveyed in very few words. This places a premium on good visual imagery
Difficult to evaluate	Audience figures are hard to measure, because the audience may be walking, driving or riding past on a bus. Traffic counts are helpful, but even so, the number of people who may have looked at the billboard will be hard to assess
Difficult to target	Segmentation is not as simple as with magazine advertising. Segmentation by ethnic group may be possible in some cities. Segmentation by age, for example, would be virtually impossible
Vulnerability	Billboards are often vandalised or defaced
Noise	The audience's mood may not be ideal. Apart from the distractions of dealing with traffic, and a preoccupation with the purpose of the journey, the outside environment may be characterised by heat, dust and noise, all of which tend to make the individual less than receptive to marketing messages. Sometimes this can be turned to the advertiser's advantage; advertising a car's air-conditioning system on a billboard located on a notorious bottleneck can work very well.
Environmental restrictions	In some countries there is strict legislation on the design, location and number of billboards. This is a response to excessive proliferation of outdoor advertising, which can be environmentally damaging in the sense that it obscures views of the countryside.

20 feet. Although the size is 48 double crowns, the poster is not made up of 48 separate sheets of paper; there may only be four or six actual sheets of paper in a 48-sheet billboard.

In the past two decades **ultravision** displays have become more widespread. These are displays which have rotating slats so that three separate advertisements can be shown on the same site. These are usually used on very busy, premium-rated sites. The movement of the signs is eye-catching, and of course the advertisers pay somewhat less than they would have to pay for sole ownership of the site. These billboards are often illuminated to increase the impact at night. Miniature versions of these displays are used in banks and building societies to advertise financial services; again, the rotation of the slats is eye-catching for people passing by, or for those queuing inside the bank.

In the UK there are over 180 outside advertising contractors, six of which account for around 82 per cent of the outdoor sites (Harrison 1993). Nationally, Mills and Allen have 29 per cent of the sites, but the distribution is not even, and in some areas local contractors have the bulk of the sites. This can make media buying difficult, since it is often necessary to deal with several contractors in order to get an even coverage nationwide.

In the UK, the audience research for billboards is carried out by **Outdoor Site Classification and Audience Research (OSCAR)**. OSCAR estimates audiences for campaigns and site locations, and provides industry statistics. The standard TV regions are used to plan billboard advertising so that multimedia campaigns are easier to plan, but within this overall structure advertisers often use geodemographic classification systems such as **A Classification of Residential Neighbourhoods (ACORN)** to fine-tune the poster location. Certain roads may be targeted within a given area, or billboards sited near key retail outlets.

Outdoor advertising offers high OTS (opportunities to see) for a relatively low cost, but the problem for a media buyer lies in comparing sites. Because OSCAR's figures are calculated on the basis of OTS, all the best sites might be along the same street. This would not be a good basis on which to buy space. OSCAR's estimates also do not take account of seasonal variations, which can be considerable, and of course the research cannot take account of a driver's route, so it is impossible to say whether an individual driver will pass one, none or all the poster sites in a given town. Although a sample of individual drivers can be monitored using computerised navigational systems, this will only be possible for a small, and therefore probably unrepresentative, sample.

On the positive side, many of the viewers of posters are bus travellers, whose routes can be fairly accurately estimated. The discrepancies arise here because it is difficult to know who gets on or off the bus at particular points on the route. A good way to overcome this problem is to put the advert inside the bus.

TRANSPORT ADVERTISING

Transport advertising falls into two categories: outside transport advertising and inside transport advertising. **Outside transport advertising** is essentially billboards and posters on the sides of buses and taxis. In some countries, advertising is also carried on the outsides of trains, but since trains are not usually easily visible by passers-by this is far less common. The advantages and disadvantages of this medium are much the same as for static billboard sites, although this time the medium is moving and the audience may or may not be. The major drawback is that there is even less control over who sees the adverts. On the other hand, there is (potentially) much greater coverage in terms of the number of people who are exposed to the adverts as the vehicle travels along its route.

In some cities it is possible to arrange for the whole vehicle to be painted, which is called **livery**. This is an extremely eye-catching medium because of the movement of the vehicle. Livery, like a lot of transport advertising, is also an example of ambient advertising. There is more on this later in the chapter.

Posters sited low down on the backs of buses are at motorists' eye level, which means that they will almost certainly be read while traffic is not moving. These sites are often used by car accessory manufacturers, emergency breakdown services and service stations.

Inside transport advertising consists of posters inside bus and train stations, and inside the vehicles themselves, and it has rules of its own. First, unlike almost any other form of advertising, the adverts can and often do contain substantial amounts of copy. The reason for this is that passengers often have nothing else to do but read the adverts while waiting for their train or bus to arrive. Also, advertising inside the vehicles themselves gives the passengers something to look at rather than each other. On crowded transport, where passengers prefer to avoid eye contact, this means that the adverts are often read several times over in the course of a journey.

For example, on the London Underground, posters are often placed on the tunnel wall opposite the platform. Many of these have three to five hundred words of detailed copy about the products being advertised, which (in any other medium) would mean that they would be skipped past, zipped or zapped. Yet tube travellers are almost grateful for having something to read while they wait.

Advertising on stations is more tightly targeted than advertising on the street because it will be seen mainly by commuters. Zoning is possible to an extent, but specific campaigns can benefit by this target audience. For example, a campaign by the UK charity the Samaritans featured posters at stations and on bus stops. Those in the suburbs read 'Can't face going to work? Call the Samaritans', whereas those in the city centres read 'Can't face going home? Call the Samaritans'. This campaign targeted depressed or suicidal people in a direct but compassionate way, leading to a substantial increase in calls to the organisation. As a side issue, many other people saw the posters which raised the profile of the organisation, which, as a registered charity, relies on contributions from the public.

Adshel, a UK agency which sells advertising space on bus shelters, ran a series of adverts in *Campaign*, the trade periodical for the advertising industry, showing bus shelters with adverts aimed at individuals. For example, one poster read, 'Pardon me, Madam. That's right, madam with the pearls, the Asprey bag and the beautiful, deep winter tan.' The adverts on the bus shelters were not 'real'; they were intended to show the potential that street advertising has for getting to specific types of consumer. Copywriters are often told to make the advertisements personal, and these adverts do that admirably.

Designing outdoor advertising

With the exception of inside transport advertising, outdoor advertising has to be designed using a minimum of copy and a maximum of imagery. The adverts are not likely to be read in detail and may be noticed only peripherally by passers-by. Icons, symbols and indices play a strong part in establishing the advert in the viewer's perception (see Chapter 1), and therefore many billboard adverts are heavily symbolic.

One problem presented by this is that the creative people will almost certainly end up using stereotypes, because this is the quickest way to convey the message. Adverts which are personalised almost inevitably use sex-specific pronouns. Whereas, in most writing, authors try to avoid using 'he' and 'she', the ad copy-writer has little choice because neutral words are less appealing (DeVoe 1956). 'He' and 'she' typically refer to someone known to the reader; 'you' is, of course, the reader, and when an inappropriate reader sees this in the copy, the message will be ignored. Myers (1994) gives the example of the famous First World War recruiting poster showing General Kitchener pointing out of the poster towards the reader, with the slogan 'Your country needs you'. Clearly an 85-year-old woman reading this would know that Kitchener was not trying to recruit her, but a man of conscription age would know that it meant him.

The symbolism in the recruiting poster is clear. Kitchener was, at the time, a charismatic and very successful general who had made a name for himself in several previous wars, including the Sudan and the Boer War. The potential recruit was being asked to identify with Kitchener, who for the purposes of the advertisement was personifying the country. The potential recruit's patriotic feelings were being linked to a sense of purpose about the war.

Language can also be used as a sign. Using French in an advertisement, for example, conveys an image of chicness or sophistication which goes beyond the actual meanings of the words in the slogan. Even non-French speakers probably understand what, for instance, 'je ne sais quoi' and 'savoir-faire' mean because these phrases are in common use in Britain. In Australia, the use of Aboriginal words (such as 'corroboree') can convey a uniquely Australian image, because the words are very specific to Australia. The same applies to slang terms, and sometimes to slang terms which are transferred across borders. For example, most British people would associate the word 'barbie' with Australia, where it is the slang term for 'barbecue'. Most Americans would associate it with Mattel's Barbie doll. Conversely, such local terms may have no meaning outside their home countries: few Britons would know the common South African word for a barbecue, which is 'braai'.

Use of accents (different pronunciation) and dialects (different words) can also convey impressions of wealth, of solid working-class earthiness, of traditional values or of modern go-getting. Accents and dialects can be conveyed in billboards by spelling the words out, and there are standard ways of spelling some dialect words (for instance, the North country 'nowt' meaning 'nothing'). This foregrounds the information and makes the communication more noticeable, a prime consideration in billboard advertising, which is largely a passive medium. Adverts using accent are more common in the UK than in most other countries, due to the wide range of regional accents.

As mentioned earlier in this chapter, billboard advertising lends itself to teaser campaigns. The essence of designing such an advert is to make the initial statement intriguing, and the denouement a logical extension of the initial statement. The overall effect should be to make the reader think 'Of course!' when the denouement comes. Dialect, language and accent can be useful here because the use of puns is common.

AIRSHIPS, BLIMPS, BANNER-TOWING AND HOT-AIR BALLOONS

Airborne advertisements have the advantages of being very eye-catching and of being visible over a large area. The message is usually confined to the brand name only, although banners towed from aircraft can carry more copy. Unfortunately, these are often illegible unless the aircraft flies too low for safety.

Probably the best-known airship is Goodyear's. In itself, the airship conveys a message, symbolising unhurried freedom from care (Bounds 1994). Airships attract attention, and therefore the brand name is seen by almost everyone it passes over.

A TV camera mounted on an airship is a device sometimes used at major sporting events and rock concerts. This means that the airship gives triple value for money: it will be filmed as part of the coverage of the event; it will be mentioned by the commentators each time the view switches to the camera in the airship; and it will be seen by the audience at the event. However, the cost of operating an airship is high – about £200,000 per month. This must be considered against the cost of alternative forms of promotion; the airship can often work out to be the cheapest option.

A smaller, cheaper and simpler alternative to the airship is the **blimp**. These inflatables cost around £20,000 and can be tethered above business premises. Although initially they were as eye-catching as airships, they have become commonplace and consequently have lost a great deal of their advertising value. As with any other medium which relies on novelty, blimps can quickly lose their impact if overused, so the best way to use them is to change their location regularly (perhaps from branch to branch of a large firm) so as to expose them to a new audience each time.

Banner-towing from light aircraft is a high impact way of getting a message across to people in a particular location. It is a popular medium at beaches, because the target audience is usually facing towards the sea and concentrated in a long, narrow area. Because of constraints on the size of banner and the height at which the aircraft can safely fly, the signs can be hard to read, so copy needs to be kept as short as possible.

An extension of banner-towing is **skywriting**, where the aircraft uses a smoke trail to write a message in the sky. This form of advertising is illegal in the UK due to the risk of collisions between aircraft, but is still legal in many other countries.

Hot-air balloons have proved extraordinarily effective in corporate advertising (see Chapter 6). The balloons can be made in the shape of the product (if the product is a simple shape, such as a can of beer), and they are often used at displays and festivals where perhaps a dozen or more balloons are flown. Their major drawback is that they are affected by the weather, and even a moderate breeze can mean that they cannot fly. In most countries their use is seasonal, and the reliability of the medium is therefore much limited.

There is, at present, little or no academic research into flying media. There are also no industry guidelines or regulatory bodies apart from the civil aviation bodies, whose concern is for safety in the air rather than advertising value. This means that the effectiveness of the media is highly debatable, although there is a strong feeling that airships, blimps, banners and balloons are all eye-catching and therefore likely to be effective.

AMBIENT ADVERTISING

Ambient advertising is a relative newcomer to the outdoor advertising scene and as such has not been researched by academics to any great extent. A precise definition of ambient advertising appears to be lacking, although examples abound.

Apart from the objectives of the campaign, the prospective 'ambient advertiser' needs to consider the relationship between the ambient medium being used, the advertised product or service, and the proximity to the point of sale. Ambient advertising makes the message become part of the surrounding environment in which the consumer operates. In ambient advertising, the medium becomes the message. For example, a campaign run on the London Underground involved replacing all the hanging straps in carriages with empty bottles of underarm deodorant. Commuters holding the straps were in a situation where their underarm odour would be obvious to fellow passengers, so the impact of the deodorant bottles was greatly heightened. In this campaign there was a clear connection between the advertised product and the ambient medium.

Ambient advertising works best when it is either close to the point of purchase or close to the location of the problem. Kellogg's NutriGrain bar was promoted as a snack for commuters who have missed breakfast, so the company arranged for the product to be advertised on bus and train tickets. Many travellers were reported as having tried the bars as a result (buying them from station newsstands). The NutriGrain campaign is an example of placing the advert close to the problem. Petrol nozzles at filling stations often carry advertising for products which are available from the filling station shop: this is an example of placing the advert close to the point of sale. Volkswagen was successful in using the nozzles to promote the fuel economy of the Golf TDI: this campaign is another example of placing the advert close to the problem. Promotional messages placed on super-market shopping carts can fulfil both functions, being close to the problem and the point of sale.

Technological advances are likely to increase both the effectiveness and the prevalence of ambient advertising. For example, the Etrema company has devel-oped a device which sticks to shop windows and turns them into loudspeakers. This means that the shop window will be able to 'speak' to customers and tell them about their contents (Grapentine 2003).

Some ambient advertising is outstanding in its impact: art installations in shopping malls or train stations can cause crowds to gather. Advertisements printed on eggs create an impact at breakfast time, and adverts printed on the rising barriers in car parks are guaranteed an audience. When Nike constructed a robotic installation showing two tennis players hitting a ball the length of the platform at Wimbledon train station to coincide with the 1997 tennis tournament, some people went to the station just to see the installation.

Table 5.2 lists some examples of ambient media.

TABLE 5.2   Ambient advertising media

Environment	Example of locations	Examples of ambient media vehicles
Retail	Shopping centres, car parks, petrol stations, supermarkets, post offices, fast-food outlets	Trolleys, tickets, takeaway lids, postcard racks, floor advertising, eggs, carrier bags
Leisure	Cinemas, sports stadia, pubs, clubs, restaurants, fitness clubs, music venues	Postcard racks, toilet wall adverts, beer mats, washroom floor adverts
Travel	The Underground, trains and buses (with vehicles and stations), bus stops, petrol and service stations, airports	Liveried trains, planes, buses, taxis, etc., petrol pump nozzles, stair riser adverts, car park barriers, tickets
Other	Aerial and mobile media	Sponsored balloons, skywriting
Academic	Schools, universities and colleges, libraries	Posters, video screens, bookmarks, payroll, litter bins
Community	Playgrounds, emergency services	Sponsorship opportunities
Corporate	Council offices, company buildings	Payroll advertising

Source: Shankar and Horton (1999)

Ambient media can be classified according to campaign objectives and proximity to the point of sale, as shown in Table 5.3.

TABLE 5.3	Classification of ambient media

| Objectives of campaign | Proximity to the point of sale | |
	High	Low
Strategic: designed to create long-term effects	Toilet walls (e.g. anti drink-drive campaigns)	Stunt ambient media designed to generate publicity, sky banners, skywriting, art installations, painted aeroplanes (e.g. blue Pepsi Concorde), railway platform advertising
Tactical: designed to create immediate responses	Petrol pump nozzles, toilet walls, in-store floor advertising, tickets, supermarket till rolls, credit card vouchers, stair risers, shopping trolleys	Ticket advertising, supermarket till rolls, credit card vouchers, betting slips

Source: Shankar and Horton (1999)

Traditional marketing communications techniques are becoming less effective as markets fragment, costs increase, audiences diminish and clutter worsens (Evans *et al.* 1996), therefore, new routes for communicating with consumers and customers are being sought, and this means in turn that ambient advertising is likely to grow. Ambient advertising offers the following advantages:

• Used close to the point of purchase, ambient campaigns are cheaper to produce than sales promotions, and (compared with price reductions) give a point-of-purchase incentive with no negative profit-reduction effects.

• Well-executed ambient campaigns enhance brand image.

• Creative campaigns often obtain press coverage, some of them being designed with this in mind.

• Ambient campaigns are very effective for activating needs.

Table 5.4 maps ambient advertising against Ehrenberg's ATRN model of advertising effects (Ehrenberg 1997; see also Barnard and Ehrenberg 1997).

TABLE 5.4   Mapping of ambient advertising against the ATRN model

Stage	Explanation	Role of ambient advertising
Awareness	Consciousness of a new brand is followed by interest	Consciousness is developed by high impact, innovative campaigns
Trial	Trial purchase of the brand may occur, perhaps with the consumer in a sceptical frame of mind	Ambient advertising close to the point of sale may be enough to make the consumer choose one brand rather than another
Reinforcement	Satisfactory use of the brand will encourage further purchase, or even establish a habitual propensity to buy the brand	Ambient advertising only really has a reminder role to play at this stage, and is probably no better than other advertising at doing this, except that the more spectacular exercises may provoke a feeling of pride by association in some consumers
Nudging	Propensity to buy may be enhanced or decreased by the 'nudging' effect of advertising – either the firm's own or that of competitors	Ambient advertising is reputed to have the ability to 'nudge' better than any other form of advertising since it has greater proximity both to the point of purchase and the point at which the need arises

To summarise the position, it would appear that environmental stimuli are important ingredients in consumers' decision-making processes right up to the point of purchase – especially for low involvement products. Therefore, being nudged by appropriately placed advertising stimuli close to the point of sale can enhance the probability of purchase. Consumers tend to exhibit little pre-purchase decision making for low involvement products (Foxall and Goldsmith 1994), and some studies have shown that 70 per cent of all decisions to purchase specific brands are made inside the store (POPAI 1995). Trolley advertising makes up to a 19 per cent difference in purchase of specific brands (Shankar 1999a), which demonstrates the power of ambient advertising in nudging consumers at the point of sale.

The ambient advertising industry is characterised by a large number of small suppliers (200 in the UK alone), with one firm handling petrol pump nozzles, another supermarket trolleys, and so on. There is no industry-wide evaluation system (as there is for TV advertising and press advertising), so there are no objective measures by which the success or failure of the campaigns can be assessed. For example, there is no organisation that can estimate how many people picked up a particular petrol nozzle and thus saw the advertisement (Shankar 1999b).

Much ambient advertising depends on surprise and novelty, so unless an advertiser can guarantee to be the first to use a particular vehicle, the choice of vehicle needs to be considered carefully. Some vehicles will almost certainly continue to work for some time to come (for example, petrol nozzle advertising) whereas others rely on surprise value to a greater extent (for example, the deodorant bottles described earlier in the chapter).

In the future, it seems that ambient media will grow. Although great creativity is involved in producing the campaigns, the impact is high and the cost is relatively low. Publicity spin-offs can generate additional interest, and the campaigns can easily be orchestrated within an integrated marketing communications approach in order to support, and be supported by, other communications tools.

CASE STUDY: JO LIVELY

In most of the developed world, governments and others recognise that there is a rapidly growing problem of obesity among children as well as adults. The availability of cheap food, the lack of exercise brought about by increasing use of cars, and the growth in sedentary entertainments such as television and electronic games, is leading to a ballooning population. Even in Australia, which has had an official government policy of encouraging participation in sport for over 50 years, there is a problem of childhood obesity.

This is where Jo Lively steps in. Jo is a cartoon character of no specific sex, the owner of a dog called Jive who chases Jo's Frisbee. Jo Lively promotes healthy living, using the slogan 'Eat well, live well, play well'. Jo is the invention of Sydney artist David Egan, who is best known for his serious artwork but who says, 'It's good to allow people to see there's another side to my work.' What is unique about the campaign is that it is not a government initiative at all – it comes from the advertising industry itself.

Advertising agencies, media owners and trade associations came together to create the Jo Lively campaign as a response to criticisms concerning the promotion of junk food and snack food to children. Almost the whole of the Australian advertising industry is involved, including the Outdoor Advertising Association of Australia (OAAA). On 21 June 2005, the OAAA launched its Jo Lively campaign on billboards throughout the country. The billboards serve three functions: they act as reminders for the TV, radio and Internet advertising; they promote the campaign to those who have not yet seen the campaign in the other media (or who perhaps are out of reach of TV broadcasts); and they drive people (primarily parents) to the Jo Lively website. The campaign included billboards and posters sited in places where children would be likely to see them. The simplicity of the slogan echoes the 'Slip, slop, slap' campaign of a few years ago, aimed at combating skin cancer, and the appeal of the cartoon character ensures that the message will resonate with children.

The campaign is likely to run for the foreseeable future. From the viewpoint of the advertising industry, it represents good PR as well as demonstrating the power of outdoor advertising, and from the viewpoint of parents and children it offers useful advice and help – most parents want their children to grow up healthy, and this campaign gives them the help they need in persuading children to eat up their vegetables!

Questions

1 Why use a billboard campaign?

2 Why should the advertising industry fund such a campaign?

3 How might fast-food companies feel about the campaign?

4 What other forms of outdoor advertising might be appropriate for the campaign?

5 What are the possible problems with using outdoor advertising for this campaign?

SUMMARY

Outdoor advertising covers the spectrum of audience involvement, from the passive medium of billboards through to the involving ambient media. At the most passive end, the giant hoardings which appear in every city are used to show brief glimpses of products, brands and corporate slogans to passers-by. This medium, although difficult to research and evaluate, is still one of the most widely used advertising methods. Further along the scale, outside transport advertising fulfils much the same function in much the same way, but this time both the medium and the audience move. Greater impact is achieved by using illuminated or rotating billboards.

Inside transport advertising has more impact because it is read by people who are waiting for, or travelling on, buses, trains and trams. Finally, the art installations and stunts of the ambient advertiser have the most impact of all, sometimes actually drawing crowds.

Key points from the chapter are as follows:

• Billboards are a relatively cheap but passive medium.

• Billboards are very effective for support advertising and for teaser campaigns.

• Audiences for outdoor advertising are difficult to measure.

• Inside transportation adverts are actually read by the audience.

• Ambient advertising makes the medium the message and builds the message into the surrounding environment.

CHAPTER QUESTIONS

1 How could billboard adverts be made more interactive?

2 What products might best be advertised on eggs? Why?

3 Why might inside transport advertising be more effective than outside transport advertising?

4 In terms of perception theory, why are billboard adverts likely to be less effective than TV advertising?

5 What factors mitigate the unreliability of hot-air balloons?

FURTHER READING

Myers, G. (1994) *Words in Ads*. London: Edward Arnold. Few textbooks give more than a passing coverage of outdoor media. For a view of the use of words in ads, this book is difficult to beat.

Ogilvy, D. (1983) *Ogilvy on Advertising*. London: Pan. This has a good section on poster advertising, admitting that posters work, but not knowing why. Ogilvy was one of the giants of the advertising industry: this book is an inspirational read!

Most general advertising books have a small section on outdoor advertising.

REFERENCES

Barnard, N. and Ehrenberg, A. (1997) 'Advertising: strongly persuasive or nudging?', *Journal of Advertising Research* January/February, **37**(1): 21–31.

Bounds, W. (1994) 'Fuji's spirits soar as its blimp is winner of a World Cup contest', *Wall Street Journal*, 21 June.

Brierley, S. (1995) *The Advertising Handbook*. London: Routledge.

DeVoe, M. (1956) *Effective Advertising Copy*. New York: Macmillan.

Ehrenberg, A. (1997) 'How do consumers buy a new brand?', *ADMAP*, March.

Evans, M., O'Malley, L. and Patterson, M. (1996) 'Direct marketing communications in the UK: a study of growth, past, present and future', *Journal of Marketing Communications*, **2**(March): 51–65.

Foxall, G. and Goldsmith, R. E. (1994) *Consumer Psychology for Marketing*. London: Routledge.

Grapentine, T. (2003) 'Window shopping', *Marketing Research*, **15**(4): 5.

Harrison, D. (1993) 'Case for a specialist', *ADMAP*, April.

Myers, G. (1994) *Words in Ads*. London: Edward Arnold.

POPAI (1995) 'Point of purchase consumer buying habits study', reprinted in Shimp, T. A. (ed.) (1997) *Advertising, Promotion and Supplemental Aspects of Integrated Marketing Communications*, 4th edn. Fort Worth, TX: Dryden Press.

Shankar, A. (1999a) 'Ambient media: advertising's new opportunity?', *International Journal of Advertising*, **18**(3).

Shankar, A. (1999b) 'Advertising's imbroglio', *Journal of Marketing Communications*, **5**(1): 1–17.

Shankar, A. and Horton, B. (1999) 'Ambient media: advertising's new media opportunity?', *International Journal of Advertising*, **18**(3): 305–22.

6 Public relations and corporate image

Objectives

After reading this chapter you should be able to:

- describe how public relations operates
- explain the basics of writing press releases
- explain how product placement works
- show how to prepare for and plan press conferences
- explain the purpose and practice of corporate image advertising
- explain the role of sponsorship in generating publicity and positive corporate image

INTRODUCTION

Public relations – PR – is about creating favourable images of the company or organisation in the minds of consumers. It is often associated with creating a news story or event that brings the product or company to the public attention, but in fact PR goes a lot further than this and uses many more tools and techniques.

PR is concerned with the long-term reputation of the organisation rather than with short-term marketing objectives. There is even some debate about whether PR belongs with marketing at all, since PR professionals do not measure their success in financial terms whereas marketers often do. This chapter looks at PR from a marketers' standpoint and concentrates mainly on those aspects which are marketing related.

PUBLIC RELATIONS

Public relations is defined as 'the planned and sustained effort to establish and maintain goodwill and mutual understanding between an organisation and its publics: customers, employees, shareholders, trade bodies, suppliers, Government officials, and society in general' (Insititute of Public Relations 1984). The PR managers have the task of coordinating all the activities that make up the public face of the organisation, and will have some or all of the following activities to handle:

- organising press conferences
- staff training workshops
- events such as annual dinners
- handling incoming criticisms or complaints
- grooming senior management for the press or for TV appearances
- internal marketing, setting the organisation's culture towards a customer orientation

The basic routes by which PR operates are word of mouth, press and TV news stories, and personal recommendation. The aim is to put the firm and its products into people's minds and conversations in a positive way. Because the information appears as news, it tends to carry more weight. PR is not advertising, because it is not paid for directly (even though there is usually some cost attached in terms of paying somebody to write the press release and also in creating a news story). Advertising can be both informative and persuasive, but PR is used for conveying information only, and it certainly should not be considered to be free advertising as the costs attached can be substantial.

Here are some examples of good PR activities:

- A press release saying that a company has developed a way of recycling rubbish from landfills to produce plastics.

- The company sponsors a major charitable or sporting event (for example, the London Marathon or a famine-relief project).

- An announcement that one of the firm's senior executives has been seconded to a major government job-creation programme.

- The Body Shop requires all its franchise operations to run projects to benefit their local communities. This gives a positive image of the company to the community, and also gives the staff pride in working for a caring firm.

- McDonald's counters the negative publicity from environmental pressure groups by running litter patrols outside its restaurants.

These examples have in common that they are newsworthy and interesting, that they put the companies concerned in a good light, and that they encourage people to talk about the companies in a positive way.

A good press release can be much more effective than advertising, for the following reasons:

- The space in the medium (newspaper, magazine or whatever) is free, so there is better use of the promotional budget.

- The message carries enhanced credibility because it is in the editorial part of the paper.

- The message is more likely to be read because, whereas readers tend to skip past the advertisements, their purpose in buying the paper is to read the news stories.

Like people, organisations have needs; a structure for these (based on Maslow's hierarchy, see Chapter 1) was developed by Pearson (1980). PR is helpful in meeting all the organisation's needs, but particularly those nearer the top of the hierarchy. Table 6.1 shows Pearson's hierarchy of organisational needs, with the lowest, most basic needs at the beginning of the table, and higher needs at the end.

TABLE 6.1	The hierarchy of organisational needs

Organisational need	Requirements	Typical PR activity
Output	Money, machines, manpower, materials	Staff programmes to attract the right people
Survival	Cash flow, profits, share performance, customers	Publicity aimed at customers; events publicising the firm and its products
Morale	Employee job satisfaction	Staff newsletters, morale-boosting activities such as staff parties etc.
Acceptability	Approval by the external stakeholders (shareholders, government, customers, suppliers, society in general)	External PR, shareholder reports, lobbying of government departments and MPs, events for suppliers and customers, favourable press releases
Leadership	Having a respected position in the company's chosen field; this could be customer satisfaction, employee involvement, industry leadership in technology, or several of these	Corporate image-building exercises, customer-care activities, publicity about new products and technological advances, sponsorship of research in universities, sponsorship of the arts

Like Maslow's hierarchy, Pearson's hierarchy is useful as a concept but less useful as a practical guide because so many firms deviate from the order in which the needs are met. For example, when Sony Corporation was founded by Akio Morita (and others) just after the Second World War, the directors decided that corporate unity and staff involvement would begin almost from day one, at a time when (due to post-war shortages) the company was having difficulty getting materials to work with and a factory to operate from. Morita arranged for the employees to have a company uniform so that the distinction between management and staff would be less obvious, and also to give the outside world a good impression of the firm (Morita *et al.* 1986). Incidentally, this also had a practical aspect – many of the employees had only ragged clothes or the remnants of their army uniforms, so Morita was able to ensure loyalty because so many of his staff literally had nothing else to wear except the company uniform.

PR activities cover a whole range of issues and should not be considered solely as a publicity device. PR has a strategic role to play in maintaining the organisation's reputation; it has a key role to play in relationship marketing (see Chapter 9) since it is concerned with building a long-term favourable image rather than gaining a quick sale. Relationship marketing is often compared to courtship and marriage: PR is concerned with making a good impression before the first 'date' and with maintaining a good relationship during the 'courtship' and 'marriage'. To extend the analogy, PR ensures that the company is wearing its best clothes and is on its best behaviour, and remembers anniversaries and birthdays.

PR and staff

PR is largely about sending information and creating the right image for organisations and products, but it is also concerned with creating favourable impressions in people's minds. It is rarely, if ever, connected with directly bringing in business, and in this respect it differs from the other tools in the promotional mix. Although most of the time and for most activities PR will be the responsibility of a press agent or PR officer, PR is the responsibility of everybody who comes into contact with people outside the organisation. This will include the 'front-liners', the people whose day-to-day work brings them into contact with outsiders. For example:

- receptionists
- telephonists
- van/lorry drivers
- warehouse staff
- serving staff in the canteen

This is apart from the marketing staff, such as salespeople, who come into contact with outsiders as part of the overt marketing effort. In a sense, everybody in the organisation must take some responsibility for PR, since everybody in the organisation goes home after work (and discusses their company with friends and families).

In this context, a bad approach to PR (but one that is all too common) is to hire somebody with a nice smile and a friendly voice to sit by the telephone to handle complaints and smooth over any problems that arise. This is a fire-fighting or **reactive PR** approach.

A better approach to PR is to encourage all the staff to feel positive about the company. This is done by ensuring that everybody knows, in simple language, what the organisation is doing, what the policies are and what the company's overall aims are. Most people would like to think they are working for a good, responsible, successful organisation; it is part of the job of PR to ensure that this is communicated to staff. This is sometimes done by using a slogan or company motto to sum up its main aim. Table 6.2 contains some examples.

TABLE 6.2	Corporate slogans

Example	Explanation
'We're Number, Two, so we try harder' (Avis)	This communicates to staff that the company is among the biggest, but that their efforts to 'try harder' are recognised and appreciated. It also conveys a valuable image to customers'
'Everything we do is driven by you' (Ford)	This emphasises the customer orientation of the company, that Ford is not aiming merely to make as much money as possible but is also looking out for customers' interests
'Your natural resource' (Great Southern Energy of Australia)	The company emphasises its rural New South Wales roots and its honesty and integrity

Internal PR uses staff newsletters, training programmes and social events to convey a positive image. Because most of the front-liners are working away from the company's headquarters, the PR process has to be handled by persuasion, not through diktat. It would be impossible for PR staff to be everywhere at once, following people around to ensure that they say and do the 'right' things. There is more on the detail of internal PR later in the chapter.

PR and the press

Usually, **external PR** communicates through the news media. Newspapers and magazines earn their money mainly through paid advertising, but they attract readers by carrying stimulating articles about topics of interest to the readership.

Figure 6.1 shows the relationship between publicity, PR and press relations. PR occupies the overall strategic role, with publicity (creating news) and press relations (ensuring that news is printed) occupying the tactical positions.

Often, a PR manager or agent will be an ex-journalist who understands what is newsworthy and what is not, and will be able to issue press releases about the company that are actually published. Table 6.3 shows the criteria according to which press releases must be produced if they are to stand a chance of being published.

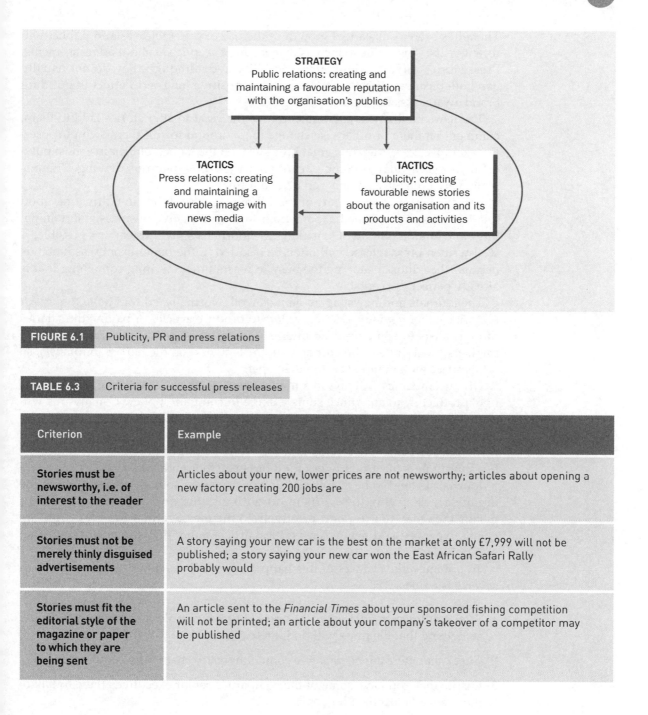

FIGURE 6.1   Publicity, PR and press relations

TABLE 6.3   Criteria for successful press releases

Criterion	Example
Stories must be newsworthy, i.e. of interest to the reader	Articles about your new, lower prices are not newsworthy; articles about opening a new factory creating 200 jobs are
Stories must not be merely thinly disguised advertisements	A story saying your new car is the best on the market at only £7,999 will not be published; a story saying your new car won the East African Safari Rally probably would
Stories must fit the editorial style of the magazine or paper to which they are being sent	An article sent to the *Financial Times* about your sponsored fishing competition will not be printed; an article about your company's takeover of a competitor may be published

There has been a substantial growth in the use of press releases and publicity in recent years. This is due to increasing consumer scepticism about advertisements. Press stories carry much greater credibility and, although they do not usually generate business directly, they do have a positive long-term effect in building brand awareness and loyalty.

The news media will, of course, reserve the right to alter stories, add to them, comment on them or otherwise change them around to suit their own purposes. For example, a press agent's great little story on the launch of Britain's most powerful sports car may become part of an article on dangerous driving. There is really very little the company can do about this.

For this reason, a large part of the PR manager's job lies in cultivating good relationships with the media. Sometimes this will involve business entertaining, but more often it will involve making the journalists' lives as easy as possible. A well-written press release will often be inserted in the paper exactly as it stands because the editorial staff are too busy to waste time rewriting something that is already perfectly acceptable.

The journals and newspapers gain as well. Normally, editors have to pay for editorial, either paying freelance writers to produce articles or paying the salaries of journalists to come up with interesting stories. A good press release can be published with little or no editing and no 'legwork' on the part of journalists, so it fills space with minimal cost to the paper.

Often companies will lay on a **media event**, such as a launch ceremony for a new product or to announce some change in company policy. Usually this will involve inviting journalists from the appropriate media, providing lunch with plenty of free drinks, and inviting questions about the new development in a formal **press conference**. This kind of event will have only a limited success, however, unless the groundwork for it has been thoroughly laid.

Journalists tend to be suspicious of media events, sometimes feeling that the organisers are trying to buy them off with a buffet and a glass of wine. This means they may not respond positively to the message that the PR people are trying to convey, and may write a critical article rather than the positive one that was hoped for.

To minimise the chances of this happening, media events should follow these seven basic rules:

1 Avoid calling a media event or press conference unless you are announcing something that the press will find interesting.

2 Check that there are no negative connotations to what you are announcing.

3 Ensure that you have some of the company's senior executives there to talk to the press, not just the PR people.

4 Only invite journalists with whom you feel you have a good working relationship.

5 Avoid being too lavish with the refreshments.

6 Ensure that your senior executives, in fact anybody who is going to speak to the press, has had some training in doing this. This is particularly important for TV.

7 Be prepared to answer all questions truthfully. Journalists are trained to spot lies and evasions.

Journalists much prefer to be able to talk directly to genuine corporate executives rather than being allowed only to talk to the PR department; however, care should be exercised in ensuring that the executives spoken to are able to handle this type of questioning. It is also a good idea to have a press office that can handle queries from journalists promptly, honestly and enthusiastically and can arrange interviews with senior personnel if necessary.

PR and other publics

PR involves dealing with the company's other **publics**, apart from consumers. These are typically the following groups:

- Shareholders, for whom the company will produce end-of-year reports, special privileges and so forth.

- Government departments, with whom the company will liaise about planned legislation or other activities.

- The workforce.

- External pressure groups such as environmentalists or lobbyists.

Pressure groups can cause problems for companies by producing adverse publicity, by picketing company plants or by encouraging boycotting of company products. This can sometimes be dealt with effectively by counter-publicity, but in other cases the company may need to change what it is doing in order to satisfy the pressure group.

Sometimes adverse publicity from pressure groups is dealt with by advertising. For example, McDonald's was attacked by environmental groups for indirectly encouraging the destruction of rainforests for the purpose of producing cheap beef. McDonald's responded with a series of full-page press adverts asserting that beef for its hamburgers comes only from sources in the countries where it is eaten, and is not imported from developing countries.

A journalist who is offered a story by a pressure group will usually respond by trying to get the other side of the story from the firm. This is partly for legal reasons, since newspapers can be sued for libel if they print stories that turn out to be untrue, but it is also because most journalists are professionals and want to ensure the accuracy and fairness of their stories. This means that a firm's press office, a PR manager or even a senior executive may be asked for comment with little or no prior warning. It is therefore advisable to be as prepared as possible beforehand, and to answer as fully as possible any questions that you are asked. However, it is better to delay comment than to say something that will make matters worse. In these circumstances it is better to say something like, 'I'm sorry, I'll have to look into that and get back to you later', than the standard 'No comment'. The former response at least gives the impression that you are trying to help, whereas 'No comment' gives the impression that you are trying to hide something.

Defensive (reactive) PR is about responding to attacks from outside the firm and counteracting them as they arise. The attacks might come from pressure groups, from investigative reporters or from MPs. The safest way to handle this type of attack is to begin by trying to understand the enemy, and to this end the following questions should be asked:

- Are they justified in their criticism?
- What facts do they have at their disposal?
- Who are they trying to influence?
- How are they trying to do it?

If the pressure group is justified in its criticisms, it may be necessary to bring about changes in the organisation in order to quell the criticism, otherwise the problem will simply continue. Good PR people will always respond in some way. As anyone who watches investigative reporters on television will know, the company managers and directors who flee with a hasty 'No comment' always look guilty, whereas the ones who are prepared to be interviewed always appear honest (until the reporter produces the irrefutable evidence, of course).

Proactive PR means setting out deliberately to influence opinion, without waiting for an attack from outside. Here the manager will decide on the following:

- Who do we need to influence?
- What do we need to influence them about?
- How can we influence them?
- How can we marshal the arguments carefully to maximise their impact?

Overall, it is probably better to be proactive rather than defensive (or reactive) because then the PR office is in control of the process and is better prepared. If the firm is planning on dumping toxic waste at a beauty spot, it is better to contact Greenpeace beforehand and get its opinion rather than suffer the inevitable protests afterwards and take a chance on being able to patch up any problems.

What PR will and won't do for a firm

The following is a list of what good PR will do for the firm:

- It helps build a positive image.
- It can counter bad publicity.
- It can improve employee motivation.
- It can greatly improve the effectiveness of both the advertising and the salesforce.

On the other hand, here are some of the things that PR will *not* do for the firm:

- It will not directly increase sales.
- It will not cover up something that is adverse for the company.
- It will not replace other promotional activities.

Ultimately, PR works best as part of a planned and integrated programme of promotional activities that includes advertising, sales promotion and personal selling. It works least well when used only occasionally and in isolation.

Internal PR

The purpose of internal PR activities is to encourage employees to take a greater interest in their own work and in the organisation's goals. This has spin-offs for the staff themselves: most people would prefer to work for an organisation with a good record and most actually like to feel involved in their work. After all, work forms the dominant part of an employee's day; it is a large part of one's life and gives one the opportunity to do something useful.

Creating pride in the organisation and in work can be done by carrying out the tasks shown in Table 6.4. These factors were identified during a research study involving 82 companies over a five-year period (Kanter 1985).

TABLE 6.4	Tasks for improving staff perception of the organisation

Task	Rationale and methods for achievement
Encourage an atmosphere of pride	Highlight the achievements of individuals, publicising these to others; use innovative staff as agents of change
Provide suitable vehicles for innovation	Have communication channels that allow innovative ideas to be disseminated and acted on across organisational boundaries
Improve lateral communication	This will improve the flow of ideas; it can be done by encouraging joint project teams, by encouraging interdepartmental social events and by exchanging people between departments where possible
Cutting down layers of hierarchy	By devolving decision making down the hierarchy and by cutting out layers of management, employees can feel more in control of what is happening within the firm
Increasing the available information regarding company plans and projects	Reducing secrecy will ensure closer involvement of those who have to implement the plans, and may also lead to a reduction in mistakes caused through unrealistic planning; the staff on the ground are usually much closer to the problem than are senior management
Ensure that the leadership is aware of its limited perspective	Running the organisation from the top is unlikely to be as effective as giving employees more control over events, provided of course that the employees are attuned to the organisation's objectives

Source: Based on Kanter (1985)

From the employee's perspective, the firm needs to supply answers to these questions (D'Aprix, quoted in Arnott 1987):

- What's my job?
- How am I doing?
- Does anybody give a damn?

Once the organisation has answered these questions, the employee will want answers to others:

- How are we doing?
- How do we fit in to the whole?
- How can I help?

The final question is, of course, the one that the management of the firm is most ready to answer. The task of answering all these questions is part of the firm's internal PR systems. The tools used for this are sometimes generated by the PR people, more often by the personnel departments of the firms concerned. Typical internal PR tools are:

- internal newsletters
- staff magazines
- staff meetings
- electronic media such as intranet systems, e-mails, web logs (blogs), chat rooms, and so forth.

As an example, chocolate manufacturer Rowntree Mackintosh established a comprehensive employee communications system during the mid 1970s and early 1980s. The company uses a team briefing process that involves all employees in finding solutions for problems at a local level. The company newspaper publishes five local editions every month; the employees receive an annual company report of their own, in addition to twice-yearly briefings on the state of the business; there is a profit-sharing scheme in place as well as quality circles to maintain standards. Senior managers report that involvement, trust and a greater level of understanding among employees have resulted in lower absenteeism and increased productivity. Also, it is difficult to find Rowntree Mackintosh employees who complain about the firm they work for – an unusual situation (Arnott 1987).

Many firms now use electronic media to communicate internally with staff. A framework for analysing the influence of new media is shown in Figure 6.2.

In Figure 6.2, the use of e-mail, Internet and intranet to disseminate information and ideas among staff will be moderated by the work climate, by mutual trust between colleagues and also between subordinates and management, by attitude to innovation, and by the degree to which everyone subscribes to the common goal of the organisation. If these factors are well coordinated, the result will be effective internal marketing. If the internal marketing is ineffective, management can analyse the problem to see which of the factors is not working as it should, and take appropriate corrective action.

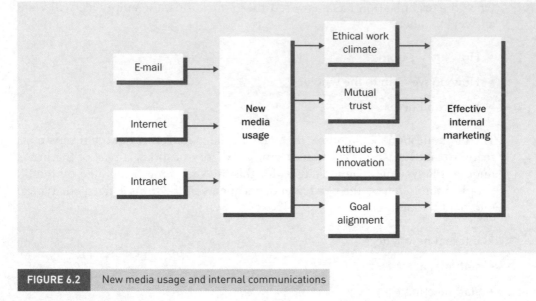

FIGURE 6.2   New media usage and internal communications

Source: Debussy *et al.* (2003)

Most importantly, the person responsible for internal PR must take the job further than merely maintaining the company noticeboard and writing a newsletter. There must be real commitment from management to the concept of good employee communications and relationships.

International public relations

As with any other form of marketing communications, PR is subject to cultural differences that alter the nature of the activities. In some cases, firms are able to transfer their PR activities without alteration, in some cases local modifications are carried out to an overall policy (as with Body Shop's community work initiatives, which are chosen by the staff in each shop); and in other cases the PR activity is, by its nature, multinational (as with Formula One racing).

There are two main ways of handling business internationally: either through a company-owned local branch, which can deal with PR on the instructions of head office in the home country; or through agents and distributors, who are rather harder to control. Part of the problem with the latter arrangement is that the local distributor has its own reputation to uphold and will usually bend its PR efforts to enhancing its own standing. This means that local representation will be chosen on the basis of what will enhance the distributor's reputation rather than that of the parent company.

The media through which PR operates exist in all countries to a greater or lesser extent (although TV is not always available everywhere in developing countries). What is less obvious is that the media may occupy different levels of importance in different countries. For example, in much of Africa, radio is far more important as a medium than newspapers, owing partly to higher levels of illiteracy and partly to large distances and poor infrastructure outside the cities.

Since TV shows and movies are often syndicated internationally, product placement will almost always be international – even when this is not the intention of the manufacturing firm. Coordinating the international effort will depend on having a suitable PR agency with branches in the countries in which the firm trades. In the absence of this, the coordinating role would have to be undertaken from head office, with consequent problems of cross-cultural misunderstanding.

In many developing countries (and indeed elsewhere), international companies are met with suspicion because of the colonial past of some of their home countries. Cultural imperialism is often suspected, and therefore the incoming firm already has difficulties establishing a good reputation. In this connection, it is useful to remember that a good, established reputation in one country is not necessarily transferable to another country, and even if the reputation remains good, this may be for other attributes.

As an example, when the Disney Corporation established EuroDisney (which later became Disneyland Paris), it made the error of assuming that European children would know what Disneyland is. Because the firm had an established reputation in the USA and 'everybody knows Disney', it assumed that this would be the case in Europe. In fact, European adults had grown up with Tin Tin, Topo Gigio and Doctor Who, rather than with Donald Duck and Mickey Mouse. Although Disney was hardly an unknown firm, the company found to its cost that it had to go through a lengthy period of educating Europeans about Disney before customers began to come to the theme park in any great numbers. In any case, the European perception of Disneyland was (and still largely is) that the park is for children only, whereas this is not the case in the USA.

Corporate image advertising is often an important part of the process. When the Australian telecommunications system was opened up to competition in the early 1990s, Optus ran a long series of TV adverts emphasising the company's commitment to Australia. This was necessary because 50 per cent of the company was foreign owned and many Australians objected to the concept of their telephone network being taken over by foreigners. The company's advertising emphasised that it was employing Australians and that it was 50 per cent Australian owned and managed. Telecom Australia (now Telstra) countered with a series of adverts emphasising its own Australian roots. At the time, Australian industry was in recession and the issue of foreign ownership of Australian assets was at the forefront of people's minds.

Word of mouth

Word of mouth is probably the most powerful communication medium in existence and can be used by marketers to good effect. The reasons for its power include the following:

- It is interactive, involving a discussion between two or more parties. This forces the recipient to think about the communication. The problem for marketers is that the interaction takes place between parties who are not usually under the control of the firm.

- It allows for feedback and confirmation of the messages.

- The source, a disinterested friend or acquaintance, carries a lot more credibility than any marketer-generated communication.

People often discuss products and services: they like to talk about their own recent purchases, to advise people considering a purchase, to show friends and family their latest acquisitions, and even to discuss controversial or interesting marketing communications. People who switch brands as a result of a referral from a friend (referral switchers) are more loyal and tend to be more satisfied with the products (Wangenheim and Bayon 2003). The same study showed that people who switch brands tend to be bigger users of word of mouth.

The problem for marketers is that people will talk about products and companies whether the firm likes it or not, and there is little that firms can do to control the process. Word-of-mouth communications can therefore be positive or negative; bad news often appears to travel twice as fast as good news, so that a great deal of word of mouth is in fact negative.

Table 6.5 shows some of the ways in which marketers can increase positive word of mouth.

TABLE 6.5   Ways to encourage positive word of mouth

Method	Explanation and examples
Press releases	A press release with a good, newsworthy story will usually stimulate discussion, particularly if it is linked to another promotion. For example, a press release announcing a sports competition for school squash players will generate word of mouth among squash players
'Bring a friend' schemes	In these schemes an existing customer is invited to recruit a friend in exchange for a small reward. In some cases the reward is given to the friend rather than to the introducer – some people feel uncomfortable about accepting a reward for 'selling' to a friend. For example, a health club might have special 'bring a friend' days when the friend is allowed to use all the facilities free for a day. This gives the member a chance to show off his or her club and encourages the friend to join

TABLE 6.5   Continued

Awards and certificates	Trophies and certificates are sometimes displayed and often talked about. For example, Laphroaig whisky distillery has a Friends of Laphroaig club in which the members (regular drinkers of the whisky) are given a square foot of land on the island of Islay and a certificate of ownership. The proud owners of this little piece of Scotland frequently mention it to their friends, especially when offering them a glass of the whisky itself. The distillers also invited the Friends of Laphroaig to nominate a friend to receive a free miniature of the whisky, on the grounds that the 'Friend' could then be sure of a 'dram' when visiting
T-shirts	Promotional clothing often receives comment from friends; designer labels, names of bands, names of tourist destinations and names of concert venues all provoke comment from friends and acquaintances.

Part of the problem for the marketer lies in identifying the opinion leaders in a given market. Journalists, influential individuals and organisations in industry, and some prominent TV pundits are easy to identify, but among the general public it usually takes careful research to identify those who are likely to be opinion leaders regarding a particular product. The main characteristics of influentials are shown in Table 6.6.

TABLE 6.6   Characteristics of influential

Characteristic	Description of influential
Demographics	Wide differences according to product category. For fashions and film-going, young women dominate. For self-medication, women with children are most influential. Generally, demography shows low correlations and is not a good predictor
Social activity	Influencers and opinion leaders are usually gregarious
General attitudes	Generally innovative and positive towards new products
Personality and lifestyle	Low correlation of personality with opinion leadership. Tends to be more fashion conscious, more socially active, more independent
Product related	Influencers are more interested in the specific product area than are others. They are active searchers and information gatherers, especially from the mass media

As we said earlier, much word of mouth communication is, unfortunately, negative. Some authorities state that dissatisfied customers tell three times as many people about the product as do satisfied customers. If true, this means that preventing negative word of mouth is actually a more pressing problem for marketers than generating positive word of mouth. Handling complaints is therefore a key issue.

Research has shown that only one-third of consumers will complain or seek redress when dissatisfied with a purchase; the remainder will boycott the goods in future, or simply complain to others, either of which is a non-optimal outcome from the viewpoint of the marketer. Consumers express dissatisfaction in one of three ways: **voice responses**, in which the customer comes back and complains; **private responses**, in which the consumer complains to friends, and **third-party responses**, which may include complaints to consumer organisations, trade associations, TV consumer programmes or even legal action (Singh 1988).

The Coca-Cola Company undertook a survey of customer communications in 1981 among customers who had complained to the company. The figures that emerged are shown in Table 6.7.

TABLE 6.7	Coca-Cola research

- More than 12 per cent told 20 or more people about the company's response
- Those who were completely satisfied told a median of 4–5 others about the experience
- Nearly 10 per cent of those who reported being completely satisfied increased their purchase of company products
- Those who thought that their complaint was unfairly dealt with told a median of 9–10 other people
- Of those who thought their complaint was unfairly dealt with, nearly one-third subsequently boycotted company products entirely, and another 45 per cent reduced their purchases

Source: Based on Coca-Cola Company (1981)

The most effective way of reducing post-purchase dissonance is to provide a product that meets the customer's expectations. This is partly a function for the manufacturer, but it is also a problem for the retailer to address, since it should be possible to ensure that the consumer's needs are fully understood before a recommendation about a product is made. As a fall-back position, however, every effort should be made to encourage the consumer to complain if things do not come up to expectations. This is why waiters always ask if the meal is all right and why shops frequently have no-quibble money-back guarantees. Ferry companies and airlines provide customer comment slips and some marketers even make follow-up telephone calls to consumers to check that the product is meeting expectations.

If the complaint is about a physical product, a simple replacement of the faulty product will usually be sufficient, but it is always better to go a step further and provide some recompense if possible.

In services marketing the problem is a little more complex because a service industry is in essence selling a promise; services cannot be returned for a replacement in the way that physical products can. Services fall into the following three categories, for the purpose of correcting complaints (Blythe 1997):

1 Services where it is appropriate to offer a repeat service, or a voucher. Examples are dry cleaners, domestic appliance repairers and takeaway food outlets.

2 Services where giving the money back will usually be sufficient. Examples are retail shops, cinemas and theatres, and video-rental companies.

3 Services where consequential losses may have to be compensated for. Examples are medical services, solicitors and hairdressers.

The above categories are not necessarily comprehensive or exclusive; sometimes it may be necessary to give the customer their money back and also make some other redress. It is important that dissatisfied customers are allowed to voice their complaint fully and that the appropriate compensation is negotiated in the light of the following factors:

• The strength of the complaint.

• The degree of blame attaching to the supplier, from the consumer's viewpoint.

• The legal and moral relationship between the supplier and the customer.

A failure to solve problems raised by post-purchase dissonance will, ultimately, lead to irreparable damage to the firm's reputation. The evidence from the Coca-Cola survey is that consumers whose complaints are resolved satisfactorily tend to become more loyal than those consumers who did not have a complaint in the first place. In the final analysis, it is always cheaper to keep an existing customer than it is to attract a new one, and therefore it behoves suppliers to give customers every chance to express problems with the service or product provision. To this end, many firms now operate free helpline numbers to allow customers to call with problems before the difficulties become too great. Ultimately, marketers aim to develop close long-term relationships with customers; this implies a two-way communications process that operates best by using the spoken word.

CORPORATE IDENTITY

Corporate identity is the outward manifestation of the organisation, a visual means of identification. It includes not only the corporate logo (the symbol that the organisation uses on all its points of public contact), but also the house style used on the company's letterheads and corporate publications, interior and exterior design of buildings, staff uniforms and vehicle livery, and packaging and products.

The recognition level of a corporate identity can be very high. McDonald's golden arches, Shell Oil's scallop shell logo, the white swirl on the Coca-Cola can and the Mickey Mouse ears of the Disney Corporation are all recognised worldwide. These images transcend language and give an immediate impression of the companies concerned.

Logos should be distinctive, easily recognisable, memorable and flexible in size so that they can be used on anything from a supertanker to a business card. This means that designing a logo can take a considerable amount of time and, once adopted, is difficult to change. For this reason, companies tend to make changes gradually; the Shell logo is updated approximately every 12 years, but the changes are usually subtle enough that the company's publics are unaware of the differences.

The remaining elements of the corporate identity should be consistent throughout the organisation, but there are exceptions; for example, HJ Heinz uses red packaging for its soups, but turquoise packaging for its baked beans. Although the shield and '57 Varieties' logo remain unchanged, the colour change enables consumers to identify the different products within the range. Maintaining a consistent approach avoids giving mixed messages to recipients and helps to avoid ambiguity (see Chapter 1).

Corporate brands are defined by six variables (Kapferer 1997). These are:

1 *Physique* – the physical aspects of the brand.

2 *Personality* – the traits which make up the corporate persona.

3 *Culture* – the shared beliefs and behaviours of the organisation.

4 *Relationships* – the relationships both inside and outside the organisation.

5 *Reflection* – the effect the corporate branding has on the organisation.

6 *Self-image* – the view the corporation has of itself.

There are six conventions in corporate branding (Knox and Bickerton 2003). These are:

1 *Brand context*. This is about setting the brand coordinates, in other words deciding what the boundaries and position of the brand should be.

2 *Brand construction*. This is about the framework for positioning the brand relative to competitors.

3 *Brand confirmation*. This is about communicating the brand's features and benefits (the brand proposition) to the target audience.

4 *Brand consistency*. This means developing consistent corporate communications so that the image of the brand is kept as uniform as possible throughout its target audiences.

5 *Brand continuity*. This refers to ensuring that the brand values are disseminated throughout the organisation.

6 *Brand conditioning*. This involves monitoring the relevance and distinctiveness of the brand.

Establishing the corporate brand is an important stage in developing an appropriate corporate image.

Corporate image

Corporate image advertising can be considered as an extension of PR. In a sense, it falls somewhere between true advertising and PR; instead of advertising specific brands or products, the advertising promotes the firm's image. Such advertising only mentions products in passing – the main thrust of the advertising is not to sell goods directly but to encourage a positive view of the firm, which is the main function of public relations.

Expenditure on corporate advertising tends to be low because the results are intangible (and seldom directly related to market share), and this makes it difficult to justify the activity to senior management. However, corporate advertising can achieve important objectives, as follows:

- To ensure that the company's activities are properly understood by its publics.

- To derive the behavioural benefits that greater knowledge and understanding can give.

- To shape the behaviour of staff, customers and other publics.

- To ensure that the company's view is communicated without the filtering (and occasionally mutating) effect of putting a press release through the editorial process.

The techniques that are used will depend on which of the firm's publics is being addressed and what the objective of the exercise is. BOC Group increased its stock market valuation by several million pounds by advertising to an audience of fewer than fifty chemical industry analysts in the City of London (Maitland 1983). Conversely, British Telecom (BT) ran a corporate image campaign on TV, billboards and in the press that cost £16 million and was intended (among other things) to improve the nation's perception of the company's technology (Newman 1986). The campaign worked: perception of BT's use of up-to-date technology rose by 15 per cent following the campaign.

The purpose of corporate advertising is basically the same as for press releases and other public relations exercises: to establish a positive image for the company. It is not directly about making sales (although sales often do increase because the favourable impression of the firm tends to spill over into a belief that the products are better, more reliable or more ethical), but it is rather about making the management task easier by smoothing the path of progress. During the 1990s, Monsanto (the giant US chemicals corporation) ran a series of press advertisements explaining its position on various issues such as the use of pesticides and the genetic engineering of food plants. The most telling aspect of the advertisements was that each one carried an address and contact telephone number for the organisations that oppose Monsanto's policies. For example, Greenpeace featured in the advertisements, with the exhortation to 'call this number for an alternative view of the problem'. The likelihood is that relatively few people actually called the number, but Monsanto effectively increased its own credibility by giving out the numbers. The firm was giving the message that it has nothing to hide.

Corporate advertising has the following characteristics:

- It is intended for long-term image building, not immediate sales.

- It rarely mentions specific brands or their features and benefits.

- It does not require any immediate response from the observer.

- The advertisements appeal to the reader's cognition rather than to affect (although the effect may be affective).

Product placement

Product placement (the placing of brands in films and TV shows) is also about creating a positive image of the firm. Firms will contribute towards the cost of producing a movie or TV programme in exchange for allowing their products to be used in the show. For example, many American films will show Coca-Cola in some form or another; either one of the characters will be drinking some or an advertising sign for Coke will appear in the background. For example, in the film *Basic Instinct* the detective and the suspect share a bourbon and Coke 'because bourbon goes great with Coke'. For a more subtle example, in *Midnight Express*, which is set in a Turkish jail where the prisoners have almost no personal possessions, one of the prisoners does possess an empty Coke bottle. It appears on the shelf behind his head while he delivers a fairly lengthy monologue. Coca-Cola spends considerable time, effort and money in ensuring that this kind of product placement happens.

In most cases the product placement is so subtle that the viewer is unaware of it on a conscious level. The product appears quite naturally, but there is a connection made via the peripheral route (see Chapter 1 for the elaboration likelihood model) and the consumer's affective response to the product becomes more positive. Because the movie star is wearing Nike trainers, or asks for a Jim Beam on the rocks, or drives an Aston Martin, the viewer associates the product with the movie and the star, and therefore assumes that the product must be a good one.

Product placement represents a relatively cheap way of obtaining some brand exposure in a mainstream medium without paying for airtime. Like any other form of promotion, it is not without cost; the firm will undoubtedly enter into negotiation with the producers of the movie or programme and there will be bargaining over who is contributing what to the overall enterprise. Sometimes firms are simply unable to meet the cost of the placement; traditionally James Bond drove an Aston Martin, but unfortunately the Aston Martin car company was unable to meet the high cost of supplying the cars for the movie *Tomorrow Never Dies*, and BMW stepped in. BMW supplied 17 cars, each worth £75,000, all of which were written off in the course of making the movie (Oakes 1997). In fact, the producers of *Tomorrow Never Dies* were approached by numerous companies which wanted their products to be associated with the cool, suave James Bond image, and they chose only those which fitted the image. Interestingly, none of the companies was British, despite the quintessential Britishness of the Bond character.

Product placement is an under-researched area academically. It tends to be the domain of major multinational firms which can afford the time to negotiate and the costs of providing the products. There is a high entry level in terms of cost because the cost of funding a movie or TV show is high, even when the firm placing the products is only meeting a fraction of the cost. On the other hand, the benefits for a company operating internationally are very great indeed. A successful movie will be screened in most countries around the world, will eventually be screened on television (perhaps for years to come) and will attract a premium audience.

From the viewpoint of the movie producers, product placement (and merchandising spin-offs) can easily cover the cost of making the movie. Even if the hit movie *Toy Story* had been a complete flop at the box office, the producers would still have shown an overall profit because of the product placement and merchandising deals.

Sponsorship

Sponsorship of the arts or sporting events is an increasingly popular way of generating positive feelings about firms. Sponsorship has been defined as 'an investment, in cash or kind, in an activity in return for access to the exploitable commercial potential associated with this activity' (Meenaghan, 1991).

The value of sponsorship in the UK grew from £4 million in 1970 (Buckley 1980) to £35 million in 1980 (Mintel 1990) and £400 million in 1993 (Mintel 1993). Much of this increase in expenditure came about because tobacco firms were severely restricted in what they were allowed to advertise and where they are allowed to advertise it; thus sponsorship of Formula One racing, horse racing and cricket matches by tobacco firms became commonplace. The recent ban on tobacco sponsorship will undoubtedly have a serious effect on these sports.

Companies sponsor for a variety of different reasons, as Table 6.8 shows, although generally their aim will be to link their name or brand with an event, person or organisation that is highly valued by their target consumers (Zafer Erdogan and Kitchen 1998).

TABLE 6.8   Reasons for sponsorship

Objectives	% Agreement	Rank
Press coverage/exposure/opportunity	84.6	1
TV coverage/exposure/opportunity	78.5	2
Promote brand awareness	78.4	3
Promote corporate image	77.0	4
Radio coverage/exposure/opportunity	72.3	5
Increase sales	63.1	6
Enhance community relations	55.4	7
Entertain clients	43.1	8
Benefit employees	36.9	9
Match competition	30.8	10
Fad/fashion	26.2	11

Source: Zafer Erdogan and Kitchen (1998)

Sponsorship is not adequate as a stand-alone policy. Although firms can run perfectly adequate PR campaigns without advertising, sponsorship will not work effectively unless the sponsoring firm is prepared and able to publicise the link. Some researchers estimate that two to three times the cost of sponsorship needs to be spent on advertising if the exercise is to be effective (Heffler 1994). In most cases, it is necessary to spell out the reasons for the firm's sponsorship of the event in order to make the link clear to the audience; merely saying 'official snack of the Triathlon' is insufficient. Since the audience is usually interested in anything about the event, it is quite possible to go into a brief explanation of the reasoning behind the sponsorship, saying, for example, 'Our snack gives energy – and that's what every triathlete needs more than anything. That's why we sponsor the Triathlon.'

Sustainable competitive advantage in the marketplace is a by-product of sponsorship (Fahy *et al.* 2004). Any enhancement of company image leads to an improved loyalty among customers, but sponsorship seems to generate feelings of gratitude among the target audience, feelings which translate into greater loyalty. Whether this is gratitude per se or whether it is affective linking is hard to say, and the answer to that question may not be of much practical importance in any case (Crimmins and Horn 1996). There are certainly spin-offs for the internal PR of the firm; most employees like to feel that they are working for a caring organisation, and sponsorship may also (on occasion) lead to free tickets or price reductions for staff of the sponsoring organisation.

Sponsorship appears to work best when there is some existing link between the sponsoring company and the event itself. In other words, a company which manufactures fishing equipment would be more successful in sponsoring a fishing competition than it would in sponsoring a painting competition. More subtly, a bank would be better off sponsoring a middle-class, 'respectable' arts event such as an opera rather than a rock concert.

The following criteria apply when considering sponsorship (Heffler 1994):

- The sponsorship must be economically viable; in other words it should be cost effective.

- The event or organisation being sponsored should be consistent with the brand image and overall marketing communications plans.

- It should offer a strong possibility of reaching the desired target audience.

- Care should be taken if the event has been sponsored before; the audience may confuse the sponsors and you may be benefiting the earlier sponsor.

Occasionally a competitor will try to divert the audience's attention to itself by implying that it is sponsoring the event; this is called ambushing (Bayless 1988). For example, during the 1998 soccer World Cup it was common for firms to use World Cup events in their advertising or sales promotions without actually sponsoring anything to do with the event itself.

CASE STUDY: LIVE8

In July 2005, the G8 group of countries (the world's wealthiest developed nations) met in Scotland, amid a flurry of protests. Besieged by protesters, the delegates were hard pressed to agree anything at all: chief among the protesting groups was the Live8 campaign led by Sir Bob Geldof, former Boomtown Rats member and long-time campaigner for African famine relief.

Sir Bob was aiming to repeat the success of the Live Aid concert of 1985, in which millions of pounds, dollars, francs, yen and marks were raised for famine relief in Ethiopia. As a pressure group, Live8 proved to be extremely powerful – Sir Bob's appeal for a million protesters to converge on Gleneagles, where the G8 conference was held, certainly worried the local police force, which feared major disturbances. Previous experience has shown that, although the majority of those who turn up are there simply to express their objections, large gatherings also attract a criminal element who go in the hope of starting a riot or preying on the protesters. Picking pockets, selling drugs, mugging the unwary or simply operating a range of fraudulent activities are only part of the problem.

At the same time, Geldof returned to his roots by organising a series of simultaneous concerts in ten cities, including London, Philadelphia, Paris, Rome and Berlin. The proceeds of the concerts will be used for aid projects in Africa, but, perhaps more importantly, the concerts promoted the cause of world poverty relief.

However, the Live8 initiative was not without its detractors. One early result of the campaign was the cancellation of the debt owed by many developing countries to members of G8. Geldof hailed this as a major breakthrough, but journalist George Monbiot, a commentator on African affairs, pointed out that the conditions attached to the cancellation of the debt might be more onerous than the debt itself. Enforced liberalisation of trade, enforced privatisation of industry and crackdowns on corrupt practices could easily be seriously counterproductive for countries without the resources or the ability to compete effectively in world markets. Monbiot went on to say, 'Bono and Geldof have made our job more difficult'. A further criticism was that the Live8 concerts had only one African musician on the bill – the musicians were predominantly white.

Some African countries are suspicious of foreign aid, seeing it as a way of controlling them – Zambia exemplified this in 2002 when it refused American food aid on the grounds that it contained genetically modified (GM) grain. Zambia saw the offer as a way of introducing GM crops into Zambia by the back door – thus making Zambian farmers dependent on further supplies of seeds from the USA. It also has to be said that, twenty years after Live Aid, people are still starving in Africa.

Meanwhile, other groups with other agendas were joining the protest. The Stop the War campaign, aimed at ending the war in Iraq, jumped on the bandwagon, running its own campaign alongside that of Live8. Other protest groups also turned up, seizing the opportunity presented by large crowds and worldwide media coverage.

Of course, the overriding aim was to publicise African poverty and move it up the agenda of the G8 meeting. In any project on this scale, there will be critics who say that it could have been done better, there will be opportunists who are either criminal or who simply want to have their own voices heard, there will be those who stand on the sidelines and suggest that the people involved have ulterior motives. What did come out of the protests was a genuine attempt by the G8 leaders to offer relief to the starving, and (in the words of the Live8 organisers) make poverty history.

Questions

1 How might the Live8 organisers have countered some of the objections?

2 What damage, if any, might be caused by the arrival of a criminal element at the protest?

3 What are the main strengths, from a PR viewpoint, of Geldof's approach?

4 What might be an appropriate image for Geldof to aim for in future events?

5 How might the Live8 impact have been made even greater?

SUMMARY

This chapter has looked at ways of improving corporate image and reputation. The basic tools for doing this are publicity, corporate advertising and sponsorship. Each of these will only work well within the context of an integrated communications strategy; they are tools for performing a specific task, and will not substitute for brand and product advertising, or indeed for any other communications tool.

The key points from the chapter are as follows;

- PR is about creating images, not making sales.

- PR is a long-term activity, with long-term pay-offs.

- Press releases are not free, nor are they advertising.

- PR is more useful at the higher end of the organisational hierarchy of needs.

- Press releases must be newsworthy, not thinly disguised adverts; they must also fit the style of the publication to which they are submitted.

- Staff in the front line may need training in PR, especially senior management.

- Corporate advertising works best as an adjunct to other communications.

- Sponsorship is not enough; it must be supported by substantial advertising and other promotions.

- Word of mouth is powerful because it has a credible source.
- Most dissatisfied customers can become loyal provided they are dealt with fairly.
- Sponsored events should be consistent with the brand and the firm.

 ## CHAPTER QUESTIONS

1 How can senior management prepare for media events?

2 What are the main pitfalls of using sponsorship for image building? How might these be avoided?

3 Why might a firm prefer to use corporate image advertising rather than press releases?

4 What are the advantages of involving pressure groups in discussions?

5 How might product placement benefit film makers?

 ## FURTHER READING

Hart, N. A. (1987) *Effective Corporate Relations*. London: McGraw-Hill. A collection of papers which together give an excellent account of applied public relations.

Hart, N. A. (1998) *Business to Business Marketing Communications*. London: Kogan Page. Very much a practitioner-based text with a strong emphasis on the practice of PR.

Hayward, R. (1998) *Public Relations for Marketing Professionals*. London: Macmillan. This is somewhat more up-to-date than Hart (1987), and gives a deeper account of PR practice, with the assumption that the reader is already familiar with the principles and practice of marketing.

Smith, P. R. (1998) *Marketing Communications: An Integrated Approach*, 2nd edn. London: Kogan Page. This has an entire chapter on word-of-mouth communications. Although it is UK-orientated, it gives some detailed and practical advice on creating positive word of mouth.

REFERENCES

Arnott, M. (1987) 'Effective employee communication', in Hart, N. A. (ed.), *Effective Corporate Relations*. London: McGraw-Hill.

Bayless, A. (1988) 'Ambush marketing is becoming a popular event at Olympic Games', *Wall Street Journal*, 8 February, p. 27.

Blythe, J. (1997) *The Essence of Consumer Behaviour*. Hemel Hempstead: Prentice Hall International.

Buckley, D. (1980) 'Who pays the piper', *Practice Review*, Spring: 10.

Coca-Cola Company (1981) *Measuring the Grapevine: Consumer Response and Word of Mouth*. Atlanta, GA: Coca-Cola Company.

Crimmins, J. and Horn, M. (1996) 'Sponsorship: from management ego trip to marketing success', *Journal of Advertising Research*, **36**(July/August): 11–21.

D'Aprix, R., quoted in Arnott, M. (1987) 'Effective employee communication', in Hart, N.A. (ed.), *Effective Corporate Relations*. London: McGraw-Hill.

Debussy, N. M., Ewing, M. T. and Pitt, L. F. (2003) 'Stakeholder theory and internal marketing communications: a framework for analysing the influence of new media', *Journal of Marketing Communications*, **9**(3): 147–61.

Fahy, J., Farrelly, F. and Quester, P. (2004) 'Competitive advantage through sponsorship: a conceptual model and research propositions', *European Journal of Marketing*, **38**(8): 1013–30.

Heffler, M. (1994) 'Making sure sponsorship meets all the parameters', *Brandweek*, May, p. 16.

Institute of Public Relations (1984) *Public Relations Practice: Its Roles and Parameters*. London: Institute of Public Relations.

Kanter, R. M. (1985) *The Change Masters: Corporate Entrepreneurs at Work*. London: Unwin.

Kapferer, J-N. (1997) *Strategic Brand Management*. London: Kogan Page.

Knox, S. and Bickerton, D. (2003) 'The six conventions of corporate branding', *European Journal of Marketing*, **37**(7): 998–1016.

Maitland, A. J. (1983) 'To see ourselves as others see us', *BOC Group Management Magazine*.

Meenaghan, J. A. (1991) 'The role of sponsorship in the marketing communication mix', *International Journal of Advertising*, **10**(1): 35–47.

Mintel (1990) *Special Report on Sponsorship*. London: Mintel.

Mintel (1993) *Special Report on Sponsorship*. London: Mintel.

Morita, A., with Reingold, E. M. and Shimomura, M. (1986) *Made in Japan*. New York: Dutton.

Newman, K. (1986) *The Selling of British Telecom*. New York: Holt, Rinehart & Winston.

Oakes, P. (1997) 'Licensed to sell', *The Guardian*, 19 December.

Pearson, A. J. (1980) *Setting Corporate Objectives as a Basis for Action*. Johannesburg: National Development and Management Foundation of South Africa.

Singh, J. (1988) 'Consumer complaint intention and behaviour: definition and taxonomical issues', *Journal of Marketing*, January: 93–107.

Wangenheim, F. and Bayon, T. (2003) 'Satisfaction, loyalty and word-of-mouth within the customer base of a utility provider: differences between stayers, switchers and referral switchers', *Journal of Consumer Behaviour*, **3**(3): 211–20.

Zafer Erdogan, B. and Kitchen, P. J. (1998) 'The interaction between advertising and sponsorship: uneasy alliance or strategic symbiosis?', *Proceedings of the 3rd Annual Conference of the Global Institute for Corporate and Marketing Communications*. Glasgow: Strathclyde Graduate Business School.

7

Branding, packaging and merchandising

Objectives

After reading this chapter you should be able to:

- explain the role of branding in the promotion and development of products
- outline the main issues around the development of a brand name for a product, and avoid the main pitfalls of doing so
- describe how brands enable a product to become fixed in the consumer's mind
- outline the possibilities for using packaging to promote other products in the range
- list the main issues affecting brand design
- explain the role of colour and package design in conveying brand values
- explain the role of merchandising in promoting sales
- describe the role of the salesforce in merchandising

INTRODUCTION

This chapter is about the communications media that surround the product itself: the branding of the product, the packaging that encloses it, and the display of the product on the retailer's shelves. From the marketer's viewpoint, these communications methods offer a relatively low cost medium for promoting products, and for positioning them in the consumer's perception. Also, and perhaps more importantly, these are the factors that influence the customer immediately before purchase; in other words, they are the last communications the marketer can make before the final purchasing decision is made. For this reason, point-of-purchase displays and materials have enjoyed a steady growth in expenditure by marketers for the past twenty years.

BRANDING

Many products are so similar to other manufacturers' products that consumers are entirely indifferent as to which one they will buy. For example, petrol is much the same whether it is sold by Shell, Esso, BP, Statoil, Elf or Repsol; such products are called commodity products because they are homogeneous commodities rather than distinct products with different benefits from the others on offer.

At first sight, water would come into the category of a commodity product. Yet any supermarket has a range of bottled waters, each with its own formulation and brand name, and each with its loyal consumers. In these cases the original commodity product (water) has been converted into a brand. **Branding** is a process of adding value to the product by use of its packaging, brand name, promotion, and position in the minds of the consumers.

DeChernatony and McDonald (1998) offer the following definition of brand:

A successful brand is an identifiable product, service, person or place, augmented in such a way that the buyer or user perceives relevant, unique added values which match their needs most closely. Furthermore, its success results from being able to sustain those added values in the face of competition.

This definition emphasises the increased value that accrues to the consumer by buying the established brand rather than a generic or commodity product. The values that are added may be in the area of reassurance of the brand's quality, they may be in the area of status (where the brand's image carries over to the consumer), or they may be in the area of convenience (making search behaviour easier).

Figure 7.1 shows the relationship between commodity products and branded products in terms of image and price.

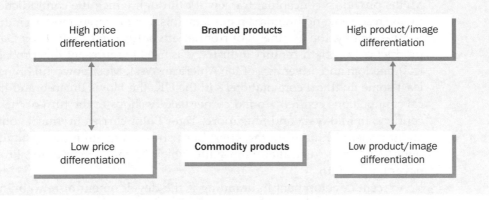

FIGURE 7.1   Commodity products versus branded products

Commodity products tend to be undifferentiated in price (for example, petrol tends to be much the same price in petrol stations within a given geographical area; a differential of even 10 per cent would be very noticeable). They also tend to have a low degree of differentiation in the product characteristics and the image. Branded goods, on the other hand, score high on both factors; since they command a premium price, this is likely to lead to an increased profit, which strengthens the case for developing a strong brand.

Brands and semiotics

In terms of semiotics (see Chapter 1) brands have four levels:

1 *A utilitarian sign*. This is about the practical aspects of the product, and includes meanings of reliability, effectiveness, fitness for the purpose and so forth.

2 *A commercial sign*. This is about the exchange values of the product, perhaps conveying meanings about value for money or cost effectiveness.

3 *A socio-cultural sign*. This is about the social effects of buying (or not buying) the product, with meanings about membership of aspirational groups or about the fitness of the product for filling social roles.

4 *A sign about the mythical values of the product*. Myths are heroic stories about the product, many of which have little basis in fact; for example the Harley Davidson motorcycle brand has a strong mythical value owing (in part) to its starring role in the films *Easy Rider* and *Electraglide in Blue*. The same is true of James Bond's Aston Martin, and several brands of beer.

Myths provide a conceptual framework through which the contradictions of life can be resolved, and brands can build on this. For example, modern industrial life is, presumably, the antithesis of frontier adventure. Yet the Harley Davidson, a product of twentieth-century industry, was used to represent the (probably mythical) freedom and adventure of the American West. Most powerful brands have at least some mythical connotations – in the UK, the Hovis bread brand has mythical connotations centred around corner bakery shops at the turn of the twentieth century; in Malaysia and Singapore, Tiger Balm carries mythical connotations about ancient Chinese apothecaries; in Australia, Vegemite carries mythical connotations about Australian family life which its main competitor, Promite, has never tapped into.

A recent development in branding is the development of retro brands. Retro brands revive old designs for products, thus tapping into mythical qualities: for example, the new-shape VW Beetle evokes images of the original Beetle, which no longer meets safety standards in most European countries. The Mini Cooper is another example. These brands rely on the following attributes for their success (Brown *et al.* 2003):

- *Allegory*. This is the brand 'story', the mythical connotations the brand has.
- *Aura*. This is the essence of the brand, the image surrounding it.
- *Arcadia*. This is the idealised community in which the brand exists: the Mini Cooper recalls the 1960s, which people (at least those who are old enough to remember the decade) think of as a decade of freedom and optimism.
- *Antinomy*. This is brand paradox, the factors which militate against the brand image.

Retro brands are very much tied into nostalgia and myth, and consequently they appeal strongly to people who find modern life stressful or unpleasant.

The association of different values with the brand name can be extremely useful when researching the acceptability of a brand's image. The importance that consumers place on these values can be researched using focus groups, with a subsequent analysis of the key signs contained within the brand, and consumers can be segmented according to their responsiveness to the particular signs contained within the brand and their relevance to the consumer's own internal values. Peer pressure can be particularly important in brand attraction, especially among young people and children: for example, branded trainers symbolise youth and wealth, whereas unbranded trainers symbolise older people and poverty (Elliott and Leonard 2003). Children can be extremely persuasive about demanding specific brands, as a fascinating survey of letters to Santa Claus illustrated (O'Cass and Clarke 2002). In this study of 422 letters to Santa Claus, children not only were very specific about which brands they wanted, they also used some meaningful request strategies (offering to behave themselves, stop fighting with their brothers and so forth) to persuade Santa Claus to bring the right brand.

Research carried out by Gordon and Valentine (1996) into retail buying behaviour showed that different retail outlets convey different meanings to consumers in terms of a continuum from planned, routine shopping through to impulse buying. Each store type met the needs differently and conveyed different meanings in terms of appropriateness of behaviour. Convenience stores conveyed an image of disorder and feelings of guilt and confusion (perhaps associated with having forgotten to buy some items in the course of the regular weekly shop). Supermarkets represented planned shopping and conveyed an image of efficient domestic management and functionality. Petrol stations carried a dual meaning of planned purchase (for petrol) and impulse buying (in the shop). Business travellers seeking a break from work, and pleasure travellers seeking to enhance the 'holiday' feeling, both indulged in impulsive behaviour motivated by the need for a treat. Finally, off-licences legitimated the purchase of alcohol, allowing shoppers to buy drinks without the uneasy feeling that other shoppers might disapprove. Off-licences also provided an environment in which people felt able to experiment with new purchases.

These signs are relevant not only for the retailers themselves in terms of their own branding, but also for branded-goods manufacturers who need to decide which outlets are most appropriate for their brands and where in the store the brand should be located. For example, snack foods and chocolate are successfully sold in petrol stations, where the travellers are often looking for a treat to break up a dull journey.

Strategic issues in branding

Adding value to the product by branding involves a great deal more than merely giving the product a catchy name. Branding is the culmination of a range of activities across the entire marketing mix, leading to a brand image which conveys a whole set of messages to the consumer (and, more importantly, to the consumer's friends and family) about quality, price, expected performance and status. For example, the Porsche brand name conveys an image of engineering excellence, reliability, sporty styling, high speed and high prices, and of wealth and success on the part of the owner. People do not buy Porsches simply as a means of transport; for that purpose a basic Ford is perfectly adequate.

Because branding involves all the elements of the marketing mix it cannot be regarded simply as a tactical tool designed to differentiate the product on the supermarket shelves. Instead, it must be regarded as the focus for the marketing effort, as a way of directing the thought processes of the management towards producing consumer satisfaction. The brand acts as a common point of contact between the producer and the consumer, as shown in Figure 7.2.

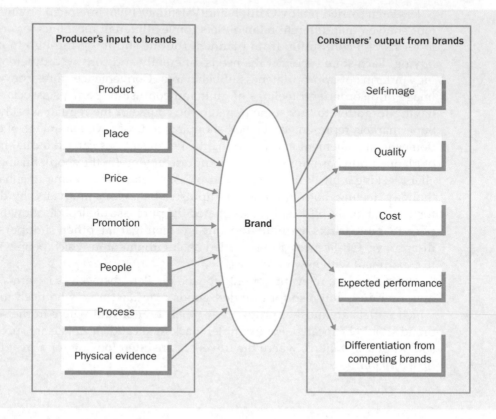

FIGURE 7.2   Brands as a contact point

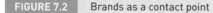

In Figure 7.2, the consumer benefits from the brand in terms of knowing what the quality will be, knowing what the expected performance will be, gaining some self-image values (for example, a prestigious product conveys prestige to the consumer by association – conversely, a low-price product might enhance a consumer's sense of frugality and ability to find good value for money).

In many cases the core product has very little to differentiate it from other products, and the brand is really the only differentiating feature. For example, Levi jeans are the world's top-selling brand of jeans, yet one would have to make a fairly close inspection to discern the difference between Levi's and and a competing brand. A famous example is the rivalry between Pepsi-Cola and Coca-Cola; in blind taste tests, most people prefer the flavour of Pepsi (which is why the Pepsi Challenge is so successful), but Coca-Cola outsells Pepsi in virtually every market. This apparent discrepancy can only be explained by the brand image which Coca-Cola has, and in taste tests where consumers are able to see which can the drink comes out of, Coca-Cola is the preferred brand.

Despite the apparently artificial nature of differentiation by branding, the benefits to the consumer are very real. Experiments show that branded analgesics work better than generic analgesics at relieving pain, even though the chemical formula is identical; this is because of the psychosomatic power of the brand.

Brands can be looked at in a number of different ways. Table 7.1 shows eight different strategic functions of brands.

TABLE 7.1	Strategic functions of brands
Function	**Explanation**
Brand as a sign of ownership	Brands were at one time a way of showing who had instigated the marketing activities for the brand. This was an attempt to protect the formulation of the product in cases where intellectual property protection was insufficient, and also to ensure that customers knew whether they were buying a manufacturer's brand or a retailer's brand
Brand as a differentiating device	A strong brand undoubtedly does differentiate the product from similar products, but having a strong brand name is not enough: the product itself also needs to be different in some way. The brand image is the communicating device that conveys the difference to the consumer
Brand as a functional device	Branding can be used to communicate functional capability. In other words, the brand conveys an image of its quality and expected performance to the consumer
Brand as a symbolic device	The symbolism of some brands enables consumers to say something about themselves. This is particularly apparent in the designer clothes industry – a very ordinary T-shirt acquires added value because the name of the designer is printed on the front. If the consumers believe that the brand's value lies in its communication ability they will spend considerable time and effort in choosing the brand that conveys the appropriate image
Brand as a risk reducer	Every purchase involves a degree of risk; the product might not perform as expected, and if it fails to do so then the vendor might not be prepared to make restitution. Buying a strongly branded product offers the consumer a degree of reassurance about both the product and the producer. Astute marketers find out what types of risk are of most concern to the customers or consumers and develop a brand presentation which addresses those risks
Brand as a shorthand device	Brands are used as a way of 'tagging' information about a product in the consumers' memories. This is particularly relevant when the brand is extended to other product categories, since the consumer's view of the parent brand is transferred to the new brand; for example, Virgin has successfully extended the brand image from records to retailing to airlines to financial services, all offering the same innovative approach and serving similar market segments

TABLE 7.1	Continued
Function	**Explanation**
Brand as a legal device	Brands give a certain amount of legal protection to the producer, since pack design and name can be protected where (often) the formulation of the product cannot. Strong branding offers some protection for the firm's intellectual property
Brand as a strategic device	The assets constituting the brand can be identified and managed so that the brand maintains and builds on the added value which it represents

Branding clearly has advantages for the manufacturer and the retailer since it helps to differentiate the product from the competitor's product. Economies of scale and scope are attributed to branding, and a brand with high sales will generate production economies (Demsetz 1973). A successful brand creates a **barrier to entry**, so that competitors find it harder to enter the market (Demsetz 1982). Brands also allow firms to compete other than on price (Mercer 1992), which clearly has advantages since the firm does not have to cut its profit margins in order to compete.

Furthermore, brands which are held in high esteem tend to be more consistent in their sales, riding over the ups and downs of the marketplace (Png and Reitman 1995). Not all brands are priced at a premium; many are competitively priced in order to take advantage of consistent sales.

Branding has advantages for the consumer: it is easy to recognise the product, and easy to identify with it; messages about the formulation and benefits are clearly conveyed, and in most cases the use of a particular brand – for example, wearing designer clothes – says something about the consumer (Bagwell and Bernheim 1996). Because most purchases involve only limited problem-solving behaviour, branding helps to reduce the decision-making time and also the effort of evaluating competing products. Consumers who either don't want to spend time on an extended information search or don't have the expertise to do so, can use the brand as an implicit guarantee of quality (Png and Reitman 1995).

Information storage and retrieval in humans is carried out by a process of 'chunking' or collecting information in substantial quantities and storing it under a single 'file name' (Buschke 1976; see also Chapter 1). In effect, the brand name provides an informational chunk; the individual is able to summon up a huge amount of information from memory using the brand name as the trigger. The more attributes a brand is linked to, the more likely it is to be purchased (Romaniuk 2003).

From a strategic viewpoint, the brand image provides a focus for the creative energies of the marketing team. Koestler (1964) suggests that creativity involves the bringing together of hitherto unrelated, yet familiar, objects to generate a creative insight. The difficulty for marketers is that product and brand development is often a team process, and as such the team needs to keep a firm picture of what the product is intended to convey – the 'personality' of the product – if it is to maintain consistency in the creative activities. One way of doing this is to use a metaphor for the product. For example, the Honda Accord developers used the metaphor 'Rugby player in a dinner suit' to achieve product coherence across the team, even though the entire creative team consisted of hundreds of people, from automotive stylists through to ad designers (Clark and Fujimoto 1990).

Brand planning is important but time consuming; often the job is given to a brand manager, many of whom are young and inexperienced. Developing the brand is a process of integrating a number of strands of business activity, so a clear idea of the brand image is essential, as is a long-term view. To see branding as merely being about design or advertising or naming is inadequate and short-sighted; successful brands are those which act as a lens through which the consumer sees the corporation and the product. Constant evaluation of the image seen through the lens is essential if the brand is to retain its status.

Brand names

When a new product has been developed, the producer will usually give it a **brand name**. A brand name is a term, symbol or design which distinguishes one seller's product from its competitors. The strategic considerations for brand naming are as follows:

- *Marketing objectives*. The brand name should fit the overall marketing objectives of the firm; for example, a firm intending to enter the youth market will need to develop brand names which appeal to a young audience.

- *Brand audit*. An estimate needs to be made of the internal and external forces such as critical success factor (also known as the unique selling proposition).

- *Brand objectives*. As with the marketing objectives, the overall intentions about the brand need to be specified.

- *Brand strategy alternatives*. The other ways of achieving the brand's objectives, and the other factors involved in its success, have a bearing on the choice of brand name.

Brand names can be protected in most countries by **registration**, but there is some protection for brands in that it is illegal to try to pass off a product as being a branded one when it isn't. For example, using a very similar brand name to a famous brand, or even using similar package design, could be regarded as passing off. This is a civil offence, not a criminal one, so it is up to the offended brand owner to take legal action.

Ries (1995) suggests that brand names should have the following characteristics:

- They should shock, that is, catch the customer's attention.

- They should be alliterative; this helps to make them memorable.

- They should connect to the product's positioning in the consumer's perceptual map.

- They should link to a visual image; again, this helps the memorability.

- They should communicate something about the product, or be capable of being used to communicate about the product.

- They should encourage the development of a nickname (for example, Bud for Budweiser Beer).

- They should be telephone- and directory-friendly.

Extending the brand

A **brand extension** is another product in the company's range which uses a similar brand name. For example, Cherry Coke is a brand extension of the original Coca-Cola. Overall **family branding** is where one brand name is used for a range of products, such as Heinz 57 Varieties, and **line family branding** is where a smaller group of brands carries a single identity, for example, Heinz soups.

In each case the aim is to convey a message of quality to the consumer by borrowing from the established reputation of the parent brand, and to appeal to the target market which is already familiar with the parent brand. Properly carried out, the establishment of a brand is a long-term project which can be expensive; this leads to an emphasis by some firms on brand extensions which are intended to maximise the return on the investment made in establishing the brand. In some cases, brands have been extended to breaking point; relatively few brands (Virgin being one example) can be extended apparently indefinitely, and even as well-established a brand as Levi Strauss jeans could not extend itself to smart suits (the company's attempt to do so in the early 1980s turned into a disaster). Brand extensions should always bear some relationship to the original brand; Virgin's ability to extend relies on the brand's image as being original and fresh-thinking, coupled with a combination of solidity and practicality.

A more recent development has been **compositioning**, in which products are grouped under a brand name to create a composite value greater than that of the components (Ruttenberg *et al.* 1995). Joint marketing and distribution alliances come under this heading. The products concerned do not necessarily come from the same producer, and may not even be in the same general category; for example, Disneyland has 'official airlines' or 'official ferry companies' to transport visitors to their theme parks. A further extension of this concept is **brand architecture**, which is concerned with setting up 'partner' brands and creating a balance between branding at the product level and corporate or banner levels (Uncles *et al.* 1995).

Within the international arena, firms have the opportunity to extend the brand across frontiers. This raises fundamental strategic issues; for example, should the brand be globalised, with the firm offering a standard package throughout the world (as does Coca-Cola), or should the brand be adapted for each market (as does Heinz)? Some firms brand globally but advertise locally (Sandler and Shani 1992), whereas others organise task groups to handle the brand on a global scale (Raffee and Kreutzer 1989).

Retailers' own brands

Retailer power has grown considerably over the past twenty years, with a prolif-eration of own-brand products. In the past, the retailer's own-brand products were usually of poorer quality than manufacturer's brands, but are now often of equal or even superior quality.

Own brands now account for up to 60 per cent of the sales in some major retail stores such as Tesco and Sainsbury in the UK, Carrefour in France (slogan: 'Carrefour – c'est aussi une marque', which translates as 'Carrefour – it's also a brand'), Coles Stores in Australia, and Quinnsworth in Ireland (Hankinson and Cowking 1997). For manufacturers this creates a problem of response: should they try to invest in the firm's brands more heavily in order to overcome the retailer's brand, or should they capitulate entirely and produce on behalf of the retailer (Quelch and Harding 1995)? Often, manufacturers will become suppliers of retailer-brand products which compete with their own branded goods. Their reasons for doing this are as follows.

- *Economies of scale.* The manufacturer may be able to buy raw materials in greater quantities, or may be able to invest in more efficient production meth-ods, if the throughput of product is increased.

- *Utilise excess capacity.* Seasonality or production synergies may make produc-tion of own-brand products attractive in some cases.

- *Base for expansion.* Supplying a retailer with own-brand goods may lead to opportunities to supply the retailer with other products in future.

- *No promotion costs.* The retailer bears all the investment in the brand (which is, of course, a brand extension of the retailer's trading name in any case).

- *No choice.* Some retailers (the UK's Marks and Spencer being an example) only trade in their own brands. Manufacturers who wish to trade with these retail-ers have no choice but to produce under the retailer's brand name.

- *Shut out the competition.* If the manufacturer does not produce goods under the retailer's brand name, another manufacturer will, and will thus gain ground.

Manufacturers with very strong branding often refuse to produce own-brand goods – Kellogg's breakfast cereals is a notable example. If the brand is strong enough, this allows the firm to promote on an 'accept no substitutes' platform.

In the past, own-brand products were cheap versions of the leading brands, but in more and more cases the retailers now have enough financial strength to fund the development of entirely new versions of products, some of which are superior to the proprietary brands and have achieved substantial market shares.

In many cases this is achieved by producing lookalike branding, where the product looks very similar to the brand leader. In the UK this led to the formation of the British Producers and Brand Owners Group which lobbied Parliament to regulate the visual and physical simulation of successful brands. In fact, research showed that few, if any, consumers accidentally pick up the wrong brand (Balabanis and Craven 1997), but some confusion is engendered. Retailers (perhaps disingenuously) claim that using similar packaging helps consumers identify products, whereas manufacturers claim that lookalikes give the impression that the products are identical. In other words, the confusion arises not at the level of picking up the wrong pack, but at the more subtle level of forming inaccurate beliefs about the lookalike's attributes based on the attributes of the leading brand (Foxman *et al.* 1992).

A further argument advanced by retailers is that the strong manufacturers' brands have created generic product categories of their own – 'Gold Blend-type' instant coffees, for example. The retailers argue that products with similar quality and specifications should look as similar as possible to the brand which first created those values – an argument that is particularly galling to manufacturers who have invested large sums of money in creating those brand values in the first place.

Creative issues in branding

Creating a brand name and a brand identity requires considerable care. The brand name conveys an image of the product even when the brand name itself has no apparent connection with the product. For example, the biscuit brand Hob Nobs conveys an image of friendliness (perhaps from 'hobnobbing') and also a rustic warmth (perhaps from 'hob') which is in perfect accord with the chunkiness of the honey oat biscuits themselves. 'Hob' is also an acronym for 'honey oat biscuit', although few consumers would make this connection.

Creating a brand name occurs through one of the following processes:

- A sudden flash of inspiration by an individual.

- Brainstorming by a team.

- Reasoned synthetic process, for example making a list of single words describing what the product is, and another list describing what it does, and assembling a brand name from the two lists.

By their very nature, brand names are ambiguous. Examples were given in Chapter 2 of cross-cultural problems caused by brand names which have different meanings in different languages, but even within a single culture brand names often have more than one interpretation. This means that brand names need to be tested with consumers before being adopted.

PACKAGING

Packaging can be considered as part of the product since the packaging can confer some of the product's benefits, or even be integral to the product's use. For example, a kitchen surface cleaner could be sold in a bottle from which the product is poured on to a cloth or directly on to the surface; it could also be sold in an aerosol spray and in a trigger-spray bottle. Although the core product (the cleaning fluid) is identical in each case, the augmented products are very different since the packaging determines the method of use.

The main purpose of packaging is to protect the contents from the outside environment and vice versa, but packaging also carries out the following functions:

- It informs customers.

- It meets legal information requirements.

- It sometimes aids the use of the product (for example, ring pulls make it easier to open a drinks can).

- It can add value to the product by being reusable as a container, a toy or even a decoration.

Packaging decisions might include such areas as **tamper resistance** (for example, paper strips around caps to prevent bottles being opened while on supermarket shelves), and **customer usage** (for example, the development of beer packaging from bottles to cans to ring pulls to non-waste ringpulls to draught beer systems). The protection of the environment has become important to consumers in recent years, so more packaging is either recyclable or biodegradable. Customer acceptability is of obvious importance; packaging must be hygienic and convenient for the consumer. Within the UK there has been a growing trend to develop packaging designs that can be legally protected under the Trade Marks Act 1994 in order to prevent imitators from making close copies of the packaging. In some cases the package design has been made expensive to copy, requiring retooling for unusual pack shapes, or expensive printing processes (Gander 1996). As described in the section above on branding, lookalike packaging has become particularly common among supermarket own-brand versions of popular products, and there has been some debate about the ethics of this. In some countries these close copies infringe copyright and patent laws (Davies 1995).

Colour in packaging

The colour of packaging can be important. For example, Heinz's use of a turquoise label for its baked beans emphasises the orange colour of the beans when the can is opened. Table 7.2 shows some of the characteristics of different colours; it should be noted that these characteristics are by no means universal, and will vary from one culture to another.

TABLE 7.2	Common characteristics associated with different colours
Colour	**Characteristics**
Yellow	A strong attention-grabber, often symbolising summer. As a background for black print it is eye-catching and makes the print easier to read, but may look 'cheap and cheerful'
Orange	Tends to be a sociable colour but is usually used mainly for products which contain oranges. Some products (and many signs) use dayglo orange as an attention-grabber; in the UK, Radion washing powder is a prime example
Red	Usually the first colour anyone thinks of, red is the prime attention-grabber. It is very widely used in packaging, denoting warmth and a premium product
Purple	Formerly associated with royalty, purple still has an upmarket image. It is the most expensive colour to produce, and has poor resistance to fading.
Blue	Very few foods are blue, so this colour is not usually associated with food packaging. It is commonly used to indicate coolness or cleanliness, so it is evident on packages of antiseptic and on cleaning materials
Green	The rise in environmentalism has led to a consequent rise in the use of green (small g) packaging. Green has a 'natural' image and is often used to denote spring. It is the national colour of Ireland and so denotes 'Irishness' in some products (for example, Irish Spring deodorant, which is an American product), and to Americans it can denote money, since dollar bills are green on the back
Pink or magenta	Formerly very much a feminine colour, pink has been widely used on cosmetics. More recently it has been used for baby products, and for some categories of household goods
White	Purity and cleanliness in most European countries and the USA, but has connections with death in Japan, where it is the colour of mourning

TABLE 7.2	Continued
Brown	In food containers, brown usually indicates strong flavours such as pickles and sauces. For gardening products, it conveys a rich earthiness
Black	Often used with gold to give an impression of exclusivity (and premium price). Otherwise it tends to be associated with death

Colours have a strong effect on perception. Research conducted in the 1960s showed that people believed that coffee from a dark brown container was stronger than coffee from a blue can, and that coffee from a yellow can was 'too weak in flavour or aroma'. In fact, the coffee in each can was identical (Dichter 1964). Of course, this type of research will not be generalisable across cultures, and (not unnaturally) respondents who are asked what differences there are between two products will try to find a difference even if they are unable to sense one. Having said that, the differences reported (or imagined) showed a remarkable consistency between respondents, with 87 per cent of them agreeing that the 'yellow' coffee was too weak.

Colour also has a dramatic effect on search times for products. Bright colours and contrasting colours make a product stand out, but consumers also use colour as a quick way of identifying the brand they are looking for (Jansson *et al*. 2004). For this reason, firms will often adopt a corporate colour, or a colour for a range of branded items: Coca-Cola uses red and white, Heinz uses red for its range of soups, Kodak uses yellow. In the UK, it has recently become possible to register corporate colours as part of a brand; although this does not mean complete exclusivity, it does make it easier for firms to sue for passing off. Colours are not international; hot, sunny countries tend to be more accepting of bright, lively colours, and in China bright colours symbolise high quality, whereas in Britain they are often associated with low price, low quality articles.

Product labelling

The term 'labelling' covers two distinct aspects of packaging. First, the term is often used to denote the information printed on the packaging (as opposed to the brand name or promotional details). Used in this sense, labelling is concerned with the sought aspects of the marketing communication which is the packaging. Second, the term is used to denote the labels which are attached to bulky or irregularly shaped products, or to clothing which needs to be handled or tried on by consumers.

Labelling serves the following functions:

- It helps the consumer to identify the product.
- It gives instructions for the use of the product so as to get the best use from it.
- It promotes alternative uses for the product (for example, bicarbonate of soda is good for deodorising fridges).
- It promotes other products in the range (for example, food products often carry a recipe which uses other products from the same manufacturer).
- It informs about sales promotions, possibly jointly with other firms or other brands belonging to the same firm.
- It gives details on contents and formulation which may reassure the consumer.
- It encourages first-time purchase by using words such as 'new' or 'improved', or even 'free sample'.

In recent years, because of the huge upsurge in world trade, it has also become necessary to consider the legal requirements of labelling, which differ from one country to the next. For instance, nutritional information may have to be in a different form for each country (in the USA, for example, food has to be labelled with the amount of fat it contains expressed as a percentage of a 2,000 calorie daily intake). During the 1990s there was a dispute within the European Union regarding the labelling of recipe products. The EU officials wanted manufacturers to label products with the proportions of each ingredient, so that consumers could judge how much sugar or fat was contained in the product. Manufacturers pointed out that this was tantamount to giving their competitors their recipes, which in many cases are carefully guarded trade secrets. Eventually the manufacturers won this argument. Often, packaging is used internationally even when advertising is not, so many firms label their products in several languages and comply with all the packaging regulations for all the countries the product will be sold in. This can mean that the package becomes extremely crowded with print.

Packaging can often be used for promotion of other products in the manufacturer's range (via recipe instructions, for example) or for joint promotions with non-competing companies. Packages can also build customer loyalty by being attractive to put on the table, or by being easy to find in a cupboard, or by being convenient to use.

Visuals in packaging

Graphics are the visual image conveyed by the pack, and include the **logo**, the print **font** and any illustrations used on the package. Not surprisingly, the graphics can affect the consumer's perception of the product at least as much as can the colour of the package. Table 7.3 shows some of the ways graphics communicate about the product.

TABLE 7.3   Effects of graphics on consumer perceptions

Effect	Explanation
Reinforce brand name or image	The colours used on the pack, and the wording of the pack, will reinforce the image. For example, old-fashioned writing will reinforce the 'traditionally made' image of a can of ginger beer
Attracts attention	An eye-catching graphic will make the product stand out; care should be taken that the image used for catching the eye is consonant with the image of the product, however
Adds aesthetic quality	Some packages are so attractive people keep them and use them as containers; this was the original idea behind putting landscapes on the tops of biscuit tins
Trigger lifestyle aspirations	Pictures on the package can show the product being used by attractive people, or can show attractive situations; mountain scenery, beaches or luxurious homes have all been used for this purpose
Add value	Christmas packs of children's sweets often have a game or puzzle printed on the back; jars of mustard sold in France often have cartoon heroes printed on them so that they can be used as children's drinking glasses; boxes of matches have puzzles or quiz questions printed on them. All these pack designs make the product worth more to the consumer without adding significantly to the cost of production
Can incorporate cues and symbols	A wooden spoon on a pack of cooking fat can invest the product with the traditional reliability of an old-fashioned kitchen (Pilditch 1973). Horizontal lines on packages suggest restfulness and quiet, vertical lines denote strength and confidence, and slanted lines suggest upward movement (left to right for western cultures, right to left for Arabic and some Oriental cultures, due to the direction of reading script). Rounded lines suggest femininity; sharp, angular lines suggest masculinity
Can encourage people to touch the pack	Yves Rocher aromatherapy oils have the letters running right round the pack so that consumers have to pick up the pack to read the writing

Packaging is the last marketing communication the firm has before the purchase decision is made, so it has an important place in the communications mix; around 40 per cent of TV advertisements feature the package, presumably to ensure that consumers know what to look for on the supermarket shelves (*Marketing News* 1987).

Evaluating packaging

Although no single evaluation method (or set of methods) will apply across all forms of packaging, four general features can be evaluated to assess the overall effectiveness of the package. These are as shown in Table 7.4, and are easily remembered using the acronym VIEW.

TABLE 7.4	Evaluating packaging effectiveness
Feature	**Explanation and examples**
Visibility	Does the package stand out from the others on the shelf?
Information	Does the package have the correct user instructions and formulation information? Does it stimulate trial purchase? Does it encourage repeat purchase? On the other hand, does the package look cluttered because it has too much information?
Emotional appeal	Does the package evoke a desired feeling or mood? Do the colour, package shape and graphics combine to give a consistent appeal? Is the balance right between the hedonic appeal of the package and the cognitive appeal?
Workability	Does the package function well? Does it protect the contents? Does it facilitate easy storage for both consumer and retailer? Does it lend itself to being given prominence by the retailer? Does it make the product easy to use? Is it environmentally friendly? Is it a practical (and economical) package to produce? In many cases these factors represent trade-offs; the ideal package from the consumer's or retailer's viewpoint might be far too expensive to produce; conversely, a cheap package may be difficult to use or store and may not protect the contents adequately

The VIEW system is useful for assessing packages, but very few packages will show well on all four aspects. VIEW should therefore be used in the context of the promotional brief and, more importantly, in the context of the other communications tools and strategies surrounding the brand. In particular, the balance between hedonic appeal and cognitive appeal will have a very large effect on the packaging policy – the packaging for a box of chocolates will differ greatly from that for a bag of flour, even though both are types of food.

New developments are always occurring in packaging technology, both in terms of new materials and in terms of new functions. For example, some packages have been developed which are able to interact with machinery and appliances. The obvious example is the printing of bar codes on packages which allow the use of laser readers at supermarket tills to speed up the checkout process. Films now come with a metal code on them which can be read by the camera so that (combined with a built-in light meter) the correct exposure can be given automatically. Packaging is even being developed that will 'tell' microwave ovens how long the food needs to be cooked for (*Brandweek* 1995).

MERCHANDISING

Merchandising is concerned with the way products are displayed in the retail outlet. The criteria used by retailers are as follows:

- Efficient use of floor space
- Visibility for consumers
- Traffic flows around the shop
- Availability of display materials and stands from the manufacturers

Merchandising is a way of promoting products at the point of sale. Some research indicates that around three-quarters of all purchasing decisions are made inside the shop, rather than before leaving home to make the purchase. Given the emphasis many people place on 'shopping around' and 'browsing', this is hardly surprising. The retailer is providing a service to customers, and therefore is operating with a unique marketing mix which may be different from that of the manufacturers whose goods are on the shelves.

The layout of the shop floor involves several trade-offs for the retailer, as shown in Table 7.5.

TABLE 7.5	Floor layout dichotomies

Display of a wide range of products	vs	Keeping aisles broad and minimising clutter
Making it easy for customers to find favourite products quickly	vs	Ensuring that new products receive prominence
Giving prominence to profitable items	vs	Having enough regularly purchased cheap items (also called known-value items) to ensure suitable customer flows

In a supermarket, customers typically move around the store in a clockwise rotation; this helps with the positioning of displays and promotional materials.

There are many merchandising tools and **point-of-purchase** materials that can be utilised. The list below is not intended to be exhaustive.

- *Stickers*. These can be placed near the display shelf or near other (preferably linked) products to direct the customer to the product being promoted.

- *Window displays*. Many stores have windows which are entirely devoted to displays of posters and goods; this was at one time the main way of displaying goods, attracting the attention of passers-by. In recent years the trend has been to minimise the window displays, since they were often seen as a psychological barrier to entering the shop. In any case, the shop's full range of goods could not be displayed.

- *Dump bins*. Piling merchandise into a cardboard or netting bin gives the impression that it is exceptionally cheap, and also encourages customers to pick up the products. It overcomes the (admittedly slight) psychological barrier of disturbing a shelf display. Obviously the merchandise needs to be fairly robust to avoid damage to the goods.

- *Posters, cut-outs and showcards*. Posters are often used in windows, and cards can be suspended from the ceiling in-store, which saves some floor space. Cut-outs (for example of the model who appears in the product's advertising) can be very striking, particularly if a life-size cut-out of a person is used; unfortunately, they tend to take up a lot of floor space.

- *Shelf space and colour blocking*. Supermarket customers scan the shelves at an average rate of four feet per second, so a product needs to have a reasonable minimum of shelf space if it is to be noticed. One way around this is to **colour-block** a section of shelf by grouping products with similar-coloured packs. Some manufacturers design the packs so that they form an eye-catching pattern when seen as a block on the supermarket shelf.

- *Branded display units*. Manufacturers supply display units for their products; typical examples are cosmetics companies, photographic film companies and battery manufacturers. In many cases the manufacturer's salesforce takes responsibility for stocking and maintaining the stands, and in a few cases the stand and the goods remain the property of the manufacturer, with the retailer taking a share of the profit in exchange for giving up the space and serving the customers. This is known as **rackjobbing**.

- *Shelf positioning*. Premium locations tend to be near (but not too near) the entrance doors, and (for impulse purchases) near the checkouts. Other locations within a store become apparent by monitoring the movements of customers, which is sometimes done by using the security cameras and recorders to track movements at different times of day.

- *In-store sampling*. This perhaps belongs more in the realm of sales promotion (see Chapter 10). Sampling involves stationing a member of staff with small samples of the product for people to try. For example, a supermarket might offer tastings of a new cheese spread. The customer feels a social obligation to compliment the product, which leads to a tendency to buy a pack of it. In-store sampling is expensive to run because of the cost of dedicating a member of staff to it, but it usually leads to a very high rate of first-time purchase.

- *Three-dimensional methods*. These range from injection-moulded three-dimensional plastic characters (often used to promote newly released videos), to hologram images, which can now be projected to give a ghostly 3D image suspended in the air. Some very ingenious cardboard engineering is sometimes used to make 3D displays which can be flatpacked for assembly on site.

- *Video walls, spotlighting and fibre optics*. These can all be used to attract attention to the product.

- **Interactive systems**. These are often used in DIY stores to demonstrate the use of a product. The customer can ask questions by using a keyboard to access expert advice on which products to buy for a particular job.

- *In-store public address*. Again, commonly used in large DIY outlets as well as supermarkets. The retailer uses the public address system to broadcast advertisements for special offers or in-store demonstrations. In some cases these advertisements are fairly sophisticated, with music or jingles, and may be pre-recorded and produced in the same way as radio advertisements.

Point-of-purchase materials have been credited with as much as 29 per cent of the business done in some commodities (POPAI News, 1990).

The retail store's external image is also important in enticing customers into the store. Apart from telling the customer what kind of store it is (often very subtle cues are used to decide whether the store is 'posh' or 'cheap and cheerful'), the customer can also sense whether the store appears friendly and easy to enter without obligation, or whether there is a psychological barrier to entry. Some psychological barriers are steps leading in, solid-looking doors, blanked-out windows, poor interior lighting and dark colours. Many supermarkets have made their doors virtually disappear altogether for this reason.

Merchandising and the salesforce

Because of the limited shelf space available for products, and also because supermarkets usually group similar products together, one of the major issues for manufacturers' salespeople is to ensure adequate shelf space for their products. This is frequently an issue for negotiation and can be easily as important as order quantities and price (if the product is moving off the shelves, the store will reorder anyway and will also be less fussy about negotiating the price). Negotiating greater shelf space is also likely to be more successful than trying to negotiate for a big point-of-purchase display – many retailers are concerned with maximising their profit per square foot and are often doubtful about giving up space for large display units.

In many cases the salesforce takes responsibility for the merchandising of the goods. This can take the form of checking the supermarket shelves to ensure that goods are displayed in the right amounts and in the right places; it can involve monitoring and replenishing stock on display stands (either on a sale-or-return basis or on a rackjobbing basis); or it can mean assembling and filling point-of-purchase materials and display stands.

Retailers are usually happy for the suppliers' salespeople to carry out these functions because it frees up the retailer's staff for other tasks and also ensures that the goods are displayed in the most effective manner (since it is clearly in the supplier's interests to do so). The salespeople are happy to merchandise the goods because it gives them the opportunity not only to maximise the sales to the consumer but also to ensure the product's prominence compared with competing brands. Since many retailers will only be carrying the two leading brands in a given product category, filling the rest of the shelf space with own brands, this can be an important issue.

Semiotics and merchandising

A study carried out for the Mammouth chain of hypermarkets in France (now owned by Auchan) identified four sets of values which consumers associate with hypermarkets (DeChernatony and McDonald 1998). These are shown in Table 7.6.

TABLE 7.6	Values associated with hypermarkets	
Values	**Explanation**	**Associations**
Convenience	Concern about finding products quickly, having known-value items always in stock, and always on the same shelves	Convenience values were associated with interchanges and avenues
Critical	Concern about the quality of the products, and value for money (not necessarily cheapness)	Critical values were associated with roundabouts and orientation maps
Utopian	Concern about the store layout being on a human scale, not seeming too overwhelming	Utopian values related to markets and public gardens
Diversionary	Concern about the capacity for browsing, or shopping for pleasure once the practical aspects have been covered	Diversionary values were associated with covered arcades and street markets

Those consumers who were concerned with convenience and critical values wanted simple, continuous space. Consumers with utopian and diversionary values preferred complex, discontinuous space. The Mammouth store designers were eventually able to come up with a design which contained areas of the store designed around each of these groups of consumers, and which allowed each group a separate entrance to the store giving direct access to their preferred space. The store design needed to be adapted somewhat to allow for operational issues such as refilling the shelves and safety concerns, but focus groups were able to give considerable help on this.

Obviously the store designers did not compel customers to use a particular entrance to the store, but after a few visits most customers gravitated to the appropriate entrance because they found that the store layout met their needs most effectively when approached from a particular direction.

Merchandising has moved on considerably in the past ten years; department store layouts from the 1940s and 1950s were intended to encourage customers to 'shop the store' by forcing them to walk past enticing displays in order to find the most regularly purchased items. This policy eventually proved counterproductive since customers who were in a hurry simply shopped elsewhere. As with any other aspect of marketing, a failure to meet the customer's needs will eventually lead to a decline in business.

CASE STUDY: VALUING BRANDS

Brands are the focusing point for marketing activity. They act as identifiers for customers and as a checkpoint for marketers to plan campaigns and design communications. Marketers talk of investing in brands, and with good reason – for many large companies, the brand represents the major part of the firm's assets. For example, in blind taste tests most people prefer Pepsi-Cola to Coca-Cola, but when they can see the bottle the reverse is the case.

Companies are valued in two ways: the balance sheet value of their assets, and the stock market value of their shares. For a firm such as the Coca-Cola Company, the stock market value is so much higher than the balance sheet value that the firm's brand apparently accounts for 95 per cent of the company's total value. In the past, accountants have used the concept of goodwill to account for this type of discrepancy, but from the viewpoint of marketers this is less than satisfactory because it does not value the marketers' input. In the UK in 1999, a new accounting standard was introduced for valuing brands: this was considered a major breakthrough for many firms because it enabled brands to be separated out from all the other considerations which make up goodwill. The accounting standard draws a distinction between intangible assets which have a limited life (for example, patents) and those which do not (for example, brands). The standard defines limited life as being less than twenty years.

Having an accounting standard for the brand has obvious advantages. Because firms now (in theory, at least) account for their brand values in a uniform way, the sale of brands to another firm becomes easier, calculating the value of the brand in franchise or licensing arrangements becomes much simpler, and accountants can produce a more representative balance sheet. From the marketer's viewpoint, however, the new system is less than satisfactory. 'Brand valuation is much like business valuation with a couple of tweaks,' Alex Batchelor of consultants Interbrand Newell and Sorrell says. 'Sure, there are judgements in it but there are judgements in everything. The accounting profession have done a wool-pulling act where people think it's a perfect science when it's not.' The reason for this statement is that the accountants rely on market research to tell them what the value of the brand should be. Market research on branding still relies heavily on judgement – but as soon as the accountants start attaching numbers to the results, they acquire a spurious credibility. Market research is essential to valuing brands because the consumer's view of the brand will determine whether it is purchased over the next few years, and also what the robustness of the brand will be, in other words how well it will stand up to competition in the long run.

Even heavy industrial companies such as BP owe 74 per cent of their value to the brand: Microsoft's stock market value is 96 per cent based on its brands. Whichever form of valuation is used, the major advantage of having a new standard is that it focuses senior management on the brand as an asset – and therefore an asset worth investing in.

Questions

1 Why do firms need to value their brands?

2 How might marketers decide what would be the most effective route for investing in a brand?

3 How might qualitative research be used to evaluate a brand?

4 What differences in investment approach might be needed to meet the differing needs of accountants and marketers?

5 What is the purpose of investing in a brand?

SUMMARY

This chapter has looked at the promotional and communications tools which immediately surround the product itself. These tools are often the most powerful in marketing as they immediately precede the purchasing decision or the act of purchase; they are a final chance to promote the product or to clarify what its characteristics are (thus avoiding later complaints), and to assure the customer of the marketer's good intentions.

Key points from this chapter are as follows:

- Branding helps consumers identify products.
- Branding helps producers to avoid price competition, to differentiate their products and create barriers to entry.
- Brands can be configured to generate marketing synergies.
- Packaging is part of the product because it bestows real benefits.
- Colour affects perception at a deep and subtle level.
- Colour coding is not universal in meaning across cultural boundaries.
- Graphics affect shelf impact and in-store customer behaviour.
- Seventy-five per cent of all purchase decisions are made in-store.
- Point-of-purchase materials may account for 29 per cent of business done.

CHAPTER QUESTIONS

1 How might brand architecture be developed to link food company brands?

2 What factors need to be taken into account when designing packaging if customer complaints are to be minimised? What might be done to the package to maximise contact with dissatisfied customers?

3 How might positive word of mouth be encouraged for a pizza delivery service?

4 What would be the issues surrounding the branding, packaging and merchandising of a baby food product?

5 Who are likely to be the most important groups of opinion leaders for the hi-fi market?

FURTHER READING

Shimp, T. (1997) *Advertising, Promotion and Supplemental Aspects of Integrated Marketing Communications*. London: Dryden Press. This has a good chapter on point-of-purchase materials.

REFERENCES

Bagwell, L. S. and Bernheim, B. D. (1996) 'Veblen effects in a theory of conspicuous consumption', *American Economic Review*, **86**: 349–73.

Balabanis, G. and Craven, S. (1997) 'Consumer confusion from own-brand lookalikes: an exploratory survey', *Journal of Marketing Management*, **13**(4).

Brandweek (1995) 'Packaging 2000', 16 October, p. 40.

Brown, S., Sherry, J.F. and Kozinetts, R.V. (2003) 'Teaching old brands new tricks: retro branding and the revival of brand meaning', *Journal of Marketing*, **67**(3): 19–33

Buschke, H. (1976) 'Learning is organised by chunking', *Journal of Verbal Learning and Verbal Behaviour*, **15**: 313–24.

Clark, K. and Fujimoto, T. (1990) 'The power of product integrity', *Business Review*, November/December: 107–18.

Davies, I. (1995) 'Look-alikes: fair or unfair competition?', *Journal of Brand Management*, 1 (October): 104–20.

DeChernatony, L. and McDonald, M. (1998) *Creating Powerful Brands*, 2nd edn. Oxford: Butterworth Heinemann.

Demsetz, H. (1973) 'Industry structure, market rivalry and public policy', *Journal of Law and Economics*, **16**(1): 1–9.

Demsetz, H. (1982) 'Barriers to entry', *American Economic Review*, **72**: 47–57.

Dichter, E. (1964) *Handbook of Consumer Motivations: The Psychology of the World of Objects*. New York: McGraw-Hill.

Elliott, R. and Leonard, C. (2003) 'Peer pressure and poverty: exploring fashion brands and consumption symbolism among children of the "British poor"', *Journal of Consumer Behaviour*, **3**(4): 347–59.

Foxman, E. R., Berger, P. W. and Cote, J. A. (1992) 'Consumer brand confusion; a conceptual framework', *Psychology and Marketing*, **19**: 123–41.

Gander, P. (1996) 'Patently obvious', *Marketing Week*, 28 June, pp. 51–5.

Gordon, W. and Valentine, V. (1996) 'Buying the brand at point of choice', *Journal of Brand Management*, **4**(1): 35–44.

Hankinson, G. and Cowking, P. (1997) 'Branding in practice: the profile and role of brand managers in the UK', *Journal of Marketing Management*, **13**(4).

Jansson, C., Marlow, N. and Bristow, M. (2004) 'The influence of colour on visual search times in cluttered environments', *Journal of Marketing Communications*, **10**(3): 183–93.

Koestler, A. (1964) *The Act of Creation*. London: Pan.

Marketing News (1987) 'Packaging plays starring role in TV commercials', *Marketing News*, 30 January, p. 6.

Mercer, D. (1992) *Marketing Management*. Oxford: Blackwell.

O'Cass, A. and Clarke, P. (2002) 'Dear Santa, do you have my brand? A study of brand requests, awareness and request styles at Christmas time', *Journal of Consumer Behaviour*, **2**(1): 37–53.

Pilditch, J. (1973) *The Silent Salesman*, 2nd edn. London: Business Books.

Png, J. P. and Reitman, D. (1995) 'Why are some products branded and others not?', *Journal of Law and Economics*, **38**: 207–24.

POPAI News (1990) 'AC Neilson research reveals cheese sales skyrocket with in-store promotions', *Marketplace*, no. 19.

Quelch, J. and Harding, D. (1995) 'Brands versus private labels; fighting to win', *Harvard Business Review*, January/February: 99–109.

Raffee, H. and Kreutzer, R. (1989) 'Organisational dimensions of global marketing', *European Journal of Marketing*, **23**(5): 43–57.

Ries, A. (1995) 'What's in a name?', *Sales and Marketing Management*, 10 (October): 36–7.

Romaniuk, J. (2003) 'Brand attributes: distribution outlets in the mind', *Journal of Marketing Communications*', **9**(2): 73–92.

Ruttenberg, A., Kavizky, A. and Oren, H. (1995) 'Compositioning – the paradigm-shift beyond positioning', *Journal of Brand Management*, 2 (December): 169–79.

Sandler, D. and Shani, D. (1992) 'Brand globally but advertise locally? An empirical investigation', *Marketing Review* 4: 18–31.

Uncles, M., Cocks, M. and Macrae, C. (1995) 'Brand architecture: reconfiguring organisations for effective brand management', *Journal of Brand Management*, 1 (October): 81–92.

8

Managing exhibitions and trade events

Objectives

After reading this chapter you should be able to:

- explain the role of exhibitions and trade fairs in the marketing communications mix
- describe ways of assessing the effectiveness of exhibition activity
- identify the main issues in planning an exhibition
- identify the strengths and weaknesses of exhibiting
- explain which marketing objectives exhibitions best address

INTRODUCTION

Exhibitions and trade shows provide a temporary forum for sellers of a product category to exhibit and demonstrate their products to prospective buyers. Agricultural shows fulfil a similar function but are usually biased more towards competitions among livestock breeders and other types of farmer rather than being purely about promoting products.

Some exhibitions exist as marketplaces where buyers and sellers meet; these are called selling exhibitions. Others (such as the London Motor Show) exist purely as showcases, with no actual buying and selling taking place at the exhibition. Some exhibitions are open to the public whereas others are business-to-business vehicles.

Considerable controversy exists as to whether exhibitions are cost effective and which promotional objectives they best address. The area is considerably under-researched by academics, and much of the existing research has been conducted by parties with vested interests who may or may not be entirely unbiased in their findings. Nonetheless, exhibitions are used by most firms at one time or another and therefore merit at least as much consideration and preparation as any other communication tool.

EXHIBITIONS IN THE COMMUNICATIONS MIX

Exhibitions and trade fairs are widely regarded as a powerful way for firms to reach a large number of potential customers face-to-face at a cost far below that of calls by salespeople. Exhibitions do, indeed, bring together buyers and sellers under one roof in a way that is unique; it is probably the closest thing most modern businesses have to the medieval marketplace which is so often held up as an example of ideal marketing practice.

Substantial sums of money are devoted to exhibitions. Exhibition expenditure is consistently higher than expenditure on radio advertising (usually around four times as high) and magazine advertising. In some years, UK expenditure on exhibitions even approaches that of expenditure on all press advertising.

Despite the widespread use of exhibitions as promotional tools (for exhibitors) and as sources of up-to-date information about the latest developments (for visitors), relatively little research has been conducted into them. This may be because research is unlikely to yield a definitive answer to the question whether exhibitions are an effective way to promote. This may in turn be because of the difficulty of reconciling the aims of exhibitors with those of visitors, or it may be because of entrenched attitudes on the part of exhibitors, non-exhibitors and exhibition managers. One of the areas in which conflict occurs is in the split between activities that directly relate to personal selling (lead generation, appointment making and closing of sales) and activities that relate to other marketing functions such as public relations, promotion, new product launches and marketing research.

Certainly, attitudes among exhibitors and non-exhibitors can be extremely polarised. There are firms that have no other promotional activity than exhibitions, so strong is their belief in the efficacy of the medium; equally, there are marketers who do not believe that exhibitions serve any useful purpose as a promotional tool.

Exhibitions and trade fairs are concerned with two main areas of marketing communications: activities directly related to making sales, and areas that relate to more general promotional activities. Some exhibitions are intended primarily as selling events, where visitors would expect to be able to buy goods directly from the exhibitors, whereas other exhibitions (called non-selling exhibitions) exist primarily to show the latest developments in the industry.

Exhibitions occupy a key role in business-to-business marketing since they allow contact with buyers who would otherwise be seen infrequently owing to geographical or time constraints. This is particularly the case with international exhibitions such as those held in Germany, where exhibitions occupy a more important role than in most other countries. In many cases these exhibitions bring together people who would otherwise not have met at all, and who might not have known of each other's existence.

Since contact at exhibitions is on neutral territory, both parties may feel more relaxed, so that the exhibition allows the relationship between buyer and seller to develop more fully and often in unexpected directions. Meetings at exhibitions can therefore be important factors in relationship marketing, and, certainly, exhibitions present opportunities for strengthening personal bonds between buyers and sales-people. Networking opportunities between exhibitors are also likely to be available; firms with complementary products may be able to make contact with each other.

Sometimes exhibitions also allow contact with clients who order only occasionally but who have strategic importance (for example, companies involved in major construction projects or defence projects).

Exhibitions and public relations

As a PR exercise, exhibitions have a great deal to offer. Although not everyone who visits an exhibition is planning to make a purchase (in fact, some research shows that buyers are in a minority at most exhibitions), it can be said that almost everyone who visits is interested in the industry exhibiting. For example, not everyone who visits the Boat Show in London each January is about to buy a yacht, but those who are not in the market are probably dreaming about buying a yacht. Many of them will crew for friends at weekends, perhaps will sail dinghies, and may one day be in a position to buy. At the very least, they will be talking to their friends about what they have seen.

There is considerable evidence that exhibitions are most useful to visitors at the information-gathering stage of the decision process rather than at the buying stage. This means that exhibitions should be regarded as a sought communication (see Chapter 3). The emphasis therefore needs to be on supplying factual information, answering queries and ensuring that the firm's products become part of the consideration set.

Research into exhibitions

As in many other areas of marketing, the bulk of the published research originates in the USA. Although there might be cause for caution when dealing with US research, on the grounds that exhibitions acquire a somewhat different nature in a large country, where comparisons exist with UK research the findings are broadly similar.

Most research into managers' perceptions of trade shows and exhibitions confirms the view that managers see exhibitions in terms of making sales. This is true of both US and UK research: even when managers do not expect to take orders at the shows, they still tend to expect to obtain leads, qualify prospects and open sales. This is particularly apparent in the staffing of stands: managers predominantly staff them with salespeople even though there is evidence to suggest that visitors do not like this (Tanner and Chonko 1995).

Shipley *et al.* (1993) identified thirteen reasons for exhibiting, of which seven were directly related to selling, with six representing non-selling activities. Table 8.1 shows their ranking of reasons for exhibiting; the mean scores refer to the scores out of seven given by the respondents.

TABLE 8.1 Reasons for exhibiting

Objective	UK (n = 124)		Overseas (n = 61)	
	Mean	Rank	Mean	Rank
Meet new customers	6.02	1	6.11	1
Enhance company image	5.62	2	5.56	2
Interact with customers	5.55	3	5.43	4
Promote existing products	5.49	4	5.51	3
Launch new products	5.11	5	4.79	5
Get competitor intelligence	3.71	6	3.90	6
Get edge on non-exhibitors	3.65	7	3.38	9
Keep up with competitors	3.61	8	3.46	8
Enhance personnel morale	3.30	9	2.82	13
Interact with distributors	3.02	10	3.89	7
General market research	2.92	11	3.10	11
Take sales orders	2.74	12	2.90	12
Meet new distributors	2.15	13	3.20	10

Source: Based on Shipley *et al.* (1993).

This research showed that taking sales orders ranked low on the list (although this depends on the nature of the exhibition itself). This is despite the fact that much of the strategy-orientated research into exhibitions focuses on the level of resources committed to participation (Bonoma 1983; Herbig *et al.* 1994), with the decision being made according to the number of sales leads the show is likely to generate (Cavanaugh 1976; Kijewski *et al.* 1992).

Trade fairs and exhibitions tend to be regarded as selling opportunities in much of the literature, particularly in the practitioner textbooks (Waterhouse 1987; Cotterell 1992), with an emphasis on the low cost per contact made, as compared with cold calling in the field. The problem with this view of exhibitions is that it does not take account of the strength of the contacts; contacts obtained in the field are likely to be stronger, if only because competitors are not present when the contact is made.

Sharland and Balogh (1996), for example, define **effectiveness** as the number of sales leads generated, followed up and successfully closed, and **efficiency** as the comparison between the cost of trade show participation versus other sales and promotion activity. Research by the Centre for Leisure and Tourism Studies (1994) showed the cost of a useful trade show contact to be £30, compared with £150 for a field call. These figures may not be comparable, since a 'useful contact' is not necessarily a qualified lead, but the general conclusion drawn by the researchers is that exhibition contacts are cheaper than field contacts.

This view of exhibitions as selling tools is certainly borne out by other UK research; managers typically talk about selling and meeting new customers, rarely about the PR value of exhibitions. In fact, in one study some managers expressed surprise that there could be any other reason for exhibiting (Blythe and Rayner 1996).

Having said that, Kerin and Cron (1987) found that non-selling activities are considered by some exhibitors to be more important than selling activities. Many firms view exhibitions as an opportunity to enhance the company image, for example, or to carry out some general marketing research – to find out what the competition is offering, for instance. Although it can be argued that the purpose of all marketing activity is, ultimately, to make sales, not all activities relate directly to the personal selling function. Therefore, although the received wisdom (and the prevailing view) is that exhibitions are tools for personal selling, not all exhibitors agree. Table 8.2 shows the importance accorded to various trade show aims by Kerin and Cron's respondents.

The dissidents may well be right. For example, there is a conflict between the exhibitors' view of exhibitions and the visitors' view. Many visitors do not have any role in purchasing (Gramman 1993), and in fact the majority have no direct role. Some are students on visits from their universities and colleges, some are competitors who are not themselves exhibiting, some are consultants or others who are trying to make contact with exhibitors in order to sell their own services. They are therefore unlikely to become qualified leads (although they might well be useful contacts).

TABLE 8.2	Importance of trade show aims	
Aim	Mean score (out of 10)	Standard deviation
Identify new prospects	5.08	1.521
Servicing current customers	4.69	1.956
Introduce new products	5.14	1.695
Selling at the show	2.79	2.294
Enhancing corporate image	5.32	1.384
New product testing	2.17	1.955
Enhancing corporate morale	3.75	1.816
Getting competitive information	4.94	1.392

Source: Kerin and Cron (1987)

In the USA, Bello and Lohtia (1993) report similar findings. Other researchers report visitors complaining of 'too much sales pitch' (Chonko *et al.* 1994); many visitors are on information-gathering expeditions rather than intending specifically to purchase anything. Moriarty and Spekman (1984) identify trade shows as being most useful to purchasers in the information-gathering and vendor selection stages of the decision-making process. Given this conflict between visitor expectations and exhibitor expectations, it is presumably up to the market-orientated exhibitor to adapt the approach on the stand (Tanner 1994). Exhibitors really need to ask themselves why the visitors come (Godar 1992), and in most cases will find that they did not come to be sold to.

It is therefore entirely possible that non-selling aims are more important (or at least more realistic) in exhibiting. The main non-selling activity that firms do report as an aim is enhancing the corporate image; for some this is the most important aim (see Table 8.2). Shipley *et al.* (1993) found that it ranked second for both domestic and overseas exhibitors, and 25 per cent of respondents in a US survey reported 'establishing a presence' as their primary goal in exhibiting (Tanner and Chonko 1995).

This background of dissent about the true value of exhibitions naturally leads some exhibitors to question whether there is a value at all, and of course some exhibitors have moved away from exhibitions and towards road shows or other means of promotion or lead generation (*Industrial Marketing* 1979; Couretas 1984). Equally, there is dissent among academics as to the value of exhibitions. Sashi and Perretty (1992) express doubts about the overall usefulness of trade shows, Bonoma (1983) is critical of them, yet Gopalakrishna *et al.* (1995) are of the opinion that trade shows are effective. Not unnaturally, the exhibition industry itself reports that exhibitions are very effective in generating sales leads and other benefits (Trade Show Bureau 1988; Exhibition Industry Federation 1989).

One area in which exhibitions have a strong role is in establishing and maintaining business-to-business relationships (Blythe 2002). In the early stages, exhibitions represent a neutral ground on which first contacts can be made. As the relationship progresses, contacts can be made at other levels in the organsiation: research shows that most visitors to exhibitions are not buyers, but many of them may have influence in the buying decision (Price and Blythe 2004). Building relationships in business-to-business markets means establishing contacts at all levels in the firm, not just between buyers and salespeople: technical people such as engineers and designers represent around 20 per cent of exhibition visitors, but they are largely ignored by most exhibitors. Placing some engineers on the stand could be an effective way of improving the levels of contact between the firms. The same applies to administrators and even buyers, since some visitors to exhibitions are actually there to sell to the exhibitors (Price and Blythe 2004).

Planning an exhibition

Although exhibitions are expensive activities, many firms do not put sufficient time and effort into planning them. In some cases this is because the management believes that the exhibition is merely a flag-waving exercise and does not expect to get anything tangible from it; in other cases the exhibition is a one-off or infrequent activity and thus imposes an extra burden on the marketing team which disrupts their usual routine.

A properly planned and executed exhibition is likely to take up six months or more in total, both in the preparation beforehand and in the follow-up activities afterwards. The first stage is to decide what the objectives of the exhibition are; this goes beyond merely deciding what the reasons are for exhibiting. The objectives need to be realistic (bearing in mind the visitor profile of the exhibition), they need to be achievable (within the context of the firm's resources), and they need to be quantifiable (and mechanisms must be in place to monitor their achievement).

Formal objective setting appears to be influenced by a combination of the importance of the activity and the ease of assessment. Most exhibitors state that personal selling is the main aim of exhibiting, or indeed the only aim; most are able to set formal objectives for taking sales orders, but the majority (more than two-thirds) are unable or unwilling to set objectives for interacting with existing customers. If most firms do not set objectives for this activity, clearly even fewer would set objectives for non-selling activities such as enhancing the company image (Blythe 1997).

The second stage of the planning process is to decide which exhibition to attend. This decision will rest on the following factors:

- The number of available exhibitions to choose from. In some industries there are only one or two suitable exhibitions each year.

- The visitor profile of the exhibition. Most exhibition organisers will provide this information based on the previous year's attendance. Obviously, information from this source will need to be treated with some circumspection – exhibition organisers are unlikely to give a negative picture.

- The cost of exhibiting.

- The availability of suitable space in a good location.

- The timing of the exhibition relative to the firm's business cycle and other communication projects.

- The profile of exhibitors (in other words, which competitors will be exhibiting and which will not).

- The prestige of the exhibition. It would be hard to imagine a British car manufacturer not exhibiting at the London Motor Show, for example.

The third stage is to plan the staffing of the exhibition stand. Most managers tend to use the salesforce here, but this has the disadvantage of taking salespeople off the road. Also, the research evidence shows that most visitors are not actually in a position to buy, but are probably engaged in the information search stage of the buying process. Unless the show is primarily a selling show, therefore, it is more productive to staff the stand with technical people, with perhaps one salesperson to handle buyers and collect leads.

The fourth stage is to plan the support promotions around the exhibition. These may include direct mailshots to potential visitors, advertising campaigns in advance of the exhibition, press releases in the trade or consumer press as appropriate, and extra activity by the salesforce both before the exhibition (inviting existing customers to visit the stand) and afterwards (following up new enquiries).

The fifth stage is to decide on the layout of the stand and its contents. Since visitors are usually information gathering, the stand needs to be eye-catching and attractive, but should also convey solid information. Exhibitions are often good places to launch new products, so the firm's latest offerings need to be on the stand. It is often useful to have an area that is away from public view so that potential customers can discuss their needs with the salesperson in private. Some refreshments can be available and the quiet area can also serve as a rest area for stand staff. Some exhibitors employ temporary staff for the exhibition period; this has the advantage of freeing up the firm's permanent staff and avoiding the disruption of routine that exhibitions often cause, but can mean that the stand is staffed with people who have no long-term commitment to the firm and its success. A way round this is to use the temporary staff for leaflet distribution around the exhibition, to encourage visitors to visit the firm's stand.

The sixth stage of planning is to arrange for follow-up activities after the exhibition. A surprising number of exhibitors fail to do this, with the result that the salesforce is unable to follow up on leads generated (Blythe and Rayner 1996). The main problem with delaying follow-ups is that the prospects will undoubtedly have contacted the firm's competitors as well (since they will almost certainly be at the same exhibition). This may mean that a delay allows the competition to get the business, so salespeople should clear their appointment books for about a month after the exhibition in order to have time to do follow-up visits.

The final stage of planning is to arrange the logistics of the exercise. This means ensuring that the equipment, furnishings, promotional material and staff are all transported to the exhibition at the right time and arrive in good condition to make the exhibition a success.

Once the exhibition is over, two activities need to be carried out: first, the follow-up sales activities (where appropriate) or follow-up promotional activities in the case of non-selling shows; second, evaluating the success of the show. This latter can be carried out by formal market research, or by counting the number of leads generated, or the number of visitors to the stand, or whatever other means are appropriate to the objectives. Research by Blythe and Rayner (1996) revealed, however, that many exhibitors do not have systems in place for evaluating their selling activities; still fewer had systems for tracking non-selling activities. The reasons given for this ranged from a belief that the variables are too vague, through to a view that the lead times involved in converting exhibition leads to sales made tracking impossible.

Undoubtedly these difficulties are perfectly valid, and for an individual firm in the field it may well be more expensive to find out the answers than it is to live with the problem.

More research is indicated into the reasons for firms not evaluating, but some possible reasons have been identified, as follows:

- The firm lacks the resources to carry out the evaluation.

- The activity is not important enough to warrant evaluation.

- The evaluation would be too difficult or expensive.

- The firm is owner managed and therefore the owner feels able to estimate the effectiveness of the exhibition without formal evaluation (Blythe 1997).

Non-evaluation of such an expensive, time consuming and (often) disruptive activity would seem to be perverse, to say the least. It would be hard to imagine a firm conducting, for example, a nationwide billboard campaign without evaluating the results, yet exhibiting represents more than double the national expenditure on billboard and outdoor advertising.

Managing the exhibition stand

Stand management is straightforward provided that the planning has been carefully carried out and the necessary equipment and staff have arrived. Stands are usually regarded as stressful environments; the noise and crowds at most exhibitions put a strain on those staffing the stand and they will therefore need frequent rest periods.

Designing the layout of the stand is an important part of the process. Most exhibitors tend to make the company name the most prominent feature, with brand names and product specifications lower on the list of priorities. This is a reasonable policy if the purpose of the stand is to raise the corporate profile, but in most cases (as research shows) the company is actually aiming to make sales or generate leads. In those circumstances, the visitors' need for solid information will dictate the design and layout of the stand.

In many cases, firms assume that visitors will recognise the company's name and will know what products are available. This is something of a leap of faith: overseas visitors to exhibitions may not be familiar with the firm and its products, and even domestic visitors may be more familiar with brand names than with company names, since the former are usually given greater promotion.

Exhibitions are tiring for the visitors as well as for the exhibitors, so visitors usually only spend significant time at a few stands. This may be as few as 10 or 12 stands, and this figure does not rise with the size of the exhibition since most visitors attend for only one day. This means that large exhibitions with many stands do not lead to an increase in the number of visitors who will see the stand; statistically, large exhibitions actually reduce the chances of particular visitors seeing a particular stand since there are more stands to choose from.

The problem of clutter is probably greater at exhibitions than in any other environment, as exhibitors all compete for the visitors' limited attention. For this reason the stand must be designed with the visitors' needs in mind as well as the exhibition's objectives. For example, if the exhibition objective is to raise corporate awareness, the company name needs to be prominent and a plentiful supply of brochures and leaflets needs to be available. Temporary promotion staff could be employed to hand out leaflets in other parts of the exhibition hall so that exhibitors who do not intend to visit the stand might be encouraged to do so, or at least go away with some information about the firm. The stand might have some kind of stunt or gimmick to raise awareness – a product demonstration or some spectacular event will attract attention.

On the other hand, if the company's aim is to make sales or generate leads, the stand should show the brand names prominently, with plenty of information on product benefits. The stand should be staffed with some technical people and some salespeople, and brochures should only be given to visitors who are prepared to leave their names and addresses (some exhibitors will only mail out brochures rather than give them out on the stand). This ensures that follow-up calls can be carried out. Promotions and stunts should be used to collect names and addresses; for example, a free draw for a prize. Special 'exhibition-only' discounts or promotions can be used, and pre-publicity can reflect this in order to get buyers on to the stand. In these circumstances, casual non-buying visitors are less important and might even be actively discouraged – although (for the reasons outlined earlier in the chapter) this may be a short-sighted policy, since most exhibitions are probably not good selling venues and the casual visitors may be the exhibitor's best future customers.

The following is a checklist for organising the stand itself:

• Ensure that displays are easily accessible and informative.

• Check that stand members have a clear brief.

• Have clear objectives in place and, where feasible, set targets for stand members.

• Have an area where prospects can be taken for a private conversation if necessary.

• Ensure an adequate supply of drinking water and other refreshments.

• Establish a rota for stand staff to ensure regular breaks.

• Have a record-keeping system for leads and useful contacts.

• Have a feedback system for visitors' comments.

• Set up some 'fun' activities for stand staff.

It is useful for stand staff to have the opportunity to tour the rest of the exhibition (this also gives them a break), and it is worthwhile to give them objectives for doing this – for example, making it the time for gathering information about competitors. Staff will need a break at least every hour – long periods of standing, smiling and relating to large numbers of people are both physically and psychologically exhausting. This requires careful planning to ensure that there are enough suitably qualified people left to staff the stand during breaks.

The main problem concerning stand staff is maintaining their motivation over the period of the show. After a few hours on the stand, the visitors seem to meld into a single mass, most of the enquiries seem like a waste of time and the smile begins to wear a little thin. For this reason it is a good idea to have some activities running that keep stand personnel interested. For example, a competition for collecting business cards, with an appropriate small prize, can motivate staff. Demonstrations throughout the day can help to break the monotony for staff as well as visitors, particularly if the demonstrations are given by stand members in rotation. Again, a small prize could be offered for the best demonstration.

Exhibitions are often held away from the firm's home base and therefore away from staff's homes and families. Sometimes it might be appropriate to allow staff to bring their partners with them, but in most cases this is problematical (after all, husbands and wives also have careers to consider, or children to look after), so every opportunity should be given for staff to telephone home, and it almost goes without saying that their accommodation and meals should be of a high standard – this compensates to a small extent for being away from home, but in any case it reflects well on the firm.

Overall, exhibitions need to be planned in fine detail, with everything leading towards the planned objectives. Choice of exhibition, pre-publicity, follow-up, stand design, staffing and choice of what to exhibit should all be decided with clear objectives in mind.

ALTERNATIVES TO EXHIBITIONS

Because of the cost and commitment attached to exhibiting, not least the disruption to the exhibitors' normal routine, firms often look for alternative routes for meeting buyers and promoting their products. Since one of the main advantages of exhibitions is the 'neutral territory' aspect, allowing buyers and sellers to discuss matters in a more relaxed way, many exhibitors are moving towards private exhibitions or road shows to exhibit their products.

Private exhibitions

Private exhibitions are sometimes run at venues near to the public exhibition and coincide with the main event. Typically, such events are held in hotels or small halls to which the buyers are invited.

The main advantages are as follows:

- The atmosphere is usually more relaxed and less frenetic than that in the main exhibition.

- No competitors are present to distract the visitors.

- The exhibitor has much more control over the environment than would be the case at the public exhibition, where the organisers may impose irksome regulations.

- Superior refreshment and reception facilities are available.

- If the event is held in a hotel, the staff will have access to their rooms and can easily take breaks.

- Sometimes the overall cost is less than taking a stand at the main exhibition.

The main drawback of the private event is that visitors will only come to it if they are given advance warning, and even then may decide only to visit the main exhibition. The invitations need to be sent out early enough that visitors can set time aside for the event, but not so early that they forget about it, and some incentive to make the necessary detour may also need to be offered. It is extremely unlikely that the list of desirable visitors will be complete – one of the main advantages of a public exhibition is that some of the visitors will be unknown to the exhibiting company and a first contact can be made.

Private exhibitions work best in situations where the company has a limited market, where the costs of the main exhibition are high and where a suitable venue is available close to the main site.

Road shows

A **road show** is a travelling exhibition that takes the product to the buyer rather than the other way round. In some cases these are run in hotels, in other cases trailers or caravans and marquees are used. Road shows are useful in cases where large numbers of buyers are concentrated in particular geographical areas, and where many of them would not make the journey to visit a national exhibition. For example, many householders would not take the trouble to visit a national Ideal Homes exhibition, but might be interested in visiting a hotel in their home town to see the latest imported furniture.

Like private exhibitions, road shows allow the exhibitor to control the environment to a large extent. Road shows can be run in conjunction with other firms, which reduces the cost and increases the interest level for the visitors. This can be particularly effective if the firms concerned are complementary rather than competing.

Also like private exhibitions, the exhibitor is entirely responsible for all the publicity. In the case of a major public exhibition, the organisers, and even the firm's competitors, will ensure that a certain minimum level of visitors will attend; in the case of a road show, the exhibitor will need to produce considerable advance publicity and even send out personalised invitations to individual buyers and prospects. This adds to the risk as well as the cost.

CASE STUDY: EAA AIRVENTURE OSHKOSH

Oshkosh is a town with an unusual name – and each year it hosts an unusual exhibition. The town's airport, Wittman Regional Airport, is taken over by thousands of aircraft enthusiasts. Over 10,000 aircraft are on display, including antique aircraft, home-made flying machines, military planes, helicopters, autogyros, commercial airliners, and microlights. At the 2005 exhibition, the world's first civilian spaceship, Spaceship One, was displayed along with its carrier aircraft, White Knight.

The exhibition-cum-festival attracts 750,000 visitors, far more than can be accommodated in local hotels, so part of the fun is camping. Thirty thousand people camp around the area, in the Camp Scholler camping area and in Aircraft Camping areas where they can camp out beside their own aircraft. Others fill up hotels, student accommodation, campsites, and even rent rooms in local houses within a 75-mile radius of Oshkosh. For a time, Oshkosh becomes the biggest city in Wisconsin.

The Oshkosh show naturally attracts a broad range of exhibitors. For the most part, visitors to the show are interested in flying for fun: having said that, many commercial and military pilots also fly light aircraft, gliders, microlights and even balloons for fun in their free time, and there are certainly some commercial and military aircraft on display. The exhibitors in 2005 included Honda Motorcycles, which ran engineering workshops for people who want to build their own aircraft, NASA, which showed off some of the technology it developed and passed on to aircraft manufacturers, the United States Air Force and the local Wisconsin National Guard, who displayed military aircraft and were on hand to answer questions, and 700 other exhibitors offering everything from aeronautical charts to kit planes. Shell Oil has pride of place, however – the centre point of the whole event is Aeroshell Square, where most of the spectacular demonstrations and displays take place.

During the period of the show, the control tower becomes the world's busiest – so much so that the radio frequencies become overloaded, so pilots respond to traffic control requests by waggling their wings rather than speaking. For one week, the airport is virtually out of action for its usual commercial flights.

Most people who fly for fun are relatively well heeled: middle-class professionals and businesspeople predominate, although there are many enthusiasts who operate home-built aircraft on shoestring budgets. This makes Oshkosh an attractive venue for all kinds of exhibitors who are not directly connected with aviation, although such exhibitors are discouraged by the organisers: this is, after all, an air-related exhibition. There is, of course, nothing to stop companies advertising in the show brochure or at various locations around the show – Oshkosh is an expensive event to put on, so all income is welcome.

For many amateur flyers, Oshkosh represents an opportunity to see the latest developments, order new equipment or even aircraft, examine a wide range of planes in an atmosphere where there is little pressure to buy, and especially to meet up with old friends from airfields throughout the world.

Questions

1 How might an exhibitor at such a large exhibition make an impact?

2 If you were a light aircraft manufacturer, how would you staff your stand at Oshkosh?

3 Why would NASA exhibit at Oshkosh?

4 Why does the US Air Force exhibit at Oshkosh?

5 Why does Honda Motorcycles offer free engineering assistance to people building their own aircraft?

CHAPTER SUMMARY

This chapter has been about exhibitions and trade shows. While most writers agree that exhibitions are a powerful communications tool, since no other medium brings so many buyers and sellers together under one roof, there are many voices of dissent.

Much of this dissent arises from the problem of defining the criteria for deciding whether an exhibition has been successful or not. A firm that sets unrealistic objectives (for example, setting sales objectives for a non-selling exhibition) or that fails to plan properly for following up the enquiries generated, is likely to blame the exhibition for lack of success. Equally, many managers place blind faith in exhibitions while not actually having any mechanisms in place for evaluating the activity.

Exhibitions require a considerable degree of commitment, not just for the week or so of the exhibition but for the months preceding and following the event. As an activity it is too expensive and too high profile to be left to chance.

Here is a list of the key points from this chapter:

- Visitor expectations and exhibitor objectives may not complement each other.

- Exhibitions are often seen as information sources by visitors; it is therefore too early in the decision-making process for selling activities to be effective.

- Visitors spend time on relatively few stands.

- The firm's exhibition-related activities will probably span a period of six months.

- Setting objectives is as important in exhibiting as anywhere else; the difficulty lies in measuring the success of the objectives.

- Stunts, gimmicks and demonstrations can help keep staff involved as well as attract visitors.

CHAPTER QUESTIONS

1 If exhibitions are such powerful medicine, why is there an increasing trend to use road shows and other promotional means instead?

2 How might a small firm maximise its impact at a major trade show, where stand space is expensive?

3 What can an exhibition do that the salesforce can't do better?

4 What possible courses of action are open to an exhibitor who finds that the event failed to meet its objectives?

FURTHER READING

Most, if not all, of the books on exhibiting are written for practitioners. This is probably due to the very small amount of research that has been carried out into exhibiting, at least within the UK and Europe. All the practitioner texts are strongly pro-exhibition; the voices of dissent are confined to academic journals and occasional practitioners.

Cotterell, P. (1992) *Exhibitions: An Exhibitor's Guide*. London: Hodder & Stoughton. A weighty book with a good section on planning for exhibitions.

Waterhouse, D. (1987) *Making the Most of Exhibitions*. Aldershot: Gower. A lively and readable guide to the practicalities of mounting an exhibition.

REFERENCES

Bello, D. C. and Lohtia, R. (1993) 'Improving trade show effectiveness by analyzing attendees', *Industrial Marketing Management*, **22**: 311–18.

Blythe, J. (1997) 'Does size matter? Objectives and measures at UK trade exhibitions', *Journal of Marketing Communications*, **3**(1).

Blythe, J. (2002) 'Using trade fairs in key account management', *Industrial Marketing Management*, **31**: 627–35.

Blythe, J. and Rayner, T. (1996) 'The evaluation of non-selling activities at British trade exhibitions – an exploratory study', *Marketing Intelligence and Planning*, **14**(5).

Bonoma, T. V. (1983) 'Get more out of your trade shows', *Harvard Business Review*, **61**(January/February): 75–83.

Cavanaugh, S. (1976) 'Setting of objectives and evaluating the effectiveness of trade show exhibits', *Journal of Marketing*, **40**(October): 100–3.

Centre for Leisure and Tourism Studies (1994) *The Exhibition Industry Research Report: The Facts 1994*. London: Centre for Leisure and Tourism Studies.

Chonko, L. B., Tanner, J. F. Jr and McKee, J. (1994) 'Matching trade show staff to prospects', *Industrial Marketing Management*, **3**: 40–3.

Cotterell, P. (1992) *Exhibitions: An Exhibitor's Guide*. London: Hodder & Stoughton.

Couretas, J. (1984) 'Trade shows and the strategic mainstream', *Business Marketing*, **69**: 64–70.

Exhibition Industry Federation (1989) *EIF Exhibition Effectiveness Survey*. London: Centre for Leisure and Tourism Studies.

Godar, S. H. (1992) 'Same time next year? Why industrial buyers go to trade shows', *Marketing: Perspectives for the 1990s* (Annual Proceedings of the Southern Marketing Association).

Gopalakrishna, S., Lilien, G. L., Williams, J. D. and Sequeira, I. K. (1995) 'Do trade shows pay off?', *Journal of Marketing*, **59**(July): 75–83.

Gramman, J. (1993) *Independent Market Research*. Birmingham: Centre Exhibitions with National Exhibition Centre.

Herbig, P., O'Hara, B. and Palumbo, F. (1994) 'Measuring trade show effectiveness: an effective exercise?', *Industrial Marketing Management*, **23**: 165–70.

Industrial Marketing (1979) 'Trade shows are usually a form of mass hysteria, Zagar says', *Industrial Marketing*, **64**: 4.

Kerin, R. A. and Cron, W. L. (1987) 'Assessing trade show functions and performance: an exploratory study', *Journal of Marketing*, **51**(July): 87–94.

Kijewski, V., Yoon, E. and Young, G. (1992) *Trade Shows: How Managers Pick their Winners*. Institute for the Study of Business Markets, Penn State University, PA.

Moriarty, R. T. and Spekman, R. E. (1984) 'An empirical investigation of the information sources used during the industrial buying process', *Journal of Marketing Research*, **21**(2): 137–47.

Price, E. and Blythe, J. (2004) 'Information source usage by trade show attendees', Proceedings of the Academy of Marketing Conference, Cheltenham, July.

Sashi, C. M. and Perretty, J. (1992) 'Do trade shows provide value?', *Industrial Marketing Management*, **21**(3): 249–55.

Sharland, A. and Balogh, P. (1996) 'The value of non-selling activities at international trade shows', *Industrial Marketing Management*, **25**(1): 59–66.

Shipley, D., Egan, C. and Wong, K. S. (1993) 'Dimensions of trade show exhibiting management', *Journal of Marketing Management*, **9**(1): 55–63.

Tanner, J. F. (1994) 'Adaptive selling at trade shows', *Journal of Personal Selling and Sales Management*, **13**: 15–24.

Tanner, J. F. and Chonko, L. B. (1995) 'Trade show objectives, management and staffing practices', *Industrial Marketing Management*, **24**: 257–64.

Trade Show Bureau (1988) *Attitudes and Opinions of Computer Executives Regarding Attendance at Information Technology Events*, Study no. 1080. East Orleans, MA: Trade Show Bureau.

Waterhouse, D. (1987) *Making the Most of Exhibitions*. Aldershot: Gower.

9 Direct and database marketing

Objectives

After reading this chapter you should be able to:

- describe the main advantages and disadvantages of database marketing
- explain the stages a company goes through to develop a fully integrated database
- explain the main driving forces in the growth of direct marketing
- describe the ways in which consumers respond to direct marketing, both positively and negatively
- explain some of the ethical issues involved in database marketing

INTRODUCTION

This chapter is about direct marketing and computer-based marketing approaches. In recent years, since the advent of cheap computers and user-friendly software, there has been an exponential growth in the use of databases for targeting and mailing directly to consumers. Computer-driven marketing systems have become all-pervasive, and both academic and practitioner interest has been directed at the 'new' methods of marketing. In fact, direct marketing has developed from the well-established mail order industry; computers have speeded up and simplified the process, but have also given marketers new techniques to use.

The terms 'direct marketing' and 'database marketing' are often used synony-mously. In fact, database marketing is only that part of direct marketing which is handled by computers; other forms of direct marketing exist which are not computer-driven, although it should be said that these are becoming rarer as the advantages of using computers mean that they are becoming ever more ubiquitous.

DATABASE MARKETING – BACKGROUND

Most people receive advertising leaflets through the post; some people receive large numbers of these leaflets. The purpose of database marketing is, ultimately, to reduce the number of these leaflets and increase the relevance of them to the recipients by ensuring that each person receives only leaflets that will be of interest, given their needs and circumstances. Database marketing is the antithesis of **junk mail**; instead of using a 'scattergun' approach of mailing anybody and everybody, the database marketer uses a carefully screened list of people who have demonstrated that they are interested in the product category, and that they are open to the direct mail approach.

Database marketing has evolved from **mail order** and direct distribution methods. In the UK, mail order began around the turn of the twentieth century; it had been popular in the USA since the mid nineteenth century, when farmers and ranchers in remote parts of the country were able to order goods through the Sears Roebuck catalogue.

In each country where mail order began, it came to fulfil a slightly different role. In the USA, it was often the only means available for people far from towns to buy consumer goods. In Germany, the mountainous nature of much of the country led to similar problems of getting to towns, and also legal restrictions on the opening hours of retail outlets meant that working people were unable to go shopping except during their lunch hours. In the UK, mail order offered credit to people who would otherwise not be able to obtain it; the system relies on local agents who are creditworthy, who are paid commission for sales to their friends and neighbours, and who are presumably in a better position to collect the money when it falls due. This meant that, in the UK, mail order targeted lower socio-economic groups, and this bias remained evident until fairly recently.

Because of this bias, mail order declined during the 1980s. The recession in the first few years of the decade meant that many traditional mail order customers lost their jobs, and consequently the number of bad debts increased; at the same time, traditional retail outlets began to offer credit, which meant that mail order firms lost the main plank in their platform.

The other root of database marketing lies in mailshots (commonly called junk mail). As postal services came into being and improved, it became possible for marketers to mail out advertising leaflets and letters to potential customers. In most cases these were actually a mass communication method, since they were mailed out indiscriminately to people who may or may not have been in the market for the products concerned. Although response rates for this type of mailing are relatively high compared with other mass methods, and therefore the exercise is often cost effective, junk mail also engenders high levels of resentment from consumers. Some estimates state that 40 per cent of consumers regard junk mail as the most irritating marketing tool. The irrelevance of many mailings accounts for this: single men being sent catalogues of women's fashions, childless couples being sent material about children's educational trusts, and the widespread use of mailings to promote pension plans and life insurance, some of which went to people who are already pensioners and therefore ineligible. These indiscriminate mailings only served to bring direct communications into disrepute.

During the 1980s the solution to this problem became available in the form of cheap, high powered computers with sufficient memory and data handling capacity to handle detailed information on consumers' buying behaviour. For the first time it was possible to refine mailing lists beyond simply a name and address and (perhaps) an estimate of income: the computers were now able to examine an individual's purchasing behaviour and send accurately targeted and informative letters rather than persuasive leaflets.

DIRECT MARKETING

Direct marketing goes beyond its original distribution-based roots to include direct communications in its remit. The American Direct Marketing Association defines direct marketing as follows:

> *Direct marketing is an interactive system of marketing which uses one or   more advertising media to effect a measurable response and/or transaction at any location.*

Direct marketing is not a mass medium; it communicates with consumers as individuals, rather than as a group of segments (Bird 1993), and it is interactive, meaning that consumers respond directly (and measurably) to direct communications. The communications are aimed (as far as is possible) only at those individuals who are likely to be interested in the offering.

Bauer and Miglautsch (1992) offer an alternative definition, accepted by the UK's Direct Marketing Association:

Direct marketing is a cybernetic marketing process which uses direct response advertising in prospecting, conversion and maintenance.

This definition shows clearly that direct marketing is neither a sophisticated mail order system nor merely a communication device like the old mailshots. It is instead a new type of marketing system, with its own marketing mix and its own set of parameters. The result of the increasing sophistication of direct marketing is a huge growth in expenditure in this area; expenditure on direct mail in the UK alone is estimated to be over £8 billion per year.

Part of the reason for this huge growth is the rapidly falling cost of information technology, and at the same time a rapid increase in the costs associated with traditional marketing approaches, particularly in personal selling. Another reason is the increasing fragmentation and individualism evident in most western cultures (Evans and Blythe 1994).

Impact of technology

Direct marketing relies on having good, up-to-date information about the individuals it seeks to approach. This implies using computer-based systems (sophisticated databases) to record information about potential customers. The other way in which computers contribute is in **desktop publishing (DTP)**: tailored communications can be sent out to prospects, personalised and of high quality.

The impact of technology in improving targeting is summarised in Table 9.1.

TABLE 9.1	Impact of technology
Technological factor	**Explanation and examples**
Addressability	Being able to identify and reach individuals (Vavra 1992)
Measurability	Knowing the purchasing behaviour of individuals (Vavra 1992)
Flexibility	The ability to appeal to each customer in a different way at a different time (Vavra 1992)
Accountability	The ability to track expenditure and assess profitability of a given event, as well as identifying the type of customer who responded (Vavra 1992)

TABLE 9.1   Continued

Technological factor	Explanation and examples
Increased processing power	The ever increasing data processing capabilities of equipment allow faster and more detailed analysis of customers and their purchasing behaviour, as well as increased capacity for holding detailed information about prospects and customers
Analytical systems	Software for rapid analysis and graphical presentation of statistics has greatly improved the ability to make sense of the data held on computer
Desktop publishing (DTP)	This is a software development which allows the production of customised, high quality documentation and promotional materials. Because the materials can be produced almost instantly, the delays caused by traditional print methods are largely eliminated
Telephone technology	Until the mid 1980s, telephones could only be used for outbound telemarketing, i.e. calls originating with the marketer. Consumers were reluctant to make long-distance calls because of the costs involved. The advent of 0800 (free) and 0345 (local rate) numbers and automatic call distributors has meant that marketers can handle large numbers of inbound calls. A recent innovation has been interactive voice response (IVR) facilities; the telephone is answered by a computer, which invites the caller either to speak or to use the touchpad on the telephone to select different options. Most calls can be handled entirely by the machine, with human (expensive) operators brought in only for non-standard problems. A major advantage is that calls are answered quickly and the lines are rarely engaged; the drawback of the system is that it is cold and impersonal, and some callers will hang up rather than speak to a machine, especially about personal matters such as finance. IVR is not much help in collecting customer information because of this
Electronic point of sale (EPOS)	EPOS has become widely accepted by retailers because of the staff savings and better customer service offered by more rapid progress through the checkouts. Coupled with the bar code system, the retailer can access product purchasing behaviour and, by linking this to loyalty cards, can develop a clear picture of the individual's tastes and preferences EFTPOS systems (electronic funds transfer at point of sale) have to an extent replaced regional bank branches as a way for customers to draw cash on credit or debit cards. This encourages purchases while in the shop as well as saving on travelling and bank charges
Smart cards	Smart cards contain a computer chip which stores information about the user's transactions. It enables the supplier to build up a much better picture of a customer's total spending patterns than would be possible with a conventional credit card or store card
Consumer research	Set meters have been used for some years to research the TV viewing habits of consumers. Recent developments in scanning technology allow much simpler meters to be used, and thus much more detailed and reliable information can be collected (Evans and Moutinho 1992).

Developing a database

Databases come in several varieties, with new ways of structuring them being developed constantly. Three of the most common examples are described in Table 9.2.

| TABLE 9.2 | Types of database |

Type of database	Explanation and examples
Hierarchical databases	Data are stored under a single criterion such as an account number. This makes it easy to record and report transactions for an individual, but hard to generate a list of, say, individuals who have bounced cheques against their accounts recently. Hierarchical databases are really derivatives of manual filing systems, and are faster but not much more sophisticated
Network databases	These use 'tags' to identify records needed for analysis. For example, a customer's records might include a tag for the postcode (so that records can be sorted geographically), another tag for the date of the last transaction (so records can be sorted by recency of use), and a set of tags for demographic variables. These databases are an improvement on hierarchical databases but are more expensive and harder to run since the user needs to understand the structure of the data to manipulate them
Relational databases	Currently the dominant system, relational databases store the data in two dimensions; the data for a given customer lies in one dimension, the data on a given attribute across all customers lies in the other dimension. For example, a bank might store information on a loan under both the customer's records and against the bank's loan records, including a record of any default or extra borrowing. A relational database allows the information to be added to both records at once, and to be accessed either way

Relational databases allow the user to make links between different tables: one-to-one, where records in one table are linked to records in another table; one-to-many, where each record is linked to many records in another table, and many-to-many, where tables can be cross-linked in complex ways.

Business managers need to ask themselves the following questions (Linton 1995):

- How will the database support business objectives?

- What is expected from the system?

- What are the main requirements?

- What applications will it be used for?

Most large firms keep the database in-house, but this can be an expensive option for small firms due to the high cost of buying sufficiently powerful hardware; such firms often contract out the database to specialist agencies. The advantages of **outsourcing** the database are as follows (Linton 1995):

- The database will not affect the capacity of the organisation's internal systems.
- There will be no need to recruit or train extra staff.
- The database will be managed by specialists.
- Outsourcing is often more cost effective owing to economies of scale.

Populating the database can occur from in-house sources (customer records, returns from sales promotions, enquiries made at exhibitions, and so forth), or records can be bought in. Lists of names and accompanying information can be bought from list brokers (and the company's own lists can be sold through list brokers). The cost varies according to the desirability of the list and the extent of the information held as well as its currency – outdated information can make the list expensive to clean. Obviously, information the company already holds is the cheapest, so building the database should begin with the firm's own records.

It is tempting to use market research records for building the database, and this is perfectly acceptable provided the respondents know that the information will be used in this way. Using such information without prior permission is likely to be construed as **sugging** – selling under the guise of market research. This is regarded as abuse of the respondents' confidentiality and is outlawed by the Market Research Society. If respondents believe that the information they give will be used to bombard them with sales pitches, they will not participate in market research in future; sugging therefore adds to the non-response problem which is the bugbear of survey research. Some lists are developed from **omnibus surveys** in which the respondents give a great deal of information about their buying habits and circumstances in exchange for a small gift or entry in a prize draw. Such questionnaires usually include a box which the respondent can tick for confidentiality.

Having obtained the list, the firm can enhance the data by adding, say, credit rating information obtained from credit reference agencies, or perhaps telephone numbers obtained from the *Yellow Pages* or residential directories. The data will need to be **profiled** (categorised) into coherent segments, and will also need to be checked periodically for accuracy. Clean lists are those with a high level of accuracy. List accuracy links closely to profitability, since fewer mailings will go astray and fewer potential customers will be missed out (Bradford 1995). The commonest errors found in databases are shown in Table 9.3.

| TABLE 9.3 | Common errors in databases |

Error	Explanation
Incorrect name	Even minor errors (incorrect initials, for example) might result in the wrong family member opening the mail or, in the case of a business, the mail might go to the wrong division of a company. Even if the mail gets to the right person, errors of this type give a poor impression
Titles	In some cases, a recipient might be irritated by the omission or addition of a title such as Dr, Professor or Reverend
Duplicate entries	Often the same person is listed under different versions of the same name. For example, Alan Reynolds might be listed as Mr A. Reynolds, Alan Reynolds, A. J. Reynolds or any combination of these. This could mean receiving several copies of the same mailing, which apart from being irritating for the recipient is also wasteful for the firm doing the mailing
Gone-aways	Sometimes mail continues to be sent to individuals who have moved away, or even died. On average in the UK, people move house about every seven years and around 640,000 a year die, so databases need constant cleaning

Ridding the list of these errors can be easy or difficult. Many companies include a form with the mailing asking whether the name and address details are correct, and this does at least show that the company is trying to get things right. 'Gone-aways' can sometimes be picked up by comparing addresses with the electoral roll, and in the UK the direct marketing industry has access to the Register of Deaths for the purpose of removing the dead from mailing lists. One of the major problems for the UK industry is that the government has placed restrictions on commercial access to the electoral roll, making it much more difficult for companies to clean their address lists.

Removing duplicate names (**de-duping**) can be carried out in six stages (Mander 1993):

1 Identify and examine key elements of name and address, for example title, initials, surname, occupation and each line of the address.

2 Form access keys. When two or more records share the same combinations of parts of names and addresses they should be identified and 'pulled'.

3 Develop a scoring system for potential duplicates. The higher the score, the greater the similarity. This allows the machine to compare records for similarity and 'pull' the most similar ones.

4 Identify the acceptable level of duplication. This gives the machine a cut-off point beyond which the records are regarded as being separate.

5 Prioritise duplicates. If two people from the same household are receiving mailings, for example, the company can decide which of them (or whether both of them) should receive the mailing.

6 Change the records. Delete unwanted records, merge data from duplicated records and so forth.

The first three stages of the process can be carried out by the computer, given suitable software; the last three require increasing involvement by a human being.

Databases and the firm

The role of the database develops strategically within the firm, as shown in Table 9.4. The process described in the table is not necessarily a tidy one, and firms may skip stages, but it does illustrate a hierarchy of commitment to the use of the database as the driving force in the company's marketing communications activities.

TABLE 9.4 Strategic position of the database

Phase of development	Explanation
Phase 1: Mystery lists	The firm regards the database as an adjunct to its main business, as a standalone operation next to its main marketing activities
Phase 2: Buyer databases	There may be several databases in use, each carrying different information. For example, the salesforce may use one database for special customers, the distribution department may have a separate database containing delivery details and scheduling, credit control may have yet another. The Phase 2 focus is on broadening the databases, defining target markets, improving list quality, segmentation, credit scoring, response handling, testing and management systems for campaign planning
Phase 3: Coordinated customer communication	Databases are amalgamated so that one database drives all the customer communication. The database is used to identify prospects within the broader market, review performance and segment the market.
Phase 4: Integrated marketing	Most functions automate within closed loops, but need each other's information for the plan–execute–monitor–report cycle. Each functional subsystem gets its information from every other subsystem within the context of the main database. Common IT architecture ensures maximum automatic feedback, combining lifetime management of customers with the management of campaigns for particular brands

Integrating all the firm's activities around a single database increases the coherence of the marketing communications and increases the possibilities for establishing relationship marketing. A single database puts the company in the position of the small corner shop: the company knows all its regular customers and can therefore anticipate and satisfy their needs much more effectively both in terms of product and in terms of communications.

Monitoring and control

Direct marketing's main appeal is that it is, by its nature, easily monitored and controlled. Because the consumers are dealt with as individuals, it is easy to see whether the individual has responded to the stimulus and in what way the response has been made. Databases help the monitoring process in the following ways (O'Malley *et al.* 1999):

- Tracking responses
- Recording speed of fulfilment of the sale
- Tracking responses in different sectors
- Comparing conversion rates to response rates
- Assessing effectiveness of media in reaching target audiences
- Comparing response levels in different media
- Recording customer data capture through the campaign

Segmentation

Direct marketers have a different approach to segmentation from that used by traditional marketers. Traditionally, segmentation is a top-down approach which begins with a mass of consumers and divides them, according to their needs, into a set of sub-markets or segments (Shani and Chalasani 1992). Direct marketers begin with individuals and group them into segments. As far as communication is concerned, it is possible for direct marketers to target individually – the 'segment of one' – but in most cases the physical product cannot be tailored to the individual so easily. Therefore some segmentation will probably always be necessary.

Demographic segmentation is an obvious candidate under a direct marketing approach. Census figures are available on CD-ROM, and most people are fairly happy to provide information about their age, sex, number and ages of children and so forth, so that data on individual customers is easy to obtain. Geographical segmentation has recently become more accessible to direct marketing owing to the development of ACORN, MOSAIC and other geographical analysis systems. ACORN stands for A Classification of Residential Neighbourhoods, and breaks down areas according to type of housing. This often has a greater relevance to the buying behaviour of the people living in the houses than does, for example, their age or income level; for this reason, marketers in general are moving away from using socio-economic groupings and other crude demographic variables for segmentation.

Direct marketing has, in common with traditional marketing, two main aims: customer acquisition and customer retention. Both these activities take on new dimensions under a direct marketing regime.

Customer acquisition

Mass marketing approaches tend not to be accurate in targeting the appropriate market. For example, golfing magazines often carry advertisements for prestige cars, on the basis that most golfers are in socio-economic group AB. Likewise, billboard and newspaper ads are shown to a very wide audience, most of whom are not prospective customers for the products advertised. The main way these advertisements target their audience is in the style of the ad itself: ads are designed to appeal to specific groups.

The problem with this approach is that it is wasteful and it contributes to advertising clutter, so that consumers (and industrial buyers) become overloaded and resistant to further appeals. This is particularly the case with 'scattergun' mailshots which are sent out indiscriminately to prospect for new customers. For this reason, companies are increasingly looking for less intrusive ways to prospect.

Firms often use press, radio or TV advertising which invites a direct response from prospective customers, for example by calling an information hotline, by sending in a coupon, or by visiting a website. These have the advantage of being sought communications rather than unsought communications (see Chapter 3), and also mean that the marketer acquires an address to respond to.

Prospects divide into the following groups (Hansotia 1997):

- Households, individuals and businesses with no prior relationship with the company
- Lapsed customers
- Customers of a parent or sister company
- Customers of strategic partners
- Enquirers

Cold prospects have never bought the product before, and their level of interest is unknown. The problem of moving these individuals from 'cold' to 'warm' is common to almost all other marketing situations. **Warm prospects** are those whose characteristics are similar to those of existing customers; **hot prospects** are those who are almost certain to have an interest in the product category or who have actually expressed an interest.

For direct marketers, warm prospects can be identified by combining databases so as to obtain a very broad profile of the individuals contained therein. Hot prospects can be identified by their responses to communications; the content of these communications is what converts a prospect from cold to hot. For this reason the response (which identifies the prospect as hot) needs to be made as easy as possible for the prospect; a freephone number, a website or a freepost facility is essential.

Figures 9.1 and 9.2 show examples of advertisements for a computer modem. Figure 9.1 is a traditional-type advertisement; Figure 9.2 is designed to elicit a direct response.

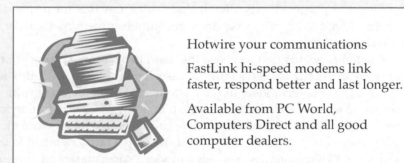

Hotwire your communications

FastLink hi-speed modems link faster, respond better and last longer.

Available from PC World, Computers Direct and all good computer dealers.

FastLink modems start from £199.

FIGURE 9.1 Traditional advertisement for a modem

Hotwire your communications

FastLink hi-speed modems link faster, respond better and last longer.

*Call **0800 785933** or visit our website **www.pear.com.uk** to find out how to trade in your existing modem for a FastLink.*

FIGURE 9.2 Direct response advert for a modem

The second advert has a freephone number and a website address; both are needed, because prospects may or may not be connected to the Web. Those who are will already have a modem, so the firm needs to offer a trade-in; this is, in effect, a discount since the second-hand market for obsolescent modems is probably limited. The first advertisement does not allow the firm to gauge responses accurately, since the interested parties are being directed to a retailer; this means that the effect of the manufacturer's advertising cannot be distinguished from the effect of the retailer's advertising, or indeed the effectiveness of the retailer's in-store salespeople. The second advertisement allows responses to be measured accurately, and also provides a set of names and addresses (or e-mail addresses or telephone numbers) which can be used in future for marketing other products which might be of interest to computer users.

Direct response adverts often include small rewards for responding; a free gift or the chance to enter a prize draw encourages prospects to make the telephone call or post the coupon.

Customer acquisition has been the main focus of marketing efforts in the past, and for many firms this is still the case. The problem with this focus is that it leads to a short-term view of the customer; existing customers are dealt with in the same way as new customers, which in many cases is irritating and could even be construed as rude. In days gone by, corner shopkeepers would know their regular customers personally, and would develop a fairly detailed knowledge of the individual's likes and dislikes. For a modern supermarket to develop this kind of knowledge requires computers, but the principle is the same; treating customers as people is more likely to build loyalty.

Customer retention

The first move in understanding ways of retaining customers is to find out why customers defect in the first place (Reichheld and Sasser 1990). A dissatisfied customer could defect (exit), complain (voice), or remain as a customer (loyalty) (Hirschman 1970). The evidence is that dissatisfied customers can become loyal, and some research suggests that customers who complain can become more loyal than those who have never had a problem with the company (Coca-Cola Company 1981).

There is considerable disagreement among academics about the meaning of loyalty and the ability of firms to influence it. The loyal customer is one who habitually buys the same brand or buys from the same company, and there is a natural presumption among marketers that any firm or brand that provides the customer with the right product at the right time and at the right price will enjoy the customer's patronage in the future.

There is an assumption that satisfied customers will also be loyal; in fact, the correlation is tenuous at best. In one study, 66 per cent of packaged goods purchasers identified a favourite brand but admitted having bought a different brand most recently (McKenzie 1995). Attitude is not necessarily a clear guide to behaviour; people are sometimes prevented by circumstances from carrying their intentions through.

Loyalty has been defined as 'the relationship between the relative attitude towards an entity and patronage behaviour' (Dick and Basu 1994). There are four categories of loyalty, as shown in Table 9.5.

TABLE 9.5	Categories of loyalty
Category	**Explanation**
No loyalty	If the consumer's relative attitude is low, and there is no evidence of patronage behaviour. Petrol buying is an example: motorists buy from the most convenient outlet, regardless of brand (Dignam 1996)
Spurious loyalty	Although there is high repeat patronage, the customer does not believe that the products are differentiated. This can come about through loyalty programmes or through persistent sales promotions. Marketers can generate real loyalty by differentiating the product from its competitors
Latent loyalty	The customer's high relative attitude towards the brand is not reflected in patronage. This is probably due to situational factors such as location of the retail outlets or pressure from family to buy another brand
Loyalty	High relative attitude plus high patronage behaviour denotes true loyalty

From a communications viewpoint, establishing a loyal relationship with customers presents particular challenges. Most importantly, loyalty is more likely to be retained if the information flow is two-way. Existing customers can be encouraged to stay loyal by sending out newsletters, information on special offers and invitations to special events. As always, communications need to be relevant to the recipient, but the company needs to categorise its communications objectives for each communication, as shown in Table 9.6.

Ideally, communication should be a dialogue. This means that customer responses need to be taken into account when the company next contacts the customer. At a simple level, a credit card customer who pays a bill late might receive a message on the next statement which mentions that the last payment was late, that normally charges would be applied but that these have been waived this time, and advising the customer of the last date of posting which would ensure the payment arriving on time. The technology for doing this is now in place: Barclay's Bank personal customers are not charged for unauthorised overdrafts unless they have a record of regularly overdrawing. The systems for waiving the charges are now automated.

TABLE 9.6	Categories of direct communication

Communication objective	Explanation and examples
To inform	If the intention is to inform, then attempts to persuade are annoying and detract from the information. For example, a film guide sent out with the bill for cable services should give a fair assessment of the films, without hype, otherwise the information will be discounted by the customer. Honesty is essential. Monthly statements and bills need to be clear and should show how the charges are arrived at
To persuade	Persuasive messages need to be tailored to the individual's needs. For example, a message sent to a regular international traveller should take account of whether the travel is for business or for pleasure, and also whether the traveller usually buys package deals or prefers to travel independently
To educate	Education implies a deeper learning process than merely being informed. Charities often need to educate their audiences about the importance of their work; such communications need to be clearly written and detailed, but can also be interactive. For example, recipients could be asked questions, and could even be invited to send in replies (with a contribution) to win a small prize

The aim of interactive communications is not so much to allow the company to get close to its customers, but rather to allow the customers the opportunity to feel close to the company. This means opening up suitable channels of easy communication for the customers: telephone hotlines, websites, e-mail addresses (with contact names), fax numbers and so forth. Such inbound communications should be treated seriously; they are the equivalent of a letter from an old friend, which, if ignored, will mean the loss of the friend. Treating customers as individuals, and communicating with them in a two-way (interactive) dialogue, is at the heart of direct marketing, and is the reason why direct marketing and relationship marketing are so closely intertwined. Research shows, however, that around 30 per cent of mailings do not include a way for the customer to respond (Darby 1997). Of those that do, 40 per cent expect the customer to pay the postage – a clear disincentive to respond.

Response to direct mail depends on four factors: subject matter, brand relationships, personality types and creative execution (TQC/Ogilvy and Mather Direct 1991). Having the right offer at the right time is essential to success; at a basic level, an insurance broker who sends out a reminder about car insurance a few weeks before the insurance falls due, and includes in the letter some alternative quotations, is more likely to get the business than one that sends out insurance offers during the currency of the existing insurance. Brand relationship refers to the customer's existing commitment to the brand; the stronger this is, the more likely the mailing will be successful. Personality type includes such factors as the customer's attitude towards direct mail in general, degree to which the customer will enter competitions or prize draws, the degree to which they value information and so forth. These personality characteristics are set out in Table 9.7.

TABLE 9.7 Personality typologies and direct mail

Type	Basic attitude	Motivation	Characteristics
Compies	Very positive	Winning competitions	Not interested in subject matter; small/extreme group
Librarians	Positive	Value information; like storing things	Litlle compulsion to respond now; like financial services
Adults	Balanced	Look for things of value; ability to discriminate	Open most mail; feel in control; quick to filter out useful and not useful
Adolescents	Negative	Dislike pressure; attack and reject authority	Defensive and rebellious; feel threatened
Cynics	Negative	Scepticism; want to prove it's a con	Fear being duped; want to show they can see through things
Conscientious objectors	Very negative	Anger; dislike intrusion	Fear manipulation; justified by rational arguments; concern for other defenceless people

Source: Based on TQC/Ogilvy and Mather Direct (1991)

Media

The media used for direct marketing fall into two main categories: addressable media, which can be directed to the individuals, and non-addressable media, which require a response from the prospective customer.

Table 9.8 shows the main types of addressable media in use.

TABLE 9.8   Addressable media

Type of medium	Advantages	Disadvantages
Direct mail: personally addressed communications delivered through the post	Can generate leads, build loyalty, improve image, generate sales, build brand awareness; can cross-sell and up-sell, build a database, and support the trade. Cost effective, easily targeted and flexible. Also offers creative opportunities – the ability to send videos, scratch-and-sniff samples and so forth	Cost per thousand is high compared with press or TV. Can easily be binned or set aside for later action, and lost. Widely used and therefore subject to clutter
Catalogues: retail publications containing a wide range of branded and unbranded goods	Catalogues are often kept by customers and referred to; this is particularly true of big-book catalogues which carry a wide range of goods. Specialogues, more closely targeted, can appeal to niche markets and usually offer a quicker delivery service. Both offer a convenient alternative to high street retailers	Very high costs of production and distribution have affected big-book catalogues in recent years. Many agents play the system by requesting catalogues, ordering the cheap (or free) promotions and then moving on to the next catalogue
Customer magazines: specially produced periodicals aimed at existing customers	Derived from in-flight magazines produced by airlines, these magazines build loyalty by raising the brand profile. Customer information can be collected from vouchers and competition returns	Expensive; although these magazines carry advertising, the revenues are rarely enough to cover the cost of production
Card decks: packs of advertising reply cards are mailed out to potential customers	Because the cost of mailing is shared among many promoters, the overall cost is relatively low. Response rates can be good if the offer is right; it is easy for customers to mail the cards back. Good for generating sales leads rather than actual sales	As with other 'omnibus' approaches, the targeting is imprecise. Response rates tend to be lower than those for dedicated mailings

TABLE 9.8	Continued	
Telemarketing: marketing over the telephone, either **outbound** (the marketer makes the call) or **inbound** (the customer makes the call)	Outbound telemarketing has been most widely used in business-to-business areas where it has been widely accepted by customers. It is a selective medium, and has most of the advantages of personal, face-to-face selling at a much lower cost. Personal relationships between caller and recipient often develop, and approaches can be tailored to suit the customer. List accuracy can be checked instantly, and monitoring can be handled easily (and often electronically). Inbound telemarketing is easy for the customer to participate in	Consumers tend to be less tolerant of outbound telemarketing, often feeling that it is intrusive. It works best when the customer already has a relationship with the organisation. Outbound calls can be inconvenient for the recipient (Murphy, 1997). Staff costs are high compared with mailing, but low compared with personal selling. Sometimes customers can be put off by the cost of inbound telemarketing unless there is a freephone number

Unaddressable media at first appear indistinguishable from traditional mass marketing media, since they are untargeted and expensive. The important distinction is that direct marketers always include a response method for the customers in order to generate two-way communication.

Direct response TV advertising (DRTV) includes a telephone number, address, fax number or (increasingly) web address which viewers can contact. The 1996 Direct Marketing Association Census indicates that 25.4 per cent of TV advertising in the UK now carries a response device of some sort, and this is likely to increase in future. The reasons for this are as follows:

- With more TV channels (terrestrial, satellite and cable), audiences are being more accurately targeted and defined.

- Traditional TV advertising is difficult to evaluate since it is almost impossible to know which of many possible stimuli caused the consumer to buy the brand. DRTV offers instantly measurable results.

- The cost of TV advertising is high, therefore as much value for money needs to be extracted from it as possible.

Table 9.9 shows some of the types of DRTV advertisements currently in use.

TABLE 9.9 DRTV advertising

Type	Explanation
Infomercial (see Chapter 4)	Lengthy advertisements full of information, designed to sell a specific product. Viewers are invited to call in and buy the product using their credit cards; the products are typically household gadgets, and the advertisements are made in the style of an in-store demonstration. In the USA, infomercials often run to half an hour and are actually TV programmes in their own right; these are illegal on terrestrial TV in the UK
Direct response commercial	More sophisticated than the infomercial, these ads are placed in off-peak time slots (to keep costs low and avoid competing with mainstream ads for the viewers' attention). Sometimes these advertisements contain a great deal of information within their 30-second limit, plus a telephone number for viewers to place their orders
Awareness ads	These are really the traditional type TV ad, but with a web address or a telephone hotline number added. Although this is only a very mild form of direct marketing, some responses are elicited and at the very least the addition of a telephone number reassures the viewer. Web addresses are useful in the case of high value items such as cars; the marketer needs to remember that website hits resulting from an awareness ad are likely to be looking for information rather than a sales pitch. In other words, the distinction between sought and unsought communications (see Chapter 1) is particularly important
Brand response TV (BRTV)	These are an attempt to increase brand awareness and integrate responses into the same advertisement. For example, the charity Oxfam integrates branded advertising with an appeal for funds; the appeal carries a telephone number for credit card donations (Darby 1996)
Home shopping channel presentations	The QVC shopping channel on satellite and cable is unusual in that there are no traditional entertainment programmes – the channel consists entirely of direct response advertisements for various products. Presenters demonstrate products, interspersed with pre-recorded infomercials. Chapter 4 has a more detailed treatment of home shopping channels.

Direct response press advertising is cheaper than TV advertising and may even be more cost effective, depending on circumstances. Because press advertising can carry a great deal of information and is a permanent medium (see Chapter 3), it is easy for a selection of response options to be offered to the reader. Targeting is somewhat better than is possible on TV owing to the wide range of specialist magazines catering to different market segments. The most important criterion for selecting press media is the receptivity of the readership to direct response advertising (Roberts and Berger 1989). Other advantages of specialist magazines are as follows (Nash 1982):

- *Economics*. The low cost per thousand (compared with mailings, for example) means that a wide audience is reachable for relatively low cost.

- *Credibility*. If the publication is well regarded by its readership, the products advertised will benefit from halo effect.

- *Lack of satisfactory lists*. Especially in the case of innovative products, a suitable list of potential customers may not exist. A specialist magazine offers the chance of reaching at least an approximation of the target market; the responses can then be used to refine a database.

Newspapers also offer benefits to direct marketers, as follows (Roberts and Berger, 1989):

- *Frequency*. Because most newspapers are published and read daily, the advertisements can be repeated to reinforce the impact.

- *Immediacy*. Advertisements can be placed on short notice, which allows the advertiser to include up-to-the-minute information.

- *Reach*. Newspapers have large circulations within their areas. Although this means that the targeting is not very accurate, it does give the marketer a lot of potential responses on which to build its own database.

- *Local shopping reference*. Many newspapers are published within a tight geographical area, so many readers use them as a reference for local shopping opportunities.

- *Fast response*. Frequency of publication, and the ephemeral nature of newspapers, means that responses tend to be quick, and also die away quickly after the advert appears. This means that monitoring and testing can be fairly accurate.

Direct response radio advertising has many of the advantages of television (see Chapter 4), but suffers from the difficulty that the response method can only be delivered aurally. This means that the listener probably needs to have a pen handy, and the telephone number (or web address) has to be repeated frequently. TV suffers less from this problem since the response mechanism can be left on-screen for the duration of the advert.

Door-to-door methods vary, from leaflets and samples put through letterboxes, to doorstep canvassers. Geodemographic segmentation techniques ensure the accuracy of the targeting, and therefore there is a great deal less wastage than is the case with broadcast or press advertising. Free samples through letterboxes can be very successful; consumers usually try them, which tends to lead to subsequent purchase (Sappal 1996). These campaigns tend to work best if they are run in conjunction with other promotional activity, for example TV advertising, particularly in the case of new products.

NON-COMPUTER DIRECT MARKETING

Not all direct marketing is carried out using computers. Producing firms have dealt direct with their final consumers for many years, and indeed before the Industrial Revolution this was the standard way of doing business.

For many firms the distribution route direct from producer to consumer creates savings and greater efficiency; in cases where wholesaling is impossible or gives no benefits, direct marketing is the obvious way of approaching the market.

Doorstep canvassing

Doorstep canvassing involves a salesperson going from house to house in a given area, knocking the doors and trying to sell to the householders. Targeting is somewhat crude, although this depends on the product; for example, a housing estate which is around ten years old is a good area to canvass for double-glazing appointments because many of the windows will be showing signs of deterioration after approximately this length of time.

Doorstep canvassing has declined greatly in recent years, although it was at one time a regular feature of most residential areas. Activities ranged from doorstep selling of brushes and household cleaners through to appointment-making for home improvement salespeople. The reasons for the decline are as follows:

- Increasing costs of labour make the costs too high.

- The increase in the number of women who work outside the home means that many houses are empty during the day.

- Rising crime rates (or at least the fear of crime) make householders reluctant to talk to strangers on the doorstep, and also make the canvassers less willing to go from house to house.

Nonetheless, when it is carried out, doorstep canvassing is a very powerful medium. Home improvement salespeople can expect to make one appointment for every ten houses they call on, and sell one in three of the resulting appointments – considering that these sales are usually high value, this is an impressive success rate.

Multilevel marketing

Also called multilevel selling, **multilevel marketing** is a system of direct marketing which relies on the personal contacts of the salesforce. Well-known examples are Herbalife, the vitamin and health food distributor, and Amway, the household cleansing products firm.

In a multilevel marketing organisation each salesperson has two areas of responsibility: first to sell the product to family, friends and work colleagues, and second to recruit more salespeople. Each salesperson is paid on a commission-only basis, with no basic salary or fringe benefits, and is regarded as self-employed; most of them sell on a part-time basis and have other jobs. Each salesperson is also paid an **override** commission of 1 or 2 per cent on the sales of each person he or she recruits. Ultimately, recruitment of other people is what makes the exercise worthwhile for most salespeople. Figure 9.3 shows a typical structure for multilevel marketing.

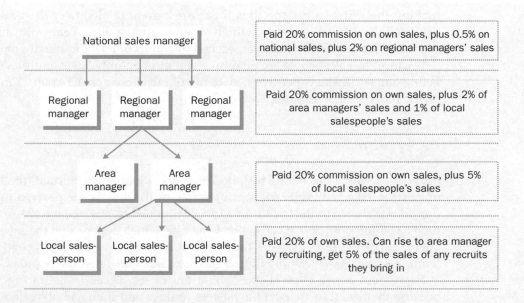

FIGURE 9.3   Multilevel marketing scheme

Multilevel marketing should not be confused with pyramid selling. In pyramid selling, each person joining the scheme is required to buy a substantial stock of the goods for sale, and recruits new people by selling them bulk stocks. Such schemes were popular in the UK in the mid 1970s, when a large number of newly redundant workers invested their redundancy payments in the schemes. Unfortunately, the end result of many pyramid selling schemes was that some people ended up with large stocks of unwanted goods which could neither be sold to consumers nor sold in bulk to other recruits. As with chain letters, pyramid schemes eventually run out of new recruits and thus fall apart, and those at the end of the chain lose their money.

Because of the large numbers of people who lost their capital (and in some cases their homes) in pyramid schemes, they were outlawed in the UK. Multilevel marketing schemes do not require the recruit to invest any money, apart from a returnable deposit on the samples and sales kit; even this deposit is strictly limited under UK law.

In most cases, multilevel salespeople earn relatively small amounts of extra money, the majority of them only using the products themselves and selling small quantities to friends and family. Few of the recruits have the necessary skills to make a success of selling in commercially viable quantities, and few companies offer sales training; the majority offer only motivational meetings and newsletters. In many cases, salespeople are recruited but never actually succeed in making their first sale. Growth is therefore a great deal slower than might be expected, and even Amway (which is now almost fifty years old and has expanded worldwide) has not yet reached the limits of its recruitment potential.

Because the salespeople are paid on a commission-only basis, multilevel marketing tends to be an expensive way to distribute goods (see Chapter 11 for more on the remuneration of salespeople).

Party plan

Party plan selling has a long history. The basis is that an individual (the hostess or host) is asked to invite friends for coffee or drinks. At the party, a range of products is shown to the friends and they are invited to buy; the hostess or host is paid a commission, or is given goods to a value which depends on the sales at the party. Tupperware is perhaps the most famous example; more recently, Ann Summers parties (which offer lingerie and sex aids) have become popular.

Party plan depends on social obligation for its success. The partygoers go because they want to support the hostess or host, and then feel obligated to buy something. The salesperson will also try to recruit new hostesses or hosts at the party, and thus the system is perpetuated.

Party plan had its heyday during the 1950s and 1960s when many women were at home all day and the parties were a welcome break from routine, and (for the hostesses) the chance to earn a little money or at least save some money on the housekeeping allowance. The lack of an army of housewives to host the parties has meant the decline of Tupperware parties; people who are out at work all day need to use their evenings to relax and certainly do not need the distraction of a party. The success of the Ann Summers parties is to some extent due to attributes of the products being sold. Most women would not want to be seen in public buying sex aids or (in many cases) sexy lingerie, so the parties offer a chance to do so in relative privacy. In addition, the parties have an inherent hedonic factor; they are thought of as 'a bit of a laugh' because the products themselves have a humorous aspect.

CONSUMER RESPONSES TO DIRECT MARKETING

As with any other marketing communications, consumers are not uniformly positive in their reactions to direct marketing. Concerns over privacy lead some consumers to subvert the process by giving false information; some say that they earn more than they actually do, some use variations of their names so that they know which company is mailing them, some lie about the number of people in their households (perhaps for security reasons – women living alone might want to invent a husband or boyfriend to deter criminals).

Many consumers feel justified in doing this because the information held about them is often inaccurate anyway. Mistakes are bound to happen, and sometimes consumers find that detrimental information is held on them; for example, a credit referencing agency might retain a record of a court judgment against an address even though the debtor has moved. The new resident might then be turned down for credit without ever knowing the real reason. In the UK it has been reported that one in five people are on one or more credit blacklists.

In the UK and in several other countries it is possible for consumers to register themselves with the Mailing Preference Service or the Telephone Preference Service. Consumers who do this will be removed from the lists of direct marketing companies, and there are penalties for firms who continue to call or send mailings to customers who have registered. The system is not perfect – it does not provide for calls or mailings originating outside the UK, nor will it prevent mailings or telephone calls from firms with whom the consumer already has a relationship (such as his or her bank or utility provider). The advantage for the consumer is, of course, fewer telephone calls and less mail, but there are advantages for the direct marketers as well, since they will not be contacting people who have no interest in buying from direct marketing companies. This will reduce costs in the long run.

Privacy issues are clearly important to consumers, and in the UK the Data Protection Act has strict provisions about the security of information. Most countries have legislation covering this issue, and direct marketers usually have to comply with the laws of all the countries in which they do business. This is particularly difficult for Internet marketing (see Chapter 12), which is by its nature worldwide; US courts regard all Internet transactions involving US residents as being within their jurisdiction no matter where the originating company resides. Since decisions of foreign courts are frequently enforceable in other countries, Internet marketers are unlikely to obtain immunity on the grounds that they do not reside in the USA.

The main areas of privacy are outlined in Table 9.10 (Westin 1967).

TABLE 9.10   Privacy issues in database marketing

Issue	Explanation and examples
Who controls customer information	In the USA some consumers believe that they have already lost control over how information is used (Schroeder 1992). Marketers tend to believe that they have the right to control information which they have gone to some trouble and expense to collect (Cespedes and Smith 1993). Consumers view this lack of control with some suspicion, often translating it as a lack of privacy; using the database to get close to customers is called **customer intimacy** (Treacy and Wiersema 1993), but when such intimacy is unwanted it causes considerable resentment
How information is collected and used	Consumers are fairly happy about giving information which is necessary for a specific purchase (for example when arranging consumer credit), but usually do not expect this information to be shared with other organisations (Cespedes and Smith 1993; Gandy 1993). UK customers tend to be protective of their personal details and object to the resale of information which they regard as theirs. On the plus side, consumers generally do not resent receiving information about products and services which interest them – nobody complains about getting discount offers on their favourite products, for example
Data security	The growth in amateur *hacking* from home PCs has increased fears of breaches in security. Keeping data 100 per cent secure is probably not possible in practice, because employees of the firm need access to the information in order to update it and handle it

Green consumers have often objected to direct mail because of the waste of paper involved: marketers are usually happy with response rates of less than 10 per cent, which means that 90 per cent or more of the mailing ends up in landfill sites. Environmental pressure groups may be slow to complain about this because they are heavy users of direct mail themselves (Bloom *et al*. 1994).

More accurate targeting will, presumably, alleviate the problem, but the problem is unlikely to disappear altogether. Even when the recipient is extremely interested in a given product category, the likelihood is that several other firms will be targeting the same individual, and only one will get the business. For example, individuals earning over £25,000 per year are targeted by credit card companies offering low or even zero interest rates for a period if the individual is prepared to transfer the balance from his or her existing credit cards on to the new one. Most of these offers will either be ignored or will be abused; the individual is able to transfer the balances between rival companies indefinitely, making substantial savings each time and even being offered cash back. There is a limit to how many credit cards an individual can use, so saturation mailings such as these can become counter-productive as well as wasteful.

Consumer response to doorstep canvassing is mixed and often inconsistent. Most people say that they do not like people coming to the door, and many people claim that they 'just slam the door in their faces', although doorstep canvassers report that such behaviour is extremely rare in practice. Yet, despite a general feeling that doorstep canvassing is a nuisance, many people do buy from doorstep salespeople or make appointments for sales presentations. Approximately one in ten door contacts leads to an appointment, and about one in three of those appointments produces a sale, so evidently some people find the process acceptable and even convenient.

Multilevel marketing meets with an equally mixed response. Many people feel obligated to help their friends by buying from them, but then admit that the products themselves are good and represent reasonable value for money. Party plan selling also provokes negative responses from people, perhaps because (like multilevel marketing) there is a feeling that it exploits a friendship in an undesirable or even unethical way.

As always, it is difficult to isolate the message from the medium; positive responses to Anne Summers parties come not from a love of party plan per se, but from the nature of the products being offered. Positive responses to double glazing salespeople come not because the individual is glad to see someone at the door, but because the house needs new windows.

CASE STUDY: ARGOS

Argos, the UK catalogue store, was founded in 1973. It is a subsidiary of Great Universal Stores plc, the UK's largest retailing company: Argos is the UK's largest general goods retailer, with a turnover of over £3 billion.

Argos runs a total of 550 stores throughout the UK, and estimates that 98 per cent of the UK population live within 10 miles of an Argos store. The company plans to open 35 more stores in the near future.

There are three basic ways to shop at Argos. The first is to visit the store, where the company's catalogues are available. The customer chooses from the catalogue, writes down the reference number of the items wanted on an order form, and hands the form to a member of staff who then brings the goods from the warehouse. Goods can be delivered via Argos Direct, or the customer can simply take them away.

The second method of purchase is via the Argos website. The website is clear, unambiguous and provides the customer with most, or all, of the necessary information to make the purchase. The customer is able to check the availability of items, and can either pay online using the secure server and have the goods delivered, or can reserve the goods and collect and pay for them in-store. This system has several purposes. First, it ensures that the customer does not have a wasted journey to the store (perhaps only to find that the item is out of stock); second, it reassures people who are concerned about the security of paying online, and third, it helps the company to keep costs down by reducing delivery costs.

The third method of shopping is perhaps the most novel. Customers can reserve items by telephone – in itself not unusual, but Argos has a system whereby customers can use text messaging from a mobile phone to send a reservation through, giving the catalogue number of the item and the address of the store from which they would like to collect the item. Argos then replies automatically with a computer-generated text to confirm whether the item is in stock, and the customer then needs only to send the word 'Reserve' to secure the item. It can then be collected by the customer. If the item is out of stock, the customer can set up an arrangement whereby Argos will automatically send a text advising when the item comes back into stock – and again, the customer can reserve the item by texting back 'Reserve'.

Argos does not have the usual approach to retail. Most retailers have stock on the shelves, allowing customers to choose what they want, take it to the checkout and pay. At Argos, the customer does much of the work of ordering, but the staff handle the actual goods, and very little effort or store space is given over to displays. The result of this is that Argos minimises the running costs of the stores, and actually runs the stores with very few staff relative to the store turnover. (In proportion to turnover, Argos runs with around 30 per cent fewer staff than supermarket chain Tesco.)

Like most retailers, Argos claims to offer the lowest prices. These claims are hard to verify when so many items are sold, and when so many special offers and discounts are available, but Argos certainly has a powerful claim to the title of cheapest retailer overall. By minimising costs, the store is able to pass on lower prices: and given the size of the turnover, the store is certainly able to carry some weight when buying stock. Consistent with keeping prices down, Argos aims to make it as easy as possible for customers to shop – and as easy as possible for goods to move out of the stores.

Questions

1 How might Argos increase its catalogue trade?

2 What is the company's position regarding online retailers (e-tailers)?

3 What other direct techniques might be open to Argos?

4 What conflicts are there in Argos's apparent strategy?

5 What threats are apparent for Argos?

SUMMARY

Direct marketing is about establishing a true dialogue between the customer and the marketer. It goes further than merely establishing a customer support system or complaints department: each of the company's communications is intended to provoke a direct and measurable response, either in terms of a purchase or in terms of information.

The essence of direct marketing is that it seeks to treat consumers as individuals rather than as segments.

The key points from this chapter are as follows:

- Direct mail is interactive, unlike indiscriminate mailshots.

- Direct marketing relies on accurate, detailed information about individuals.

- The structure of a database dictates its usefulness.

- Market research information can only be used with respondents' knowledge and permission.

- Incorrect names, titles or addresses are annoying to the recipient and wasteful to the company.

- Direct marketing makes monitoring and control easy.

- Direct marketing communications may need more than one response mechanism for customers to use.

- Direct marketing communications seek to establish a true dialogue.

- Interactive communication is intended to allow the customer to get close to the company, not to allow the company to become intimate with the customer.

- Even unaddressable media should include a contact mechanism for customers' responses.

- Media should be selected for customer receptivity to direct marketing approaches.

- Respondents do not always tell marketers the truth; if checking procedures can be built into the database, they should be used.

- Databases are never entirely secure, so confidentiality can never be wholly guaranteed.

CHAPTER QUESTIONS

1 What is the difference between direct marketing and junk mail?

2 How might database marketers avoid accusations of invasion of privacy?

3 Why do direct marketers segment bottom-up?

4 Why is customer retention gaining precedence over customer acquisition?

5 How can marketers help the customer get close to the firm?

FURTHER READING

Relatively few textbooks have been published on the subject of direct marketing, perhaps because the concept is relatively new. There has been a great deal of academic research into the topic, however, and the references at the end of the chapter give a selection from this research and comment.

O'Malley, L., Patterson, M. and Evans, M. (2004) *Exploring Direct and Customer Relationship Marketing*. London: Thomson Learning. This contains very comprehensive coverage of the subject from three of the leading academics in the field.

Tapp, A. (2004) *Principles of Direct and Database Marketing*. Harlow: Financial Times Prentice Hall. This is a readable and comprehensive text with a particularly useful section on using direct marketing to analyse the marketing situation.

REFERENCES

Bauer, C. and Miglautsch, J. (1992) 'A conceptual definition of direct marketing', *Journal of Direct Marketing*, **6**(Spring): 7–17.

Bird, D. (1993) *Commonsense Direct Marketing*, 3rd edn. London: Kogan Page.

Bloom, P. N., Adler, R. and Milne, G. R. (1994) 'Identifying the legal and ethical risks and costs of using new information technologies to support marketing programmes', in Blattberg, R. C., Glazer, R. and Little, J. D. C. (eds), *The Marketing Information Revolution*. Boston, MA: Harvard Business School Press, pp. 289–305.

Bradford, G. (1995) 'Targeting technology', *ADMAP*, January: 32–4.

Cespedes, F. V. and Smith, H. J. (1993) 'Database marketing: new rules for policy and practice', *Sloan Management Review*, Summer: 7–22.

Coca-Cola Company (1981) *Measuring the Grapevine: Consumer Response and Word-of-Mouth*. Atlanta, GA: Coca-Cola Company.

Darby, I. (1996) 'Calling for attention', *Marketing Direct*, September: 58–64.

Darby, I. (1997) 'Marketers suffer lack of response', *Marketing Direct*, July/August: 10.

Dick, A. S. and Basu, K. (1994) 'Customer loyalty: toward an integrated framework', *Journal of the Academy of Marketing Science*, **22**(2): 99–113.

Dignam, C. (1996) 'Being smart is not the only redeeming feature', *Marketing Direct*, September: 51–6.

Evans, M. J. and Blythe, J. W. D. (1994) 'Fashion: a new paradigm of consumer behaviour', *Journal of Consumer Studies and Home Economics*, **18**: 229–37.

Evans, M. J. and Moutinho, L. (1992) *Applied Marketing Research*. Harlow: Addison-Wesley.

Gandy, O. H. (1993) *The Panoptic Sort: A Political Economy of Personal Information*. Boulder, CO: Westview Press.

Hansotia, B. J. (1997) 'Enhancing firm value through prospect and customer lifestyle enhancement', *Journal of Database Marketing*, **4**(4): 351–2.

Hirschman, A. O. (1970) *Exit, Voice and Loyalty: Responses to Decline in Firms, Organisations and States*. Cambridge, MA: Harvard University Press.

Linton, I. (1995) *Database Marketing: Know What your Customer Wants*. London: Pitman.

Mander, G. (1993) 'De-duplication', *Journal of Database Marketing*, **1**(2): 150–61.

McKenzie, S. (1995) 'Distinguishing marks', *Marketing Week*, 17 November, pp. 13–15.

Murphy, J. A. (1997) 'Coming in from the cold', *Marketing Direct*, June: 51–2.

Nash, E. L. (1982) *Direct Marketing: Strategy, Planning, Execution*. New York: McGraw-Hill.

O'Malley, L., Patterson, M. and Evans, M. J. (1999) *Exploring Direct Marketing*. London: ITP.

Reichheld, F. F. and Sasser, W. E. (1990) 'Zero defects: quality comes to service', *Harvard Business Review*, September/October: 105–11.

Roberts, M. L. and Berger, P. D. (1989) *Direct Marketing Management*. Englewood Cliffs, NJ: Prentice-Hall.

Sappal, P. (1996) 'Sampling the market', *Direct Response*, November: 63–4.

Schroeder, D. (1992) 'Life, liberty and the pursuit of privacy', *American Demographics*, June: 20.

Shani, D. and Chalasani, S. (1992) 'Exploring niches using relationship marketing', *Journal of Services Marketing*, **6**(4): 43–52.

TQC/Ogilvy and Mather Direct (1991), cited in *Positive Response: The Prospects for Direct Mail*, Henley Centre, p. 83.

Treacy, M. and Wiersema, F. (1993) 'Customer intimacy and other value disciplines', *Harvard Business Review*, **71**(1): 84–93.

Vavra, T. (1992) *Aftermarketing*. Homewood, IL: Irwin.

Westin, A. (1967) *Privacy and Freedom*. New York: Atheneum.

10 Sales promotion

Objectives

After reading this chapter you should be able to:

- describe the advantages and disadvantages of different types of sales promotion
- categorise sales promotions
- choose which sales promotion would be most effective in a given situation
- plan a sales promotion
- explain how sales promotions can (and should) be integrated with other marketing communications

INTRODUCTION

The term 'sales promotion' covers a wide range of activities intended to provide a short-term increase in sales. Some sales promotions are aimed at retailers, some at consumers and yet others at wholesalers, but in all cases the intention is to provide an extra incentive to buy, or stock, a specific brand or product range.

SALES PROMOTION

Sales promotion has many guises, from money-off vouchers to free travel opportunities. Its purpose is to create a temporary increase in sales by bringing purchasing decisions forward and adding some immediacy to the decision-making process. Table 10.1 shows some of the techniques of sales promotion and when they should be used to greatest effect.

TABLE 10.1　Sales promotion techniques

Sales promotion technique	When to use to best effect
Free 'taster' samples in supermarkets	When a new product has been launched on the market. This technique works by allowing the consumer to experience the product first-hand, and also places the consumer under a small obligation to buy the product. The technique is effective but expensive
Money-off vouchers in press advertisements	Has the advantage that the company can check the effectiveness of the advertising by monitoring which vouchers came from which publications. It tends to lead to short-term brand switching; when the offer ends, consumers frequently revert to their usual brand
Two for the price of one	May encourage short-term brand switching. Appeals to the price-sensitive consumer, who will switch to the next cheap offer next time. Can be useful for rewarding and encouraging existing customers
Piggy-backing with another product	For example, putting a free jar of coffee whitener on to a jar of instant coffee. Good for encouraging purchasers of the coffee to try the whitener. Can be very successful in building brand penetration since the consumer's loyalty is to the coffee, not to the whitener. Will not usually encourage brand switching between the 'free sample' brand and its competitors. Can also use vouchers on the backs of labels of other products (see co-marketing in Chapter 8)

TABLE 10.1	Continued
Instant lottery or scratchcards	Commonly used in petrol stations. The intention is to develop a habit among motorists of stopping at the particular petrol station. In the UK, for legal reasons, these promotions cannot require a purchase to be made or be linked to spending a specific amount, but few people would have the courage to ask for a card without buying anything
Free gift with each purchase	Often used for children's cereals. Can be good for encouraging brand switching, and is more likely to lead to permanent adoption of the brand because consumers do not usually switch brands when buying for children. This is because children are not price sensitive and will want their favourite brand

Sales promotion is often useful for low value items and is most effective when used as part of an integrated promotion campaign. This is because advertising and PR build sales in the long term, whereas sales promotion and personal selling tend to be better for making quick increases in sales. The combination of the two was at one time thought to lead to the **ratchet effect**: sales get a quick boost from sales promotions, then build gradually over the life of an ad campaign (Moran 1978). This is not necessarily the case, for reasons that will become clear later in the chapter.

Care needs to be taken with sales promotions. First, a sales promotion that is repeated too often can become part of the consumer's expectations. For example, fast-food restaurant chain Pizzaland's promotional offer of a second pizza for a penny was so widely used that some consumers would not go to Pizzaland unless they had a voucher for the penny pizza. Pizzaland was eventually taken over by Pizza Hut and now no longer exists. Second, brand switching as a result of a sales promotion is usually temporary so it is unlikely that long-term business will be built by a short-term sales promotion (Ehrenberg *et al*. 1994). Third, the promotion will benefit consumers who would have bought the product anyway, so a proportion of the spend will in effect have been wasted (though this is true of most promotional tools). Good targeting can help overcome this.

Sales promotions can be carried out from manufacturer to intermediary (**trade promotions**), from retailer to consumer (**retailer promotions**), or direct from the manufacturer to the consumer (**manufacturer promotions**).

Trade promotions can be used for the following purposes:

- To *increase stock levels*. The more stock the intermediary holds, the more commitment there will be to selling the stock and the less space there is for competitors' stock (Curhan and Knopp 1987).

- To *gain more or better shelf space*. The more eye-catching the position of the product in the shop, the more likely it is to sell, and a trade promotion can encourage the retailer to give the product greater prominence.

- *New product launch*. New products always carry an element of risk for retailers as well as manufacturers. This means that the manufacturer may need to give the retailer an extra incentive to stock the product at all.

- To *even out fluctuating sales*. Seasonal offers may be used to encourage retailers to stock the products during slack periods. For example, the toy industry sells 80 per cent of its production over the Christmas period, so it is common for firms to offer extra incentives to retailers to stock up during the rest of the year.

- To *counter the competition*. Aggressive sales promotion can sometimes force a competitor's product off the retailer's shelves, or at least cause the retailer to drive a harder bargain with a competitor (Frankel and Phillips 1986).

Retailer promotions are used to attempt the following:

- To *increase store traffic*. Almost any kind of sales promotion will increase the number of people who come into the shop, but retailers would commonly have special events or seasonal sales.

- To *increase frequency and amount of purchase*. This is probably the commonest use of sales promotions; examples are two-for-one offers, buy one get discount off another product, and so forth.

- To *increase store loyalty*. **Loyalty cards** are the main example of this (although these have other uses – see Chapter 12). Using the loyalty card enables the customer to build up points that can be redeemed against products. Provided the cards offer real economic benefits to customers, they increase both loyalty and spending in-store (Verhoef 2003).

- To *increase own-brand sales*. Most large retailers have their own brands, which often have larger profit margins than the equivalent national brands. Own brands sometimes suffer from a perception of lower quality and therefore sales promotion effort may need to be increased.

- To *even out busy periods*. Seasonal sales are the obvious examples, but some retailers also promote at busy times in order to ensure a larger share of the market.

Manufacturer promotions are carried out for the following reasons:

- *To encourage trial*. When launching a new product the manufacturer may send out free samples to households or may give away samples with an existing product.

- *To expand usage*. Sales promotion can be used to encourage reinvention of the product for other uses.

- *To attract new customers*. This is sometimes called **trial impact**.

- *To trade up*. Sales promotions can encourage customers to buy the larger pack or more expensive version of the product. This is called **image reinforcement**.

- *To load up.* Encouraging customers to stock up on a product (perhaps in order to collect coupons) in effect blocks out the competition for a period. This is sometimes called **customer holding** (where it rewards existing customers) or **customer loading** (where it encourages stockpiling).

Sales promotions can be carried out in conjunction with other organisations, which can considerably increase the impact; a free sample of tonic water fixed to a bottle of gin can increase the sales of both products.

Sales promotion expenditure has tended to increase in recent years, with a consequent decline in advertising expenditures. The reason for this is that pull strategies are becoming less effective as advertising clutter increases (Achenbaum and Mitchel 1987). Table 10.2 is a reminder of the differences between push and pull strategies.

TABLE 10.2	Push versus pull strategies

- **Push strategies** involve promoting the product only to the next link down the distribution channel; this means selling hard to the wholesalers and letting the wholesalers in their turn sell hard to the retailers, who then push the product out to the consumers. This method has the advantage of being cheap and relatively straightforward, and could be justified on the grounds that each member of the distribution chain is most familiar with the ways of marketing to the next member down the chain. On the other hand, it really cannot be said to be consumer-orientated. **Pull strategies** involve focusing effort on the consumer, on the basis that an increase in consumer demand for the product will pull it through the distribution chain.

- A **push strategy** emphasises personal selling, sales promotions and advertising aimed at the members of the distribution channel. A **pull strategy** is aimed at the final consumers and emphasises consumer advertising and strong merchandising. Most launch strategies would involve elements of both push and pull. For example, retailers tend to be positive about TV advertising and will stock a product if they know there is to be a TV campaign aimed at consumers. The retailers believe that the campaign will stimulate demand for the product, thus generating sales; it is equally possible that the act of displaying the product prominently is what generates the sales, however.

- If the distribution channels are properly managed and are cooperating well, a pull strategy is indicated; in other words, greater effort can be devoted to stimulating consumer demand, since the other channel members are likely to cooperate in any case. If the channel is uncoordinated or is dominated by the wholesalers or retailers, a push strategy is more likely to work since the channel members will need to be convinced to carry the product line. Again, there will always be elements of both push and pull in any promotional strategy because channel members and consumers both need to move up the hierarchy of communications effects.

One of the main benefits of sales promotion as a technique is that it deflects attention away from price as a competitive tool, particularly if the promotion is not of the money-off variety. Sales promotions can be extremely creative; Table 10.3 describes some examples of classic sales promotions.

TABLE 10.3	Examples of creative sales promotion

- Osram long-life lightbulbs, developed in the early 1970s, were originally intended for industrial applications, where the cost of changing the bulbs often exceeds the cost of the bulb itself. Although the bulbs lasted four times as long as ordinary bulbs, they cost twice as much; the problem was that finance directors often set a fixed price for lightbulbs so the maintenance department were not allowed to pay the premium price of the bulb. Osram's answer was to mail the finance directors a cash box, with a letter saying that there was information inside on how to save 50 per cent on lightbulb replacement. The key to the box was mailed to the maintenance managers. This meant that both parties had to meet to be able to access the information and were thus able to have a discussion about the merits of the new bulbs.

- When Ramada Hotels opened its new Manchester hotel in the mid 1980s it put a plastic duck in each guest bathroom, with a note explaining that the guest could keep the duck as a gift or, for £2.50 plus the cost of mailing, the duck could be sent in a special small crate to any address in the world. This not only resulted in many people receiving a duck through the post from Ramada Hotels, it actually made a profit because the cost of the crates was a lot less than £2.50.

- Shell Oil ran a promotion called 'Make Money' in which customers at its petrol stations were given half 'banknotes' with face values ranging between £1 and £10,000. Customers who could match both halves could redeem them for the face value – which meant that they remained loyal to Shell in the hope of winning the cash. This promotion has been very widely copied, since it has the strength of the 'near win' behind it – each holder of half a banknote imagines that the other half is waiting at the next petrol station.

Creating a sales promotion campaign depends on having clear objectives and on understanding clearly what the marketer wants people to do. This has been stated as: 'Who do I want to do what?' (Cummins 1998). For example, an objective stated as, 'to increase sales', is not clear enough as a basis for any solid creative effort. If, on the other hand, the objective is 'to get existing customers to recommend the product to their friends', the brief is much clearer.

Most sales promotions involve the consumer in doing something: filling in a form, scratching out a scratchcard, collecting items towards a prize and so forth. These activities are called **mechanics** and need as much careful thought as the remainder of the promotion. Here are some of the issues involved:

- Does the mechanic involve a task that might be considered too much trouble? This can work both ways: on the one hand, many potential customers may just give up on the promotion; on the other hand, those who persevere are obviously very keen and are, or will become, committed to the product.

- What will be the feelings of the person undertaking the mechanic? Embarrassing or personally obtrusive mechanics should be avoided.

- Will the customer understand all the rules? Again, if the intention is to appeal to a particular target group, the rules could be made comprehensible only to that group (perhaps by asking quiz questions).

- Should the mechanic be immediate (for example an in-store coupon) or delayed (a coupon against a future purchase)?

- Is the mechanic restricted by law? Many mechanics (usually anything that involves gambling) are outlawed in some countries.

- Does the offer look too good to be true? Sometimes this has turned out to be the case – the notorious Hoover free-flights promotion is an example – but in any event, it is likely to be counterproductive if the consumers are looking for a catch.

In general, sales promotions involve giving something away. What is given away needs to be useful to the consumer, relevant to the product being promoted and not too expensive for the firm concerned. According to D'Astous and Landreville (2003), there are four characteristics of successful sales promotions:

1 *Attractiveness*. The promotional gift should be desirable in itself.

2 *Fit to product category*. The better the gift fits with the product being given away, the better.

3 *Reception delay*. If there is to be a long delay between making the purchase and receiving the gift, the take-up by consumers is likely to be less than it would be if the gift arrives quickly or is attached to the product.

4 *Value*. The greater the value of the gift to the consumer, the more likely he or she is to take up the offer.

These factors interact, but some are more important than others. Attractiveness has an effect, for example, but even an unattractive gift will work if it fits well with the product.

Off-the-shelf promotions

Off-the-shelf offers are those provided by suppliers which are specifically organised around providing sales promotions. As an example, a very common sales promotion is to offer free hotel accommodation to customers. Typically, the customers are supplied with vouchers from a specialist firm, the vouchers being valid for accommodation at a stated group of hotels. Usually the small print on the voucher states that the customer must pay for breakfast and dinner at the hotel; sometimes the price of these is high enough to compensate the hotel for the 'free' room.

The rationale behind such schemes is simple: they enable hotels to fill rooms that would otherwise be empty, and therefore receive some revenue rather than none. Also, the guests may return at a later date and pay the full price. Some of these schemes have come into disrepute, however, because some hotels offer discounts that are equally generous (for example at weekends when they have no business guests) or offer a downgraded service to the 'voucher' guests.

Other examples of the genre include discount vouchers for holidays, books containing vouchers for discounts on goods bought from specific shops (often given to students who open bank accounts), and discount schemes that involve collecting vouchers from newspapers or box tops.

Off-the-shelf schemes are very much two-way. The firm offering the promotion gains because customers want the discounts, and the firm giving the discounts gains because of the extra business coming in. This does require a great deal of trust on the part of both parties, however; a voucher for a reduced price on a theme park, for example, might not seem to be a bargain if the park offers a similar discount on the same day to anyone who turns up. Equally, the voucher should not carry oppressive restrictions in the small print.

The essence of all of these promotions is to provide something valuable to the consumer at a very low cost to the promoter. If a marketer is able to strike a deal with an airline to provide two flights for the price of one, this might save the customer £70 at a cost to the marketer of £10. Promotions work by satisfying the business needs of the third parties – the hoteliers, airlines and retailers that redeem the vouchers. Most of the promotions in this category are brokered by specialist firms which negotiate with the firms which will redeem the vouchers, then sell the vouchers to the marketers who wish to run the promotion.

Joint promotions

In most cases, sales promotions involve some loss of profit, since they involve giving something extra to the customer. **Joint promotions** offer a way of sharing the cost with another firm and at the same time increasing the impact of the promotion. The key to success in this area (as in most areas of marketing) lies in understanding the consumers and the ways they use the product.

Most joint promotions are short term and are often based on free samples of new products or new versions of existing products. In some cases they can be run very cheaply. A sachet of shampoo sent out with bars of cosmetic soap costs the soap company very little, but adds value to the product. Equally, as a way of distributing samples of the shampoo to known cosmetic soap buyers, the technique would be hard to beat.

Another form of joint promotion is to link the product to a charity or cause. The charity is given a proportion of the sales of the product or is helped in some other way. The advantage to the promoter (apart from increased sales) is an improved image. UK supermarket retailer Tescos regularly runs a 'Computers for Schools' scheme whereby a voucher is given to the customer for each £10 spent. The vouchers are passed on to the customers' children's school, where they can be exchanged for computers. The scheme is run in conjunction with computer manufacturers, which supply the machines at a large discount. This is worthwhile for the computer company, since the children will learn on their equipment and are thus more likely to buy similar machines for use at home.

Occasionally, firms form **phantom partnerships**. These involve linking the product to an event in the news without actually stating a connection. For example, some firms who appeared at the Australian motor racing Grand Prix implied a sponsorship connection without actually sponsoring anything (Meenaghan 1991). During the 2002 soccer World Cup, many firms ran football-related promotions. Apart from those firms that were sponsoring matches, these firms were careful not to mention the World Cup in their promotions, since this would have been a breach of copyright. Such arrangements border on ambush marketing (see Chapter 6).

The main element necessary to joint promotions is marketing synergy between the products involved. The products must be complementary rather than competitive, and must appeal to the same target audience.

Price promotions

Price is the most obvious competitive weapon – and like most weapons, it carries risks to the user as well as the target. The main risk of using price discounts is that competitors can easily retaliate in kind, leading to a price war that is damaging to both parties and ultimately weakens the industry, leaving it open to attack from less immediate competitors.

Immediate discounts are discounts available at the time of purchase. There are five forms, as shown in Table 10.4.

TABLE 10.4 Immediate discounts

Type of discount	Explanation and examples
Seasonal discounts	Designed to boost sales in off-peak times, these were originally intended to dispose of end-of-season stocks. Nowadays they have become a traditional way of boosting trade, with some goods being manufactured specifically for the sales. In Christian countries the January sales, immediately after Christmas, are a typical example; in southern India the Onam sales (around September) are another example
Multibuys	The 'buy one get one free' type of promotion is actually a price promotion, since the consumer is getting more goods for the same price. A study by London Business School found that 95 per cent of multibuys are bought by only 27 per cent of households – who then promptly switch to a competitor's brand when the multibuy ends. Of course, in the meantime the consumer has stocks of the product on hand, which in effect excludes the competitor
Banded packs	Similar to multibuys except that the goods are wrapped together in an outer wrapper. This means that the consumer is forced to buy two or more. The advantage is that the offer is under the manufacturer's control rather than the retailer's

| TABLE 10.4 | Continued |

Type of discount	Explanation and examples
Reduced shelf price	Used by retailers to sell off stock that is approaching its sell-by date or which is outmoded; the reduced price is indicated by a sticker on the shelf or by putting the stock on a special 'Reduced' counter. Sometimes these can reduce the willingness of the customer to pay the normal price; many people cruise the supermarket shelves near to closing time looking for last-minute bargains
Extra-fill packs	Packs are produced with slogans such as '25% Extra Free'. The advantage is that the extra cost of the product is small compared with the extra value it gives the customer. This type of promotion was widely used in the UK when cans of lager were switched over from the old half-pint (imperial) size to the larger half-litre (metric) size. Breweries decided that the best way to handle the transition period was to sell at the old price per can, but give the consumers the bigger cans. In some ways this backfired, since consumers expected the discount to continue, with the result that nearly all cans of lager seemed to have extra-fill offers on a more or less permanent basis

Delayed discounts are offers which are not available at the point of purchase, but which can be redeemed later. Typical examples are coupons that give a discount off the next purchase of the product, and offers that require box-top collection. The advantage for the manufacturer is that many people buy the product intending to make use of the coupons, but forget to redeem them. This keeps the cost low. The drawback is the substantial amount of administrative effort that has to go into redemption – often a special temporary office has to be set up to handle the demand. Also, it is often hard to calculate what the demand will be, which makes it difficult to ensure that sufficient stocks of the 'free gift' product are on hand. Equally, the costs are hard to calculate.

Coupons printed in newspapers or distributed through letterboxes can be highly effective in promoting trial purchase. As with delayed discounts, many (or most) of the coupons are never redeemed, but the promotion is often used to gauge the effectiveness of different media. Coupons can be coded so that the firm can tell which newspaper or magazine they came from, which gives a good indication of the appeal of the offer to the readers. The redemption rate is very small from newspapers (typically 4 per cent or less), whereas locally distributed leaflets can achieve redemption rates of better than 25 per cent in some cases. The highest redemption rates occur with in-store coupons, either distributed by hand to customers as they enter the shop or placed at strategic points around the store. In-store coupons are often used in conjunction with in-store tastings.

Three problems arise from coupon-based promotions: the difficulty of estimating the redemption rate (and therefore the overall cost) in advance; the problem of fraudulent redemption (cutting coupons from batches of newspapers and redeeming them through a retailer who is an accomplice); and misredemption of coupons against other products. Coupon redemption relies heavily on the cooperation of retailers in policing the conditions under which they are redeemed; many retailers will accept any coupon against any product, which defeats the object of the promotion. This does not apply to offers where the manufacturer takes responsibility for redeeming the coupons, but this escalates the costs of the exercise considerably.

Reduced-interest finance deals

Low interest offers or 0 per cent finance remain popular promotions for major purchases such as cars, white electrical goods, furniture and other high value items. The purpose of the exercise is to bring the buying decision forward: individuals who are planning a major purchase may want to wait until they have the money saved up, but a 0 per cent credit offer removes this objection.

The problem for the retailer lies in calculating the overall cost of these deals. The calculation is not simply one of making up the interest payments; bad debts have to be considered, as well as the cost of repossessing goods if the payments are not met. For these reasons, most retailers use a finance company to run the schemes, paying the finance charges themselves. The finance company checks credit ratings, collects the payments and even handles repossessions when necessary. Finance companies use the following criteria when assessing the retailer:

- The goods need to be durable, identifiable and movable (in case of repossession).

- The goods should have a resale value greater than the outstanding debt; this means there must be an established second-hand market for the goods.

- The retailer must be a reliable, well-established business.

Some companies, predominantly car manufacturers, are large enough to establish their own subsidiary finance companies. These finance companies operate on exactly the same basis as the mainstream finance houses and banks but they deal only with one firm's products. This is therefore not a route that is available to most retailers.

Premium promotions

Typically, **premium promotions** consist of a free gift with each purchase. For example, in one promotion Fosters gave away a free coolbag with each six-pack of lager. The bag related to the product, had a high perceived value to the consumer, but was cheap to produce; additionally, the brand name emblazoned on the side of the bag was an extra promotional aid.

Sending in proofs of purchase for a free gift also falls into this category. The number of proofs of purchase needed will reflect the frequency of purchase of the product; more proofs can be required for frequently purchased products than for infrequent purchases. The biggest problem lies in gauging the rate of redemption, which could be embarrassingly high or low. Most such offers include the disclaimer 'While stocks last', but it would still be embarrassing for the promoter to run out of stocks of the premium and to have to supply a (possibly disappointing) alternative to consumers. In the UK, the Sales Promotion Code clearly states that promoters should take all reasonable steps to prevent disappointment of this sort, but in any case it is common sense to take precautions not to annoy the paying customers.

Self-liquidating offers are those in which the customer pays all or almost all of the costs of the promotion. These promotions are of the 'Send only £5.99 for a set of kitchen knives' type; they rely on the promoter being able to obtain stocks of the kitchen knives at a bargain price. For example, Kimberly-Clark, manufacturers of Kleenex tissues, makes the bulk of its sales during the winter months, when colds and 'flu boost the amount of sneezing and hence the number of tissues used. During the winter of 2004/2005, the company ran a sales promotion in which customers were offered 'snuggle bags' at a price of only £5.99 plus proof of purchase of Kleenex tissues. The snuggle bags were made of fleece, were the size and shape of a sleeping bag, and contained pockets for cold remedies, hot water bottles and, of course, Kleenex tissues. The bags were intended to be used by cold sufferers to snuggle up on the sofa or in bed. The wholesale cost of the bags was low enough that the sales promotion paid for itself, and it was very effective in increasing sales and also improving loyalty.

In recent years these promotions have fallen out of favour owing to the widespread availability of bargain-price goods. Finding top-notch bargains to offer has therefore become much more difficult, and since the consumer has to go to some trouble to obtain the goods, redemption rates have become low. The most successful examples in recent years have been those involving promotional goods such as T-shirts with the company name on or watches overprinted with the brand name; these goods have been specially manufactured for the promotion and have the additional benefit of publicising the brand name whenever the consumer wears them. These promotions are also called brand extension offers.

Prize promotions

Prize promotions are a form of gambling and, as such, are illegal in some countries. The exceptions are competitions which require a degree of skill on the part of the participant. Table 10.5 shows the different types of prize promotion available.

All prize promotions are hedged about with legal restrictions, and since these restrictions vary greatly from one country to another it is usually difficult or impossible to transfer the promotion across national boundaries.

TABLE 10.5   Prize promotions

Promotion	Explanation and examples
Competitions	The prize is offered for the successful exercise of a mental or physical skill. For example, the contestant is invited to think of a slogan for the product. Sometimes these competitions produce very real slogans
Free draws	Prizes are distributed by random chance. The consumer is usually invited to send in an entry with an individual code number for a later draw. These are commonly used to encourage the return of guarantee cards or market research questionnaires
Instant wins	A predetermined number of winning tickets is distributed. The mechanics for this vary: sometimes the winning number is underneath the ringpull of a can, so that the consumer has to open the can to find out whether it is a prize-winner, or sometimes the promotion is in the form of a scratchcard. Scratchcards have become more popular in recent years because they involve the player in the action of scratching off the covering to reveal the symbols; this gives the opportunity to ensure a 'near win', perhaps by having two out of the three symbols match up. Near wins are known to encourage players to try again
Games	These give the appearance of needing skill but actually rely more on chance. For example, some advertisements for holiday destinations require the reader to answer questions about the destination in order to enter a prize draw; in fact, the answers to the question are contained in the advertisement. The object of the exercise is to encourage the reader to read the advertisement thoroughly
Lotteries	These require the participant to buy a ticket to enter, and are strictly regulated in most countries (and illegal in some). They are often used in small-scale situations such as charity events

INTEGRATING SALES PROMOTIONS WITH OTHER COMMUNICATIONS TOOLS

Sales promotions are often accused of being ineffective because the temporary increase in sales is offset by a subsequent drop. This view is based on the following assumptions:

1 Loyal consumers will stock up on the product while the promotion is on, and will therefore not need to buy any more for some time afterwards.

2 Some consumers who switch brands will switch back again as soon as another offer comes along from a competitor (Krishna *et al.* 1991).

3 There is a hard core of loyal consumers who will not switch brands, no matter what incentives are offered.

Although there is strong evidence that sales promotions do provide only a temporary increase in sales, the above assumptions are not always true. Although consumers may stock up on the product, this probably means that they will use more (particularly if the promotion is accompanied by an ad campaign) and may even give away product to their friends because it was such a good bargain (Wansink and Deshpande 1994). Second, not all brand switchers switch back again; sometimes they prefer the new brand, and even habitual switchers will not switch back unless there is some incentive to do so. Therefore even if the competition responds in some other way (for example, stronger advertising campaigns), the brand switchers may stay loyal to the new brand.

Third, even the hard core of customers for the rival brand will need to switch brands eventually, if only because their existing brand reaches the end of the product lifecycle and is discontinued. Product lifecycles are growing ever shorter, so this scenario is likely to be repeated ever more frequently.

Much of the effort behind integrating sales promotion with other forms of communication is intended to promote the ratchet effect. The increase in sales generated by the sales promotion is supported by advertising, publicity and personal selling so that sales remain at the new, higher level.

Sales promotions can also support other communications functions: a clever or controversial promotion can generate publicity; a promotion requiring names and addresses can generate a database (see Chapter 9); and a good sales promotion gives the salesforce a lever to sell goods into the retailers. Even advertising can benefit by having something more forceful to say, and coupon redemption rates give a good indication of the effectiveness of different media.

Ultimately, as with any form of communication, sales promotion needs to be fitted in around the marketer's other activities. Clarity of objectives, consistency between the different tools used and a suitable evaluation system are all essential, but a good supporting advertising campaign and a set of suitable press releases to accompany the promotion will ensure maximum benefit from the promotion and reap long-term benefits from what is essentially a short-term tool.

BUSINESS-TO-BUSINESS SALES PROMOTIONS

Sales promotion works equally well in the business-to-business environment. Trade promotions can follow similar patterns to consumer promotions, giving extra goods (common in the food industry, particularly snack foods, where retailers are offered extra packs rather than a discount) or discounted prices.

In some cases, the sales promotion can help to increase sales of other products in the range. For example, German hair cosmetics company Goldwell quickly established a large share in the UK professional hairdressing products market by the creative use of sales promotion. The sales reps were authorised to give away samples of the firm's products as sales promotions, but with the proviso that the 'free gift' was to be a product that the salon concerned was not currently using. Thus, a salon buying an extra quantity of hair conditioners would be given a box of setting lotions or some bottles of perm lotion. Often the salon's stylists would try the new products as a result of having them on hand (perhaps even as a result of running out of the usual products) and might become converted to their use in future.

This example shows that sales promotion can be used strategically as well as tactically. Giving salons free samples of the products fulfilled the following objectives:

- The salons were given the opportunity to try the new products, ultimately expanding the range of products used on or sold to each customer.

- Salon owners would increase stocks of Goldwell products in order to acquire the free stock, so stocking levels would increase.

- Loyalty towards Goldwell products steadily increased as salons became more committed to stocking the products and more able consequently to benefit from the offers.

- The products were not being discounted, so the perception of brand quality remained high.

Some sales promotions offer gifts to the buyer, for example attendance at an 'industry seminar' in an exotic location. This is a somewhat dangerous practice, since such gifts might be construed as bribery; the only circumstances in which promotions of this type would be acceptable are when the buyer's employers are aware of what is being offered and have sanctioned the deal, or where the buyer is also the owner of the business (as is the case with many small firms). Bribery only occurs when the buyer is acting against the employer's best interests in order to gain a personal advantage; it is perfectly acceptable to give a gift to a buyer provided the employer is aware of what is happening, or provided the gift is not linked to a requirement to purchase. Business gifts of this sort (for example a bottle of whisky at Christmas) are not sales promotions since they are not linked to specific purchases of goods. They are, of course, useful in developing and maintaining good business relationships.

CASE STUDY: LANSON CHAMPAGNE

Champagne Lanson is one of the most widely respected producers of champagne in France. The company has been in existence since 1760, producing its wines in the Champagne region. Only wines from this region may be called champagne, so Lanson's authenticity is guaranteed by the French government.

Lanson's policy has always been to innovate, however. Unlike many champagne houses, Lanson has been prepared to experiment with new production methods, and also with new marketing techniques. Champagne has always been regarded as an upmarket wine, to be drunk on special occasions and at celebrations: Lanson decided to break the mould by introducing a small bottle (20 cl) which could be sold across the bar in pubs and nightclubs.

The idea caught on rapidly, with the drink becoming popular with a largely female audience. The 'smart' way to drink the product was through a straw, almost as if the champagne were a soft drink: this tends to encourage the drinker to drink more quickly, and also increases the rate at which the alcohol is absorbed. In situations such as nightclubs, where a standard male approach is to offer to buy a woman a drink, the product proved extremely popular.

However, Lanson realised that sales needed a boost. Following the old principle of promoting in a rising market, the company wanted to ensure that it had a substantial share of the market before competitors could enter, so it decided to run a sales promotion. Lanson called in Dynamix, a young, creative sales promotion agency based in Oldham in Lancashire.

Dynamix realised that the market for the small Lanson bottles is young, fun-seeking and probably consisted of relatively heavy drinkers. The promotion route chosen was to introduce an 'instant win' in participating pubs and clubs. Everyone who bought the Lanson champagne was given a foil-wrapped straw (in itself a useful promotional tool). Random straws gave an 'instant win' of a magnum of Lanson champagne, which could either be drunk on the premises or could be taken home. Additionally, a few straws provided an instant win of £1,000.

In order to comply with UK law on sales promotions, people who did not purchase the product were allowed to ask for one straw per day. Although few people actually had the courage to do this, the company is required to make this offer so that the competition is in effect a free-entry lottery.

After a trial run in a limited number of outlets, the company decided to roll out the promotion nationally. The huge success of the promotion ensured Lanson an exclusive market in small, 'fun-size' bottles of champagne, effectively cutting out other champagne producers fom this lucrative new market.

Questions

1 How does Lanson reconcile the upmarket image of champagne with the downmarket image of nightclubs and pubs?

2 Why use an instant-win rather than a money-off promotion?

3 How might Lanson build on the promotion in future?

4 How might you expect the ratchet effect to operate in this promotion?

5 Could a similar promotion work for soft drinks?

SUMMARY

'Sales promotion' is a term that covers a wide range of activities, some of which scarcely look like marketing communications at all. Yet sales promotion is a growing field, often outstripping advertising in terms of expenditure, and certainly occupying a central position in the thinking of most marketers involved in FMCG (fast-moving consumer goods) markets.

Here are the key points from the chapter:

- Other tools will help the ratchet effect.
- Sales promotion is particularly good for encouraging first-time purchase.
- Sales promotion needs to be used sparingly; frequent repetition causes it to become integral to the product.
- Mechanics need to be simple, clear, legal and non-embarrassing.
- Off-the-shelf promotions benefit both promoter and redeemer.
- Joint promotions spread the cost.
- Coupons rely on the cooperation of retailers, so they work best when the channels of distribution are well integrated.
- Sales promotions are not only supported by other communications tools but can also be supportive in themselves.

CHAPTER QUESTIONS

1 How might sales promotion be used in the launch of a new nightclub?

2 What are the main reasons for the growth in sales promotion at the expense of advertising?

3 What might be an appropriate self-liquidating promotion for hot-dog sausages? Give three examples, with reasons.

4 What might be an appropriate partner for a firm manufacturing canned meats such as corned beef and chopped pork? Give three examples, with reasons.

5 How does sales promotion help the salesforce to sell?

FURTHER READING

Brown, C. (1993) *The Sales Promotion Handbook*. London: Kogan Page. A practitioner's book, but of the 'quick reference' variety. It has some useful checklists.

Cummins, J. (1998) *Sales Promotion: How to Create and Implement Campaigns that Really Work*. London: Kogan Page. A lively and clearly written book, again aimed at practitioners.

Toop, A. (1992) *European Sales Promotion*. London: Kogan Page. Over forty fascinating case studies from across Europe. The case studies are all explained in detail, and although some of them are a little elderly now, the principles remain the same – and they outline some very creative ideas.

REFERENCES

Achenbaum, A. A. and Mitchel, F. K. (1987) 'Pulling away from push marketing', *Harvard Business Review*, **65**(May/June): 38–40.

Cummins, J. (1998) *Sales Promotion: How to Create and Implement Campaigns that Really Work*. London: Kogan Page.

Curhan, R. C. and Knopp, R. J. (1987) 'Obtaining retailer support for trade deals: key success factors', *Journal of Advertising Research*, **27**(December/January): 51–60.

D'Astous, A. and Landreville, V. (2003) 'An experimental investigation of factors affecting consumers' perception of sales promotions', *European Journal of Marketing*, **37**(11): 1746–61.

Ehrenberg, A. S. C., Hammond, K. and Goodhart, G. J. (1994) 'The after-effects of price-related consumer promotions', *Journal of Advertising Research*, **34**(July/August): 11–21.

Frankel, B. and Phillips, W. J. (1986) 'Escaping the parity trap', *Marketing Communications*, November: 93–100.

Krishna, A., Currim, I. S. and Shoemaker, R. W. (1991) 'Consumer perceptions of promotional activity', *Journal of Marketing*, **552**(April): 4–16.

Meenaghan, J. A. (1991) 'The role of sponsorship in the marketing communication mix', *International Journal of Advertising*, **10**(1): 35–47.

Moran, W. T. (1978) 'Insights from pricing research', in Bailey, E. B. (ed.), *Pricing Practices and Strategies*. New York: The Conference Board.

Verhoef, P. C. (2003) 'Understanding the effect of customer relationship management efforts on customer retention and customer share development', *Journal of Marketing*, **67**(4): 30–45.

Wansink, B. and Deshpande, R. (1994) 'Out of sight, out of mind: pantry stockpiling and brand-use frequency', *Marketing Letters*, **5**(1): 91–100.

11 Personal selling and sales management

Objectives

After reading this chapter you should be able to:

- describe the main techniques of selling
- explain the role of personal selling within the overall marketing communications mix
- explain why salespeople may not regard themselves primarily as communicators
- describe ways to organise a sales team
- explain the advantages and disadvantages of personal selling, both in terms of communications and in terms of the broader marketing context
- outline the main issues surrounding the management of the salesforce

INTRODUCTION

Personal selling is often regarded as the most powerful weapon in the marketer's armoury. No other technique is as powerful as a salesperson sitting with a prospective customer and developing solutions to the customer's problems based on the firm's product range.

On the other hand, personal selling is also widely regarded as being an expensive option; and certainly, based on the number of contacts made and the level of information passed on by salespeople, this would appear to be very much the case. Salespeople, on the other hand, do not regard themselves as mere communications devices in the employ of the marketing department. Most would regard their problem-solving role as what sets them apart from the communications mix, and there is even some debate as to whether personal selling is primarily a communications activity at all.

After looking at personal selling in some detail, this chapter goes on to consider the problems associated with managing the sales function, both from the viewpoint of the marketing manager and from the viewpoint of the sales manager.

PERSONAL SELLING AND THE COMMUNICATIONS MIX

Personal selling is usually considered to be part of the promotional mix, along with sales promotion, advertising and publicity. Each of the other elements is usually one-way communication, but personal selling is unique in that it always offers two-way communication with the prospective customer. This is partly what makes personal selling such a powerful instrument: the salesperson can clarify points, answer queries and raise the profile of issues that seem to be of greatest interest to the prospect.

As with other forms of marketing communication, selling works best as part of an integrated campaign. Salespeople find it a great deal easier to call on prospects who have already heard something about the company through advertising, publicity or exhibition activities, and many salespeople regard it as the main duty of the marketing department to deliver warm **leads** (or even hot ones). See Chapter 9 for more on the strength of leads.

Personal selling as practised should not be confused with the selling concept. The latter is often cited as a stage in the development of marketing and assumes the following:

- that customers will not ordinarily buy enough of the product without a persuasive sales talk;

- that customers can be fooled into buying more of a product than they need if the salesperson is clever enough;

- that the customer won't mind being fooled and will still be glad to see the salesperson again;

- that customers' **objections** to the product or the company are artificial obstacles to be overcome rather than genuine problems to be solved.

These assumptions contrast with those of the marketing concept, which attempts to anticipate customers' needs and solve their problems profitably.

The selling concept can still be found in many companies and is often confused with the practice of selling, but it is a corporate philosophy rather than a set of tactics. Most professional salespeople would reject the selling concept as not only incorrect but also personally offensive, since they do not wish to be associated with the fast-talking, glib liars so often portrayed in fiction.

Salespeople and marketers often have divergent views about the relationship between selling and marketing and this is occasionally a source of conflict between them (Dewsnap and Jobber 1998).

A marketer's view of personal selling

Peter Drucker's famous quote that 'the aim of marketing is to make selling superfluous' has certainly hit home with marketers (Drucker 1973). Drucker says that there will always be some need for selling, but that marketing's aim is to produce products that are so ideally suited to the customer that the product 'sells itself'. This view of personal selling has coloured marketing thinking for 30 years and is often coupled with Levitt's statement that 'selling focuses on the needs of the seller; marketing on the needs of the buyer' (Levitt 1960). The net result is that marketers have tended to adopt a suspicious view of selling; at worst, salespeople are viewed as dinosaurs, forever wedded to the selling concept (which has little to do with the practice of selling), and at best they are viewed as a necessary evil, filling in the gaps in the communications mix.

On the positive side, salespeople are believed to be able to find, inform and persuade customers in a way that has yet to be bettered by any other communications medium. Personal selling has been variously defined as follows:

Personal selling is about finding, informing, persuading and at times servicing customers through the personal, two-way communication that is its strength. It means helping customers to articulate their needs, tailoring persuasive selling messages to answer those needs, then handling customers' responses or concerns in order to arrive at a mutually valued exchange.

(Brassington and Pettitt 2002)

Personal selling is the process of informing customers and persuading them to purchase products through personal communication in an exchange situation.

(Dibb *et al.* 1998)

Selling is a function which is concerned with identifying the specific needs, desires and problems of individual customers and providing satisfaction of these through benefit or solution in order to facilitate profitable business transactions.

(Cooper 1997)

The provision of information and the element of persuasion are paramount in these descriptions of personal selling. For the marketer, personal selling is one of several possible options available for communicating the company's messages to the customers; it has the major advantage that the message can be tailored to fit the **prospect**'s need for information. Marketers appear to be working to the model shown in Figure 11.1.

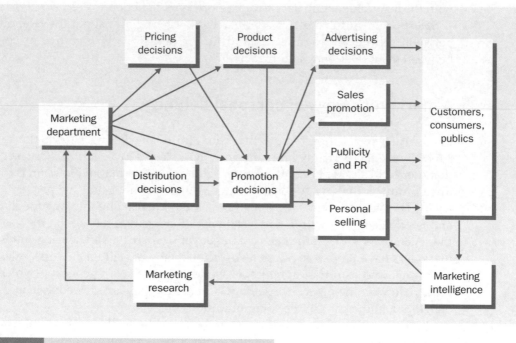

FIGURE 11.1   Marketer's view of the role of personal selling

Feedback for decision making can come from two sources: marketing research and the salesforce. Since market researchers are paid by the hour not by the result, the information obtained from marketing research is often assumed to be unbiased, objective and untainted by a desire to maximise earnings, unlike the information from the salesforce, which is often assumed to be subjective and therefore less reliable. For example, Gordon *et al.* (1997) found that the salesforce could not be relied on as a source of information for new product development.

Although marketers are unanimous in agreeing that selling is the most powerful promotional tool, all agree that it is also the most expensive. It should perhaps be noted that none of the authorities cited above goes so far as to say that selling is not cost effective, but most say that it is an expensive option. This raises the question: 'expensive in terms of what?' Presumably something that is costly but works is better value than something that is low cost but does not work.

Because of the supposed high cost of personal selling and the oft-expressed view that there are many other ways of communicating with customers, marketers will inevitably be looking for ways of eliminating the salesforce. Database marketing (see Chapter 9) is one of several approaches that have been proposed as a way of carrying out the 'tailored' communication function of personal selling without actually needing a salesforce. For example, Peppers and Rogers (1995) define database marketing as one-to-one marketing using technology to develop relationships with individual customers. Copulsky and Wolf (1990) show that firms seek to deliver differentiated messages to potential customers through channels based on the consumers' characteristics and preferences.

Equally, it has been claimed that the detailed information that the salesforce can provide on individual customers can be replaced by low cost databases (Dwyer *et al*. 1987), and that combinations of databases can fill in gaps in that knowledge. Ultimately, some marketers believe that individual customers can be described in great detail, at least in terms of buying habits (Evans 1994). To summarise the marketer's view, the salesforce functions and their potential replacements are shown in Table 11.1.

TABLE 11.1   Replacements for salesforce functions

Salesforce function	Marketer's replacement method
Prospecting	Bought-in database; database combination
Evaluating prospects	Database scrutiny, credit referencing technology, response to direct mail
Preparing	Combining databases to find the most effective approach to the individual customer
Approaching the customer	Initial mailing, Internet advertisement, direct-response advertising
Making the presentation	Tailored direct mail, interactive Internet or e-mail negotiation
Overcoming objections	Interactive computer-based (Internet-based) information system
Closing	Internet-based close, credit transfer, e-mail order forms
Following up	Direct mail

At first sight, the marketer's view of personal selling appears to allow for replacement of selling with other (often IT-based) techniques. In light of the statements made in many marketing texts about the high cost of personal selling, this viewpoint is wholly understandable. Clearly, a mailing that contacts 5,000 good prospects for a cost of £15,000 is a great deal cheaper than a sales representative who would contact around half that number of prospects in a year at a cost of £50,000. There is little doubt that traditional salesforces are under pressure from direct channels and key account management systems (Piercy and Lane 2003).

Overall, it would appear that Drucker's view that selling will ultimately become superfluous, and Levitt's view that selling is about the needs of the seller, have encouraged marketers to view selling as 'the enemy'.

In fairness, Levitt's statement may have been misconstrued. It would certainly be true to say that the selling *concept* focuses on the needs of the seller. It should also be pointed out that Drucker's statement about the obsolescence of selling could equally be applied to advertising, to publicity or to sales promotion. The Drucker ideal appears to concentrate on perfect product development, which is either some way in the future or buried in the past along with Platonic idealism and the product concept.

Undoubtedly, personal selling does have a major communications element, involving as it does a two-way dialogue between salesperson and prospect, but there is a great deal more to personal selling than this. An examination of what salespeople actually do will clarify this.

The salesperson's view of personal selling

Research into sales practice shows a somewhat different picture of the salesperson's view from that conveyed by most marketing texts.

First, the emphasis in selling practice is not on telling, but on asking. The salesperson's role in the sales presentation is characterised not by a persuasive sales talk, but by asking appropriate questions to find out the prospect's needs and to lead the discussion and negotiation in a particular direction. DeCormier and Jobber (1993) found a total of 13 different types of question in use by salespeople. Rackham (1991) categorised questions along four dimensions: situation, problem, implication and need-payoff. In each case the emphasis is on asking the prospect about his or her situation, with a view to finding a solution from among the salesperson's portfolio of products. Note that the needs of the buyer are paramount, that the salesperson is asking questions and that the marketing department's 'message' is not relevant to this core process. The social aspect of the interaction is also important, since in many cases the salesperson is seeking to build a long-term relationship, not make a single sale (Geiger and Turley 2005).

This problem-solving approach to selling is by no means new. Sales trainers and writers have emphasised the problem-solving aspects of selling for many years, and salespeople are advised to allow the customer to do most of the talking (Lund 1979).

Salespeople sometimes follow the NASA model for preparing a sales presentation. This model is as follows:

N is for *needs*. The salesperson asks the prospect about his or her needs and problems.

A is for *acceptance*. Having ascertained the needs, the salesperson confirms them with the prospect, thus getting the prospect's acceptance of the problem.

S is for *solution*. The salesperson shows the prospect how the solution will meet his or her problem.

A is for *acceptance* again. This time the salesperson is seeking the prospect's acceptance of the proposed solution.

The NASA system places the emphasis on finding solutions to the prospect's problem. Interestingly, this is what marketers tell us is the main role of marketing. In fact, examining what a salesperson actually does in the course of a presentation shows very close parallels with what marketers do (Table 11.2).

TABLE 11.2   Comparison of marketers' and salespeople's activities

Marketer's activities	Salesperson's activities
• Research into the needs of consumers	• Needs analysis based on situation and problem questions
• Gap analysis	• Analysis of needs to identify problems
• New product development, designed to meet consumers' needs	• Selection from among the existing range of products to find the closest fit for the prospect's needs
• Pricing: selecting an appropriate price which meets the consumer's and the firm's expectations	• Price negotiation: negotiating a price which meets the customer's and the firm's expectations
• Promotion: designing an appropriate promotion strategy that will equate to the consumer's psychological and behavioural characteristics	• Promotion: explaining the features and benefits of the product in terms of the customer's needs, psychology and behavioural characteristics
• Distribution decisions: ensuring that the product is in a convenient place for the consumer to buy it	• Distribution negotiations: ensuring that the product reaches the customer in the right quantities and at the right time

In the case of services, the marketer and the salesperson will also be concerned with the people, process and physical evidence (Booms and Bitner 1981). Again, the relationship is close; for example, it is common practice for salespeople to leave something with the customer once the sale is closed (a copy of the order, a brochure about the product or such like).

So far, selling and marketing appear to be similar; the main difference is that selling is concerned with individuals and individual relationships, whereas marketing is concerned with market segments. Admittedly, direct marketing and database marketing seek to target ever shrinking segments by using information technology. Salespeople already do this, face-to-face and in real time, without the benefit of the marketing department's range of resources.

For salespeople, then, the model of the relationship between marketing and sales will look more like that shown in Figure 11.2. In this model, the salesforce does the real work of finding out the customer's needs and fulfilling them, and the marketing department exists mainly to provide back-up services. Marketers provide information to the salesforce and to the production department, but the salesforce exists to solve customers' problems using products supplied by production.

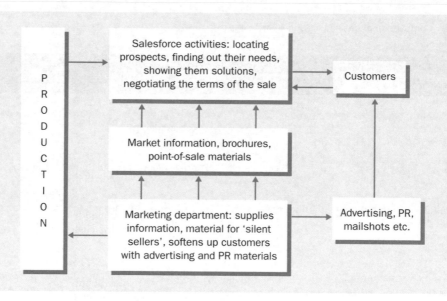

FIGURE 11.2   Salesperson's model of the relationship between marketing and selling

For the salesperson adopting this model, the marketing department occupies a subservient role. Since the salesforce is in the 'front line', dealing directly with customers, it is clear that every other department in the firm depends on salespeople to bring in the business. They are, in fact, the only department that brings in money; everything else merely generates costs. Sales training programmes sometimes emphasise this: salespeople are told that the average salesperson supports five other jobs; they are told that 'nothing happens until somebody sells something'; they are encouraged to think of themselves as the most important people in the firm. Furthermore, research has shown that many salespeople are defensive of their good relationships with customers even when this conflicts with instructions from the marketing department, since it is easier for salespeople to find a new company to work for than it is to find new customers (Anderson and Robertson 1995).

While there may be some justification for this, it is equally true to say that salespeople would have nothing to sell were it not for the efforts of the production department, would have no pay packet and no invoicing without the finance department, would have no deliveries without the shipping department, and so on. Salespeople may be given a false view of their own importance, but trainers may do this in order to counteract the often negative image and low status that selling has in the eyes of other departments.

In this model, the salesforce collects information about the customer from the marketing department's research and directly from the customer. Product, price, delivery, sales promotion and the use of advertising and PR materials (contained in the salesperson's **silent seller**) are all used in negotiation with the customer, with the aim of obtaining an optimum solution for both parties in terms of both information exchange and product/price exchange.

For many salespeople, the marketing department also paves the way for a sales call by providing publicity and advertising. It is easier for a salesperson to make a call knowing that the prospect has heard of the company and has some favourable impressions. For the salesperson, the marketing department performs a support function, providing a set of products to choose from, a price structure to negotiate around, a distribution system that can be tailored to suit the customer and promotional back-up in the form of advertising and publicity. Sales promotions are used as ways of closing sales (as deal makers), but the basic problem solving and decision making are done by the salespeople when they are with the customer.

In fact, it is this problem-solving and decision-making function that distinguishes the salesforce from other 'promotional tools'. Salespeople do not think of themselves as being primarily communicators; they think of themselves as primarily decision makers.

If salespeople are correct in this view, then it would clearly be impossible to replace them with a database (at least, given the current state of the art). A computer can hold and manipulate information very effectively, but it is unable to solve problems creatively or negotiate effectively, or indeed establish a long-term relationship on a human level. A human being is necessary for these functions. Since these human beings would be dealing with sales, it might be convenient to call them salespeople.

A customer's view of personal selling

Salespeople have a bad reputation, largely undeserved, for being pushy and manipulative. Although there are undoubtedly salespeople who do overpersuade and try to pressurise customers into buying, this approach is usually fairly unproductive for the following reasons:

- In most cases the salesperson will be calling again and would not want to be met with a firmly closed door.

- Most selling takes place in a business-to-business environment, where buyers are generally professionals and are trained to resist a pushy approach.

- Bullying customers into signing for goods only leads to cancellations once the salesperson is gone.

- This type of high-pressure approach is too demanding on the salesperson to be sustainable for a long period.

For these reasons, salespeople find that it is easier and more beneficial to begin by finding out the customer's needs and then to apply a solution to those needs based on the firm's product range. Although marketers commonly speak of 'the product', it is rarely the case that a salesperson will have only one product to offer; in many cases, salespeople even have the capacity to vary products or tailor them to fit the customer's needs.

Salespeople will, of course, have considerable knowledge about the products in the range and probably of the industry in general. The customer can therefore 'pick the salesperson's brains' for useful information to help in problem solving. The customer's knowledge of his or her unique situation combines with the salesperson's knowledge of products and industry to generate a creative solution. This is shown in Figure 11.3.

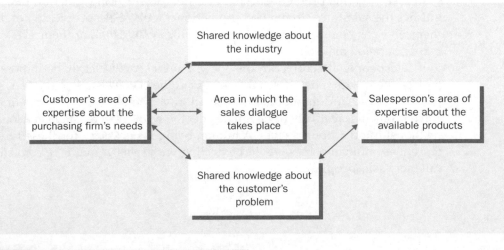

FIGURE 11.3   Areas of knowledge and the sales dialogue

For the customer, the salesperson is a source of information, a source of help in problem solving and an advocate back to the supplying company. Good salespeople are also adept at helping their customers through the decision-making process; often this is the hardest part of making a sale.

PERSONAL SELLING IN PRACTICE

Because personal selling is a labour-intensive activity, large numbers of people are employed in the profession. According to one study, over 300,000 people are employed as professional salespeople in the UK alone (Abberton Associates 1991). Virtually every product available has, at some stage, been sold by a salesperson to a prospect in a face-to-face transaction, and personal selling is a common route into a career in marketing.

The sales cycle

Table 11.3 shows the activities that comprise the **sales cycle**. This process is regarded as a cycle because the salesperson will often use the follow-up call to prospect for more business, looking either for repeat orders from the same customer or for ideas on other prospects to call on. Typically, salespeople will have several cycles running at once and will be spending part of their time on prospecting, part on follow-ups, part on presentations, and so forth.

TABLE 11.3　The sales cycle

Activity	Explanation
Prospecting	Sourcing information that enables the salesperson to identify potential buyers
Appointment making	Selecting the right person to deal with within the target firm and arranging a mutually convenient time to meet
Preparation	Researching the target company, checking the route for getting there, planning the diary etc
Ice breaking	Establishing human contact by asking some general, information-gathering questions of the prospect. This puts both parties at their ease

▶

TABLE 11.3 Continued

Activity	Explanation
Needs identification	This is the most crucial part of the sale. The salesperson asks questions that identify the prospect's needs for the product category and brings those needs to the forefront of the prospect's mind
Presentation	The explanation of the salesperson's proposed solution to the problem
Negotiation and objection handling	Dealing with problems raised by the presentation and discussion of these with the prospect
Closing the sale	Obtaining a decision from the prospect
Processing the order	Ensuring that the customer's order is dealt with efficiently by the supplier and in the terms agreed with the customer. This is a good time for the salesperson to run some self-evaluation to learn from the sales meeting
Follow-up	Checking with the customer after delivery to ensure that he or she is happy with the product and the firm. This aspect is often neglected by salespeople, perhaps because of fears that the customer may be dissatisfied with the product or service received.

Salespeople determine a prospect's needs in two ways. First, they often carry out some desk research, or pre-call preparation, to identify firms and individuals who might have a need for one or more of the firm's products. The next (and usually more important) stage of the information-gathering process is to ask questions of the prospect. In most cases, these questions are categorised as either closed or open. **Closed questions** are those with only a yes or no answer; **open questions** are those with a range of possible answers and typically begin with who, what, when, where, how or why.

Questions also help to lead the prospect towards the sale. Here is an example:

Salesperson: What's the maintenance bill like on your present machine?

Prospect: Around £14–16,000 a year.

Salesperson: Wow! So if I could show you a way of cutting that back by 30 per cent, would you be interested?

The question about the annual maintenance bill raises the issue in the prospect's mind as well as giving the salesperson some information on which to base the presentation. The first question is an open question and is used to open the sale; the second is a closed question, which helps to close the sale.

This categorisation of questions as either open or closed was developed in the 1920s by E. K. Strong. More recently, Rackham (1991) has developed a slightly more complex model for major account selling. As mentioned earlier, he divides questions into situation questions (about the prospect's present circumstances), problem questions (about problems, difficulties and dissatisfactions), implication questions (about the consequences and effects of these difficulties), and need-payoff questions (about the benefits that would accrue from solving the problems). This model provides the more detailed information that the salesperson needs to handle a major sale.

In each case, the salesperson is accumulating information that is used to solve the prospect's problem. During the presentation, the salesperson develops a solution to the problem and explains it to the prospect in terms of the prospect's needs, both for the product and for information about it.

During the course of the presentation, prospects will often raise objections; for example, they may not like some aspect of the product. Although objections are often seen as barriers to making the sale, good salespeople recognise them as requests for further information. Provided the objection is successfully answered, the negotiation can continue until a mutually acceptable solution is reached. Objections can be handled in the following way:

1 Repeat the objection back to the prospect, to confirm that the salesperson has understood what the objection is.

2 Isolate the objection, in other words, confirm that it is the only problem with the product.

3 Apologise for not having explained properly. This avoids making the prospect lose face or feel silly.

4 If the objection is false (i.e. doesn't have any basis in fact), explain how the product actually meets the problem. Alternatively (if the objection is real), show how the benefits of the product outweigh the disadvantages.

5 Confirm with the prospect that the objection has been overcome.

Once all the objections have been answered, the sale can be closed. Closing techniques are ways of helping the prospect over the decision-making hurdle. Perhaps surprisingly, most people are reluctant to make decisions, even more so if they are professional buyers. This is perhaps because of the risks attached to making a mistake, but whatever the reason, buyers often need some help in agreeing to the order. Salespeople use a number of closing techniques to achieve this; Table 11.4 has some examples.

TABLE 11.4   Examples of closing techniques

Technique	Explanation	Example
Alternative close	The prospect is offered two alternatives, each of which leads to the order	'Would you like them in red or in green?'
Order-book close	The salesperson writes down each feature in the order book as it is agreed during the presentation	'OK, you want the green ones, you want four gross, and your best delivery day is Thursday. If you'll just autograph this for me, we'll get it moving for you.'
Immediate gain close	The prospect is shown that the sooner he or she agrees to the deal, the sooner he or she will get the benefits of the product	'Fine. So the sooner we get this paperwork sorted, the sooner you'll start making those savings'

There are many other closing techniques. Salespeople will typically use whichever one seems most appropriate to the situation.

Salespeople usually don't ask prospects to 'sign' the order. This has negative connotations; it is better to ask people to 'OK that for me' or 'Autograph this for me'.

The astute reader will have recognised that the sequence of events in Table 11.4 ties in closely with the NASA model described earlier. During the face-to-face part of the salesperson's job the prospect's needs always come first, followed by acceptance of the needs, followed by the presentation of the solution to the need problem. Acceptance of the solution, or rejection of it, determines whether the sale goes ahead or not.

Having closed the sale, salespeople will usually leave the prospect with some physical evidence of the transaction: a copy order form, perhaps some information about the product, or even some samples if the product is of an appropriate type. A few polite words with the buyer, perhaps to pave the way for the next meeting, will help to cement the sale. Selling is very much a social process and is as much about the personalities involved as it is about the products and economics of the deal.

Having closed the sale and cemented the order, the salesperson will need to ensure that the order is correctly processed through the system. Many salespeople end up fulfilling a progress-chasing role, which should ideally be carried out by someone else. In the interests of good relations, salespeople often prefer to keep a personal check on the progress of orders through the system, and also like to make follow-up visits to customers to ensure that everything was carried out according to the agreement reached during the sales presentation.

Closing the sale is mainly a matter of getting a decision from the prospect. In many business-to-business situations this will not happen immediately, and other decision makers may become involved so that a sale may stretch over weeks, months or even years. In these circumstances, the role of the salesperson becomes even more crucial; the techniques of major account management need to be brought to bear.

Major account management

Major accounts (or key accounts as they are also known) have the following characteristics (Donaldson 1998):

- They account for a significant proportion of existing or potential business for the firm.

- They form part of a supply chain in which efficiency is enhanced by cooperation rather than conflict.

- Working interdependently with these customers, rather than independently, has benefits in lower transaction costs, better quality or joint product development – perhaps all three.

- Supply involves not just product but other service aspects, whether technical support, 'just-in-time' manufacturing or market development potential.

- There are advantages to both parties in close, open relationships rather than a focus on transaction efficiency.

Customers can be classified in terms of their relationship with the firm, as shown in Table 11.5.

TABLE 11.5 The relational development model

Stage	Explanation
Pre-key account management (KAM)	The preparation and identification of potential key accounts, now and in the future. The decision is based on the nature of the exchange; if it is low value and in essence transactional, KAM is unlikely to be necessary
Early KAM	An initial order has been received and the emphasis is now on building on that order to develop a longer-term and more strategic relationship. Opportunities for increasing the firm's involvement with the customer are being sought: for example, setting up training programmes, offering technical support or carrying out joint promotions

TABLE 11.5	Continued

Stage	Explanation
Mid-KAM	At this stage the buyer is becoming committed to the firm, although other competitors may still be involved. The buyer will expect to be given preferential treatment, but will also be prepared to give some preferential treatment in return. Negotiation is important at this stage; the future relationship between the parties will depend largely on what is agreed at this time
Partnership KAM	This develops from the mid-KAM stage. At this point each party is committed to the other, there is open discussion of needs and wants and a number of joint initiatives will be undertaken
Synergistic KAM	At this level, the companies are almost synonymous with one another, but there has not actually been a merger. The problem now becomes one of internal and external coordination to ensure the achievement of mutual objectives. In a sense, the salesforce is no longer involved at this stage; all the staff of both firms will be involved directly or indirectly in ensuring a close fit between the firms

Source: Millman and Wilson (1995). Republished with permission, Emerald Group Publishing Limited

As firms move through these stages, the level of involvement with the customer increases and becomes more complex and the relationship becomes more collaborative. Salespeople are crucial to the process because interpersonal trust is a key factor in deepening the relationship: in fact, it is interpersonal trust which enables weaker firms to trade effectively with stronger firms (Narayandas and Rangan 2004).

Managing the process begins with salespeople, but as the firms move through the stages of KAM other staff become involved – brand managers, distribution managers, production managers and so forth – until virtually all the executive specialists in each firm will have some involvement. Consequently, salespeople need to occupy a much greater strategic and planning role than they would in a transaction-based selling environment.

MANAGEMENT OF THE SELLING PROCESS AND FUNCTION

Much of the time, however, the salesforce is out of sight of the management, so the selling process is largely self-managed. From a manager's viewpoint this can be problematical: supervision is difficult and often impossible, and salespeople are encouraged to be creative and independent in their work. They are usually paid by results and are often working towards quotas, and therefore do not always take kindly to being told to do something differently.

A marketing perspective of the selling process

Salespeople often do not want to convey a set 'corporate message' since the evidence is that a 'canned presentation' is unlikely to result in a sale. The freedom to be creative in tailoring the message to the customer is what marks salespeople out from TV commercials.

Salespeople tend to regard marketing as a support function, generating leads and softening up prospects prior to the salesperson's visit. Salespeople will also expect the marketing department to supply samples, brochures, leaflets, testimonials and other printed material to show prospects or to leave with customers.

Salespeople often have more sympathy for the customer's point of view than for the company's – after all, they spend more time with customers. This can be problematical in that salespeople will tend to think that the products are too expensive and that the production people are uncooperative in not being prepared (or able) to adapt the product to meet customers' requirements. Having said that, salespeople are at the front line, they are in daily contact with the customers, and they are therefore a rich source of information if handled correctly.

Strategic view of the selling process

From a strategic viewpoint, the management issues revolve around determining the salesforce size, sales forecasting and budgeting, choices about the type of salesforce organisation, decisions about the use of information technology and communications systems, and territory management.

Salesforce size

Calculating the appropriate size of a salesforce is a complex procedure; there is unlikely to be a single straightforward answer, and the answer, once found, is unlikely to be a permanent solution since the business world is too dynamic. The decisions will depend on the type of work the salespeople are expected to carry out (which includes the burden of paperwork, the amount of time spent on customer support, the amount of time it takes to demonstrate the products and so forth) and the nature of the task facing the firm (servicing existing customers as opposed to finding new ones, for example). Three methods of determining salesforce size are as follows:

- *Workload method.* This is the most common technique used. It begins by calculating the total working time available per salesperson, then calculating the division of that time into selling tasks, making allowances for travel time, waiting time and breaks. The company's customers are then divided into account types (large, medium and small, perhaps, or new, growing and established), and the appropriate call lengths and frequencies established for those accounts.

Company workload needed to achieve these figures can be calculated and divided by the amount of time available for calls; this gives the number of salespeople needed. The main drawback of this method is that it assumes that all salespeople and all accounts are equal; in fact, there are marked differences in the performance and potential of each.

- *Sales potential method*. Using the management's sales forecasts for the products in the range and the average productivity level per person, the number of salespeople needed can be calculated. The drawback with this method is that it is difficult to be accurate about sales forecasting, and often equally difficult to be accurate about salesforce productivity.

- *Incremental method*. If new salespeople would generate extra revenue to an extent greater than the extra cost of employing them, then they should be recruited. This has the advantage that extra salespeople will be profitable, but there remains the problem of assessing the salesperson's potential.

Shapiro (1979) developed a six-stage process for structuring the salesforce, as follows:

1 Analyse organisational needs. The organisation should be based on the tasks to be accomplished and a clear sales strategy should be specified. The customers (or at least types of customer) to be approached, the call frequency and the selling tasks should be established to focus the salesforce purpose.

2 Structure the salesforce at the bottom level. The organisation should be designed to manage the salesforce rather than the salesforce being designed to fit the management structure.

3 Once the structure has been established at salesperson level, further change should be confined to the management level. The salesperson level is task determined, so presumably meets the prime purposes of the organisation.

4 Integrate units and staff support into the structure. This can be done during the previous stage, but not before.

5 Develop control systems to support the structure. These include measurement, evaluation, feedback and reward.

6 Allocate the staff according to the job to be done.

Unfortunately, organisations are seldom formed from scratch. This means that there will be structures in place and vested interests among existing staff members; carrying out major changes will almost always disrupt routines and usually demotivates some or all of the staff. Also, the decisions made in the course of the six stages will follow marketing decisions based on the role of personal selling in the firm's marketing mix.

Sales forecasting

A detailed examination of sales forecasting is beyond the scope of this book, but a brief introduction to it may make some of the salesforce management issues clearer. Market research is frequently used to estimate the level of sales that a particular product might have. Market research is often effective in estimating consumer response to product offerings but is unable to predict competitive responses or changing circumstances accurately.

Sometimes a consensus of opinion is sought from the salesforce and the management as to how well a product might sell. The main drawbacks with this method are that salespeople tend to be overoptimistic and at the same time are more interested in overachieving the targets than in ensuring accuracy – thus they are often tempted to put in a low estimate of sales potential.

Objective techniques include time series analysis (looking at past sales and extrapolating them into the future) and causal methods (which look at economic indicators, industry buying patterns and so forth). Most 'objective' techniques are considerably less objective than would at first appear – even in the interpretation of past sales results a degree of judgement needs to be exercised by the analyst, particularly in deciding which factors are likely to cause a future fluctuation in the figures.

Type of organisation

It is not always necessary to employ a salesforce directly. Many firms use manufacturers' agents as a cheaper alternative. An agent operates as an independent business and may well act for more than one firm, though usually not for firms that compete directly. In general, agents operate on a commission-only basis, so if there are no sales there is no cost to the firm. This shifts the risk away from the firm and on to the agent, so commission rates will often need to be quite high.

The main advantage of using agents is that they are able to cover territories that might not be economically viable for an employed salesperson (for example, sparsely populated areas), and they often develop specialist expertise in dealing with specific markets.

Anderson (1985) found that companies were more likely to use their own salesforces rather than agents in the following circumstances:

- when there was a large investment in company-specific resources such as plant, equipment and promotional expenses in a market;

- when sales performance was difficult to evaluate;

- when there was a high combination of environmental uncertainty and transaction-specific assets;

- when the price–quality combination was favourable (the product line was attractive);

- when non-selling activities were important.

It transpired from Anderson's study that travel time, company size and the nature of the products were less important than anticipated.

Using agents certainly has advantages but does not absolve the sales manager from the need to make decisions about territories, targets, training and motivation. In some ways these issues become even more important when using agents, who are, after all, not reliant on any individual firm for their livelihood.

Information technology

Information technology (IT) and computer-based management systems are revolutionising sales management and, to an extent, sales practice. User-friendly software and cheap personal computers allow management to collect and manipulate data more easily in order to support decision making.

The growth in the use of IT is due to the following factors:

- Cheap, powerful computers are available.

- Integration of computers and telecommunications has increased the speed and convenience of communications, notably through the use of e-mail and computer/fax interfaces.

- Software has developed to the point where most managers are able to operate their own computer systems to an extent that would not have been thought possible 25 years ago.

- Reliable laptop computers and car-based telecommunications systems exist.

- Computers are increasingly accepted and used, particularly among young, educated professionals.

The ways in which sales management information systems help sales managers are shown in Table 11.6.

TABLE 11.6	Sales management information systems

Functional area	Explanation
Sales reporting and analysis	Collecting and analysing call reports, levels of actual sales compared with budgeted sales, analysis of sales by market segment, and profit dimensions of sales performances. These figures can be calculated according to individual salespeople, teams or the entire salesforce
Sales planning	Identifying leads, classifying prospects (segmenting the market) and building up customer profiles. These can be assessed across a variety of criteria including organisation type, buying pattern, creditworthiness and size of average order
Future options and projections	Computer modelling enables the manager to try different options and predict possible future scenarios. Although this is unlikely to provide the definitive answer to problems, it can often help in rejecting some alternatives and in clarifying the manager's thinking

As with any other management tool, there are problems attached to the use of sales management information systems. First, there is the problem of information overload: sometimes so much information is generated that it becomes impossible to wade through it all and arrive at a coherent decision. Second, computers sometimes give a spurious credibility to results which have been obtained from inaccurate input data – what computer experts call GIGO (garbage in, garbage out).

Third, developing the systems usually means that sales managers have to come into contact with IT experts. Since neither of these groups is likely to know enough about the other's specialism to be able to comment or make suggestions, it may take some time for them to work out an optimum system. The exigencies of making the system compatible with the rest of the firm's systems may compel the IT expert to make inappropriate compromises.

Fourth, management requirements change rapidly. Changes in the market, the type of products being sold, the size of the firm or the management structure may mean that the information requirements change frequently, and the system needs to change with it.

Fifth, there is the problem of technophobia. Some salespeople (and managers) do not trust computers and are almost hoping that the system will fail. This can become a self-fulfilling prophecy as the salespeople concerned fail to provide the appropriate data at the right time.

Assessing the costs and benefits of using IT can also be problematical since the costs are easily identified but the benefits often are not.

Information systems and telecommunications

In some cases, regular face-to-face sales calls are not efficient in terms of using salesforce time, so the salespeople will use the telephone to maintain contact with customers between normal sales visits. In these circumstances, salespeople need to have rapid access to information about the customers so that telephone selling can be carried out in the most effective way. There is more on telemarketing in Chapter 12, but from a sales management viewpoint it is necessary to arrange access to PCs for salespeople who use the telephone in this way, and, equally importantly, to ensure that the salesforce has been adequately trained in the use of the system.

Teleconferencing systems using e-mail and webcams are growing in popularity. The main advantage is the time saved by not travelling, but many people who have used these methods feel that something is lost if there is no face-to-face contact. Subtleties of gesture and intonation are not as clear when seen on a screen, so for most types of sales presentation a physical presence is usually more effective. This is not to say that webcam-based systems may not become more widely used as people grow more familiar with the medium.

Telemarketing systems (where the telephone substantially replaces the personal call) can be a great deal more cost effective than personal calls and often yield the desired outcome provided the person being called already has some kind of relationship with the calling company. Unsolicited cold calls by telephone are a great deal less effective than personal visits. Because of the relatively low cost of telephoning, an improved customer support can be offered, and many firms also operate inbound telemarketing systems for customer support, the so-called helplines.

Sales territory management

Sales territory management involves ensuring that each member of the salesforce has a reasonably equal chance of making sales. Clearly, a home improvement salesperson in a major city will have an easier task than one in a rural area, simply because of the shorter distances between prospects; such a salesperson would spend more time in presentations and less time driving. On the other hand, the city salesperson would probably face more competition and might also have to cover poorer householders who would be less likely to spend much money on improvements.

Territories can be divided geographically or by industry. IBM divides territories by industry, for example, so that salespeople get to know the problems and needs of the specific industry for which they have responsibility. IBM salespeople might be given responsibility for banks, or insurance companies, or local government departments. This sometimes means that salespeople have greater distances to travel in order to present IBM products than if they were assigned a particular territory, but they are more able to make sensible recommendations and give useful advice. Geographical territories are the more common, however, since they minimise travel time and maximise selling time.

It is virtually impossible to create exactly equal territories. Thus it is important to discuss decisions with salespeople in order to ensure that they feel they are being treated fairly. For example, some salespeople may be quite happy to accept a rural territory because they like to live and work in the country, even if it means earning less.

Conclusion

Selling is much more than a communications function. It involves all the elements of marketing but on a small scale; salespeople see themselves as strategists rather than tacticians and there is considerable merit in this view. Salespeople therefore need to be consulted, rather than told, and their opinions deserve respect. As one managing director put it: 'They've got the numbers on their heads, so they've got the right to call the shots.'

A sales manager's perspective of the selling process

Sales managers are responsible for recruitment, training, motivating, controlling and evaluating salesforce activities, and managing sales territories.

Recruitment

Recruitment is complicated by the fact that there is no generally applicable set of personality traits that go to make up the ideal salesperson. This is because the sales task varies greatly from one firm to another, and the sales manager will need to draw up a specific set of desirable traits for the task in hand. This will involve analysing the company's successful salespeople and also the less successful ones, to find out what the differences are between them.

Some companies take the view that almost anybody can be trained to sell and therefore their selection procedures are somewhat limited or even non-existent; other companies are extremely selective and subject potential recruits to a rigorous selection procedure.

Sources of potential recruits are advertising, employment agencies, recommendations from existing sales staff, colleges and universities, and internal appointments from other departments.

Training

Training can be long or short, depending on the product and the market. Table 11.7 illustrates the dimensions of the problem.

TABLE 11.7	Factors relating to length of training of sales staff

Factors indicating long training	Factors indicating short training
• Complex, technical products	• Simple products
• Industrial markets with professional buyers	• Household, consumer markets
• High order values (from the customer's viewpoint)	• Low order values
• High recruitment costs	• Low recruitment costs
• Inexperienced recruits – for example recruited direct from university	• Experienced recruits from the same industry

The role the salesperson is required to take on will also affect the length of training: **missionary** salespeople will take longer to train than **order takers**, and **closers** will take longer than **telephone canvassers**.

Typically, training falls into two sections: **classroom training**, in which the recruits are taught about the company and the products and may be given some grounding in sales techniques; and **field training**, which is an ongoing training programme carried out in front of real customers in the field. Field training is often the province of sales managers, but classroom training can be carried out by other company personnel (in some large firms there will be specialists who do nothing else but train salespeople).

People tend to learn best by performing the task, so most sales training programmes involve substantial field training, either by sending out **rookies** (trainees) with experienced salespeople, or by the 'in at the deep end' approach of sending rookies out on their own fairly early in their careers. The latter method is indicated if there are plenty of possible customers for the product; the view is that a few mistakes (lost sales) won't matter. In industrial selling, however, it is often the case that there are fewer potential customers and therefore the loss of even one or two could be serious. In these circumstances, it would be better to give rookies a long period of working alongside more experienced salespeople.

The degree to which salespeople are motivated to learn is influenced by many factors, including their perception of the organisation's willingness to change (Rangajaran *et al.* 2004).

Ultimately, salespeople will lose more sales than they get. In most industries, fewer than half the presentations given result in a sale; a typical proportion would be one in three.

Payment

Salesforce remuneration traditionally has a commission element, but it is perfectly feasible to use either a *straight salary*, or a *commission-only* method. Although it is commonly supposed that a commission-only salesperson will be highly motivated to work hard, since otherwise he or she will not earn any money, this is not necessarily the case. Salespeople who are paid solely by commission will sometimes decide that they have earned enough for this month and will give themselves a holiday; the company has very little moral power to compel them to work since there is no basic salary being paid. Conversely, a salesperson who is paid salary only may feel obligated to work in order to justify the salary.

Herzberg (1966) says that the payment method must be seen to be fair if demotivation is to be avoided; the payment method is not in itself a good motivator. Salespeople are out on the road for most of their working lives and do not see what other salespeople are doing, whether they are competent at the job, whether they are getting some kind of unfair advantage, even whether they are working at all. In these circumstances, a commission system does at least reassure the salesperson that extra effort brings extra rewards. Salespeople also judge pay fairness on factors such as the supervisory behaviour of their managers, trust between themselves and the manager, and fair treatment in their negotiations and explanations with the sales manager (Ramaswamy and Singh 2003).

Table 11.8 shows the trade-offs between commission only and salary only; of course, most firms have a mixture of salary and commission.

TABLE 11.8   Trade-offs in salespeople's pay packages

Mainly salary	Mainly commission
• Where order values are high	• Where order values are low
• Where the sales cycle is long	• Where the sales cycle is short
• Where staff turnover is low	• Where staff turnover is high
• Where sales staff are carefully selected against narrow criteria	• Where selection criteria for staff are broad
• For new staff or staff who have to develop new territories	• For situations where aggressive selling is indicated (e.g. selling unsought goods)
• Where sales territories are seriously unequal in terms of sales potential	• Where sales territories are substantially the same

Motivation

Perhaps surprisingly, motivation tends to come from sources other than payment. The classic view of motivation was proposed by Maslow (1954) and is illustrated in his hierarchy of needs (see Chapter 1).

The hierarchy of needs theory postulates that people will fulfil the needs at the lower end of the pyramid before they move on to addressing needs at the upper end. Thus, once a salesperson has assured his or her basic survival needs, these cease to be motivators; the individual will then be moving on to esteem or belonging needs. For this reason, sales managers usually have a battery of motivational devices to keep the salespeople keen.

For rookies, the award of a company tie might address the need to belong; for more senior salespeople, membership of a Millionaire's Club (salespeople who have sold more than a million pounds' worth of product) might address esteem needs. Many sales managers offer prizes for salespeople's spouses or partners. This can be a powerful incentive since salespeople often work unusual hours and thus have disrupted home lives; the spouse or partner is sometimes neglected in favour of the job, so a prize aimed at them can help assuage the salesperson's natural feelings of guilt.

Major account sales management

Managing key accounts differs from the traditional small-sales approach. Typically, managers of salesforces who deal in small, one-off sales will take an **activity management** approach. This involves requiring the salesforce to achieve activity levels in terms of call rates, closing rates, order values and so forth. By doing this, the manager gives each salesperson a clear target for each day, week and month. This in turn makes it easy for the salespeople to plan their presentations and consequently to achieve the targets.

Major accounts, on the other hand, take longer to sell to because there are more decision makers involved and the decisions themselves are weightier. Clearly, a firm considering the purchase of a multimillion-pound head office building will need longer to reach the decision than it would when considering the purchase of a new photocopier for the personnel department. Major sales therefore require patience rather than drive; skill and strategy rather than energy and enthusiasm; many call-backs rather than strong closes. Managers who concentrate on activity management in such circumstances merely encourage salespeople to go for smaller, easier orders rather than the lucrative major contracts.

Managers will frequently help their salespeople to close business in circumstances where there is pressure on activity levels. This tends to mean that the manager goes with the salesperson to help close business quite late in the selling cycle, usually after four or five calls have already been made. However, research has shown that helping salespeople in the early part of the selling cycle helps them to close the sale in fewer calls (Rackham 1991).

It is vital to the company that its salespeople in major account selling work effectively. Their skills may be honed in the following ways:

- *Coaching*. Observing the salesperson in operation and giving suitable feedback.

- *Selling skills training*. Classroom sessions to improve the salesperson's problem-solving and communication skills.

- *Account strategy and account reviews*. Discussion with the manager of the current status of the sale, the personalities involved and so on, in order to improve the selling approach.

- *Effectiveness modelling*. Looking at past performance and previous experience in order to develop 'best practice' rules.

Major account selling will involve more negotiation, more creativity and longer relationship building than small-account sales. Its management clearly has to be handled very differently.

Sales managers do not necessarily need to be the best salespeople in the world. They need to be competent at selling and to have the analytical skills necessary to coach other salespeople, but the main skills required lie in the ability to motivate and control a salesforce, and to be diplomatic in handling the interface between the salespeople and the rest of the company.

CASE STUDY: Co-operative Funeral Service

The Co-operative Society in the UK has a long history. The business is owned by its members, who are also its customers, so the profits of the business are redistributed among those who support it. Originally started as a way of combating the unfair trading practices engaged in by many nineteenth-century businesses, the Co-operative Movement has been a reassuring presence in the UK high street for 150 years.

One of the services provided by the Co-operative Society is a funeral service. This service was originally founded to reassure people that the cost of a decent funeral would not leave their families in debt or under unacceptable financial pressure. The Co-op was trusted to price fairly, in an industry where unscrupulous funeral directors had been known to take advantage of the bereaved.

In the twenty-first century, the bad practices of the nineteenth century have been legislated out of existence or have been curtailed by consumer pressure and trade associations. The funeral business has cleaned up its act, but the Co-op is still in the market with over 600 funeral homes nationwide. Competition is tougher, and some people see a Co-op funeral as a downmarket option: the Co-op has to work hard to retain its share of the market.

The Co-op has put a number of initiatives in place, including a national discussion forum, The Funeralcare Forum. The insights from this forum have enabled the Co-op to make some significant changes in its approach to the market.

The Co-op found out that 75 per cent of first contacts with a funeral home are by telephone. It realised that this was the key point at which the sale would be made or broken: once someone has chosen a funeral home, he or she is unlikely to switch later. People expect to be dealt with sympathetically and in a professional manner, and for the funeral home to be businesslike without seeming unsympathetic or mercenary. Callers are unlikely to have much, or indeed any, experience of arranging a funeral, so they will need to be given clear guidance from the very start of the call. Clearly, hard-sell techniques are entirely inappropriate.

To the uninitiated, funeral services seem to be all much the same, but in fact the Co-op offers a wide range of services and products. Coffins range from a solid wood coffin with a carving of the Last Supper on the side, through a wickerwork coffin, to a coffin made of recycled cardboard. Caskets, boxes for ashes, and (most difficult to deal with) children's coffins, are all available. The Co-op also arranges flowers, funeral gowns for the deceased, and of course makes the arrangements for collecting the body and booking the funeral service. Arranging a funeral is a complex affair and staff need to be well informed to handle the process.

All the staff involved, whether receptionists, funeral directors, drivers or administrators, need to have the same professionalism and sympathetic approach, but the people answering the telephones are clearly key salespeople. The Co-op therefore called in TACK sales trainers to run courses in telephone selling.

Over 800 Co-op staff received sales training over a two-year period. The course covered issues such as:

- planning individual calls;
- handling complaints;
- establishing customer needs and motivations by careful probing;
- gaining customer interest from the beginning of the call;
- adapting the style of the call to meet the situation and personality of the customer.

Those who attended the course were almost universally positive about it. 'I am a far better salesperson now,' one said. 'It shows in my bonuses.' Another stated, 'My sales figures have jumped from between £10K and £11K up to £14K.'

On the face of it, the idea that funerals need to be sold seems odd. On the other hand, it is a time when people have very specific and clearly defined needs, and in particular need a great deal of guidance through what is a stressful and upsetting experience. Sympathetic and professional salespeople are a key element in the process.

Questions

1 What needs might a recently bereaved person have?

2 How can a salesperson close a sale for a funeral?

3 Which types of closing technique would be appropriate, and which would not?

4 What other sales training might be worth considering?

5 What type of remuneration would you expect funeral salespeople to receive?

SUMMARY

This chapter has looked at the selling function as it relates to marketing communication, and the management of personal selling from both a marketing communications viewpoint and a sales management viewpoint.

Here are the key points from the chapter:

- Selling is more about problem solving than it is about communications.
- Salespeople have a lot of information about customers, but it may be difficult to obtain it from them.
- Databases can replace the communications role of selling but not the problem solving.
- Personal selling is about listening, not about talking.
- Salespeople can get a new company more easily than they can get a new client base.
- Most people do not like to make major decisions.
- Commission-only remuneration systems are often not good for the salesperson's morale or motivation.
- Major account selling needs to be effective rather than efficient; quality is much more important than quantity.
- Training is most effective when the trainee does things rather than merely listens.

CHAPTER QUESTIONS

1 If selling is about problem solving, why do most marketers include it under promotion?

2 How can salespeople ensure that they are offering the right product to the client?

3 Why should sales managers accompany salespeople on visits?

4 Why are salespeople paid commission as well as a salary when other employees are only paid a salary?

5 Why is it that salespeople often take the customer's side in disputes with the company?

FURTHER READING

Bettger, F. (1949) *How I Raised Myself from Failure to Success in Selling*. New York: World's Work. Anecdotes of a highly successful American salesman. This book is out of print at present, but if you can find a copy in a library or second-hand bookshop it makes riveting bedtime reading. A real classic.

Blythe, J. (2005) *Sales and Key-Account Management*. London: Thomson Learning. This book goes into the subject in great detail.

Cooper, S. (1997) *Selling: A Practical Approach*. London: Financial Times Pitman Publishing. A good, clear account of selling and sales management, with a lot of practical examples and tips from practising sales managers.

Lancaster, G. and Jobber, D. (2003) *Selling and Sales Management*, 6e. Harlow: Financial Times Prentice Hall. This book takes an academic approach to the subject, with plenty of references to current research and academic thinking. It remains a readable and accessible text, however.

REFERENCES

Abberton Associates (1991) *Balancing the Salesforce Equation: The Changing Role of the Sales Organisation in the 1990s*. Thame, Oxon: CPM Field Marketing.

Anderson, E. (1985) 'The salesperson as outside agent or employee: a transaction cost analysis', *Marketing Science*, **4**(3): 234–54.

Anderson, E. and Robertson, T. S. (1995) 'Inducing multi-line salespeople to adopt house brands', *Journal of Marketing*, **59**(2): 16–31.

Booms, B. H. and Bitner, M. J. (1981) 'Marketing strategies and organisation structures for service firms', in Donnelly, J. and George, W. R. (eds), *Marketing of Services*. Chicago: American Marketing Association.

Brassington, F. and Pettitt, S. (2002) *Principles of Marketing*. Harlow: Financial Times Pitman Publishing.

Cooper, S. (1997) *Selling: Principles, Practice and Management*. London: Financial Times Pitman Publishing.

Copulsky, J. R. and Wolf, M. J. (1990) 'Relationship marketing: positioning for the future', *Journal of Business Strategies*, **11**(4): 16–20.

DeCormier, R. and Jobber, D. (1993) 'The counsellor selling method: concepts, constructs, and effectiveness', *Journal of Personal Selling and Sales Management*, **13**(4): 39–60.

Dewsnap, B. and Jobber, D. (1998) 'The sales and marketing interface: is it working?', *Proceedings of the Academy of Marketing Conference*, Sheffield.

Dibb, S., Simkin, L., Pride, W. M. and Ferrell, O. C. (1998) *Marketing Concepts and Strategies*, 2nd European edn. London: Houghton Mifflin.

Donaldson, B. (1998) *Sales Management Theory and Practice*. London: Macmillan Business.

Drucker, P. F. (1973) *Management: Tasks, Responsibilities, Practices*. New York: Harper & Row.

Dwyer, R. F., Schurr, P. H. and Oh, S. (1987) 'Developing buyer–seller relationships', *Journal of Marketing*, **51**(April): 11–27.

Evans, M. J. (1994) 'Domesday marketing?', *Journal of Marketing Management*, **10**(5): 409–31.

Geiger, S. and Turley, D. (2005) 'Socialising behaviours in business-to-business selling: an exploratory study from the Republic of Ireland', *Industrial Marketing Management*, **34**(3): 263–73.

Gordon, G. L., Schoenbachler, D. D., Kaminski, P. F. and Brouchous, K. A. (1997) 'New product development: using the salesforce to identify opportunities', *Journal of Business and Industrial Marketing*, **12**(1): 33–50.

Herzberg, F. (1966) *Work and the Nature of Man*. London: William Collins.

Levitt, T. (1960) 'Marketing myopia', *Harvard Business Review*, July/August: 45–56.

Lund, P. R. (1979) *Compelling Selling*. London: Macmillan.

Maslow, A. (1954) *Motivation and Personality*. New York: Harper & Row.

Millman, T. and Wilson, K. (1995) 'From key account selling to key account management', *Journal of Marketing Practice*, **1**(1): 9–21.

Narayandas, D. and Rangan, V.K. (2004) 'Building and sustaining buyer-seller relationships in mature industrial markets', *Journal of Marketing*, **68**(3): 63–77.

Peppers, D. and Rogers, M. (1995) 'A new marketing paradigm: share of customer, not market share', *Planning Review*, **23**(2): 14–18.

Piercy, N.F. and Lane, N. (2003) 'Transformation of the traditional salesforce: imperatives for intelligence, interface and integration', *Journal of Marketing Management*, **19**: 563–82.

Rackham, N. (1991) *The Management of Major Sales*. Aldershot: Gower.

Ramaswamy, S.N. and Singh, J. (2003) 'Antecedents and consequences of merit pay fairness for industrial salespeople', *Journal of Marketing*, **67**(4): 46–66.

Rangajaran, D., Chonko, L.B., Jones, E. and Roberts, J.A. (2004) 'Organsiational variables, sales force perceptions of readiness for change, learning, and performance among boundary-spanning teams: a conceptual framework and propositions for research', *Industrial Marketing Management*, **33**(4): 289–305.

Shapiro, B. P. (1979) 'Account management and sales organisation: new developments in practice', in *Sales Management: New Developments from Behavioural and Decision Model Research*. American Marketing Association/MSI Proceedings.

Twenty-first century marketing communications

Objectives

After reading this chapter you should be able to:

- describe some of the trends in communications technology
- explain the potential impact of the World Wide Web on communications
- describe the potential implications of the new media
- explain the impact of social changes on marketing communications
- outline the main features of the twenty-first-century marketplace

INTRODUCTION

This chapter is about some of the trends that will shape marketing communications in the twenty-first century. Advances in communications technology, increased interaction between buyer and producer, and increasing integration of marketing communications will all lead to changes in both the level and the impact of communications. Changes in social conditions and in levels of wealth will also change the availability and effectiveness of communication. Advances in the way communication is viewed and analysed will lead to greater clarity and accuracy of communication, and improved targeting will reduce its quantity and the resulting clutter.

NEW MEDIA

The term 'new media' encompasses a wide range of (usually) computer-based or electronic media that were not in existence 30 years ago and, in most cases, were not in existence even 10 years ago. The most obvious new medium is the **Internet** and that portion of it known as the **World Wide Web**, but other new media exist: interactive kiosks in hardware stores, laser projection and the ambient media discussed in Chapter 5 were all virtually unknown or indeed non-existent before 1990.

It seems likely that other new media will appear as technology advances, and some of these possibilities are explored later in the chapter.

The Internet and the World Wide Web

The Internet has evolved from a specialised (and limited) network intended to link professional researchers into a truly worldwide communications tool. Marketers have not been slow to see the possibilities, particularly in business-to-business marketing, and this has sometimes resulted in exaggerated claims being made for the efficiency and usefulness of the Net.

A subdivision of the Internet is the World Wide Web, which allows access to documents whatever the operating format of the computers involved. The Web is the main commercial arm of the Internet; users can gain access to information, documents, commercial messages, virtual shopping sites, bulletin boards and other sources of information very easily using commercially available **search engines**. Commercial use of the Web falls into two main categories: *traffic control* sites such as search engines, servers and even the telephone and cable companies which charge for access, and *destination* sites, which are the pages the user is looking for. Destination sites are further subdivided into **presence sites**, **online storefronts** and content sites (see Table 12.1).

TABLE 12.1 Categorisation of destination sites

Type of site	Explanation and examples
Presence site	These often look like a conventional advert. A presence site is a homepage with a persuasive, or at least entertaining, format, with perhaps some **hyperlinks** to other pages that offer more detailed factual information. These sites are becoming rare as consumers expect more interaction from websites
Online storefronts	These offer the capability for consumers to buy directly from the firm operating the site. A storefront typically has details of products, often with pictures or, in the case of music or software, with free trials available, and the consumer is able to buy directly using a credit card. These sites are extremely interactive
Content sites	These provide the consumer with the actual product, usually information or online publishing (newspapers and books). Content sites can carry music, time-sensitive news, stock market information, and graphics

This is, of course, a gross simplification. The Web is not only very complex but is also dynamic; new features appear regularly, as might be expected in a medium that covers almost the entire world and is used predominantly by well-educated, inventive people.

Internet-based marketing usually revolves around a firm's website. This is a page on the Web which can be accessed by Web subscribers and which contains information and directions to other pages of interest. A website can contain a sales pitch, solid information about a product or company, and an e-mail address to ask questions or buy the product using a credit card. Websites often carry detailed pictures of the products they promote and, since it is possible to use e-mail to contact the firm, it is possible to conduct sales negotiations and close a sale online.

The advantages of this are obvious, particularly for small firms which need to access a global market. The Net is open 24 hours a day and can be accessed from anywhere in the world; this means that the users (potential customers) are as local as the next room. Small firms therefore do not need to establish a presence in the country to which they hope to export, nor do they need to employ international sales staff, nor do they need to worry about exchange rates. The computer can be set up to give prices in whichever currency the company thinks is appropriate and the prices can be revised instantly to reflect exchange rate fluctuations. The communication itself is virtually instantaneous.

Much of the academic focus on the Web has been on the often-spectacular successes of consumer-targeted pages. As is often the case, industrial marketing has been overshadowed by its consumer counterpart. Berthon *et al.* (1998) postulate that the Web can be treated as if it were an electronic trade show (see Chapter 8) that is very large, international and hosting a very wide range of exhibitors. As with a trade show, the central problem is how to convert the casual visitors (surfers) into interested contacts and, eventually, into purchasers. If this is the case, then the Web will be of most use during the search phase of the buying cycle. Since much of the search can be carried out by using search engines, it seems likely that buyers will go to the Web as a main resource for searching. This implies that the selling firm should ensure that its website is easy to find, and is compatible with the instructions that the buyers are likely to give to the search engines.

The Internet, and the Web in particular, is much more than an extension of the existing marketing communications tools. Marketers have not always adapted their thinking appropriately to this and continue to use their websites as advertisements (represented by presence sites) or as brochures (which is the state of most so-called interactive sites). Since most 'interactive' sites actually only allow the customer to search the site for information, and to make purchases online, the site is only being used in the same way as a mail order brochure.

Recent developments in technology allow websites to negotiate with the customer and to learn from customer-led events such as purchasing behaviour. Furthermore, the growing use of automated search robots (called bots) which can be programmed by the customer to seek out products and prices will compel website owners to be more interactive in their approach.

The Net currently operates under its own rules; there is little or no international law to govern its use (or abuse). The governments of Europe and the USA are working on joint legislation to control the Internet, but any attempts to do so will need to be international, and will need to involve most countries of the world, since the Internet has no solid existence in any one country. The people who place materials on the Internet do have a real existence, of course, but international law would need to be enacted to enable a prosecution to take place in a country other than the one in which the crime is committed. The main stumbling block for such legislation would be the lack of an agreement on what is and is not acceptable behaviour: pornography is an obvious example of something which is acceptable in some countries and wholly unacceptable in others, but less obvious examples might include political propaganda or libellous materials.

For example, Net subscribers have registered objections to what they see as unfair marketing practices by using **bulletin boards** to blacklist companies or to give offensive messages about companies. Some of these have bordered on the libellous, but there is no way of finding out who has put the notices on the board, and since the libeller might be halfway across the planet there is very little prospect of successfully suing for damages. Most major companies' websites are shadowed by anonymous counterculture sites which carry scurrilous stories about the companies concerned. This type of website plays a major role in PR and news gathering. Environmental pressure groups, charitable organisations, self-help groups and others have all used websites to raise the profile of their causes, and some have had remarkable successes as a result. For example, McDonald's employees in the UK have established their own website to communicate about issues of relevance to them (bearing in mind that McDonald's does not allow them to join a union). The website has proved extremely popular with employees, who use it as an outlet for their grievances. Other consumers tend to visit these sites once they know they exist, but in fact the sites tend to have varying effects on visitors depending on what their attitude towards complaining behaviour happens to be (Bailey 2004). All in all, the consumer has most of the real power on the Web.

Internet marketing has the characteristics outlined in Table 12.2.

TABLE 12.2	Characteristics of the Internet as a marketing tool
Characteristic	**Explanation**
Communication style	The style is interactive and is either synchronous (happens immediately) or asynchronous (there are significant time delays between message and response)
Social presence	The feeling is that the communications are taking place at a personal level. Social presence is influenced by the characteristics of the channel: a telephone is more personal than a newspaper advert, for example. Internet communications have relatively high social presence if they are synchronous, particularly as the recipient is usually within his or her home environment when the communication takes place
Consumer control of contact	Because consumers are able to control the time and place at which they access the information, they are more willing to participate in the process of getting information from a machine (Carson *et al.* 1996)
Consumer control of content	If consumers can control the content of the message to some extent, the communication becomes truly interactive (Anderson 1996). For example, a consumer accessing a website can use a hyperlink to move to another page or can skip past information. An e-mail address allows customers to ask specific questions and thus tailor the communications

Current thinking is that the effect of increased use of the Net for marketing purposes will eventually lead to a new environment for marketing. The speed of information flow within firms, especially those operating globally, will mean greater possibilities for real-time negotiations between firms. The rapid growth in virtual shopping (accessing catalogues on the Internet) means that consumers can buy goods anywhere in the world and have them shipped – or, in the case of computer software, simply downloaded – which means that global competition will reach unprecedented levels. Perhaps unsurprisingly, high-tech firms tend to place much more importance on Web-based marketing (Traynor and Traynor 2004).

A recent development is **webcasting**, the automatic delivery of items of interest direct to the individual's PC. Webcasting involves the subscriber in stating in advance what type of information he or she is interested in and having this automatically delivered by the webcaster, thus avoiding the time and effort spent in searching the Net using a search engine. Full participation in e-marketplaces requires companies to integrate their internal and external supply chain activities and to share strategic information (Eng 2004).

Self-selection of messages depends on the consumer's level of involvement (Carson *et al.* 1996), and since the Net represents sought communication the messages should be informative rather than persuasive. Web adverts are effective in communicating implicit meanings: they outperform print advertising for low involvement products, for customers who are negative towards the product, and for light Internet users (Dahlen *et al.* 2004).

The Web is not merely a simulation of the real world, it is an alternative to it in which consumers can have the illusion of being present in a computer-mediated environment (Hoffman and Novak 1996). Consumers have a role in creating the communications themselves: bulletin boards attract users, and the success of the board attracts more users and adds credibility to the site. This means that more consumers will see the marketer's messages. Bulletin boards of newsgroups allow marketers to monitor the success of word-of-mouth campaigns and can also be directly useful in market research; Web users' comments are often useful in assessing consumer attitudes. Integrating the Internet with database marketing techniques allows firms to develop one-to-one customer relationship marketing (O'Leary *et al.* 2004). Events and media can be sponsored effectively on the Internet (Drennan and Cornwell 2004).

Research possibilities inherent in the Web include virtual focus groups and rapid concept testing of new products. There are drawbacks, however: most surveys conducted on the Internet suffer from serious sampling bias since the survey respondents in effect self-select, and not everyone is online (Ray 2003). Also, people are often unwilling to provide financial information on what is seen to be a public medium: incentives offered by researchers are not very effective, and respondents are often cynical about such offers (Ward *et al.* 2005).

A further use of the Net is for internal networks (intranets) within the firm to replace or supplement internal communications such as staff newsletters. Intranet communications can have a stronger effect than paper versions because they are rather harder to ignore; the staff member is more likely to read an e-mail than to open a staff newsletter, and the e-mail version is also quicker and cheaper to produce and distribute. In some organisations, paper memos and newsletters have virtually disappeared (although so many people make hard copies of their e-mails that the paperless office is still some way off).

Consumer search behaviour on the web

Research conducted in Belgium by Muylle *et al.* (1998) shows that search behaviour operates on three levels:

- *Macro*. This embraces the complete interaction between the individual and the machine, from switching on to leaving the Net.

- *Meso*. Each macro-level search includes at least one meso-level search. All meso search behaviour is characterised by the same objective, to find a particular source of information. The meso search level is usually shaped by the nature of the search engine being used, so its nature, duration and outcomes in terms of consumer satisfaction will depend on the search engines available to the individual.

- *Micro*. At the micro level a single website is being read, scanned or navigated according to its complexity. This is the point at which the individual is interested in the hard information contained in the website.

Meso-level search behaviour involves surfing the Net for interesting hyperlinks; this is where the main decisions about what to look for are made. The individual typically skims across a number of pages, selecting hyperlinks that look as if they might be interesting, rather than reading all the possibilities. Marketers therefore need to concentrate on making their own hyperlinks as interesting as possible so that surfers are tempted to look further. **Banner** design is of paramount importance; the Belgian research showed that banners were clicked on only if no hard information was present (that is, no hyperlinks were available). A further moderating factor in Internet behaviour is the length of time the individual has to wait for information to download: in many cases people become impatient and leave the site. Interestingly, the degree of impatience is based on a perception of time, which varies according to a number of factors, including screen colour. Relaxing colours tend to make people think they are waiting for longer than is in fact the case (Gorn *et al.* 2004).

The consumer's search objective determines the navigational behaviour undertaken. In some cases the consumer's level of purposiveness is low: he or she has no particular objective in view and is just **surfing** the Net to see what's new in a number of areas. In other cases the consumer is looking for something specific and therefore has a high level of purposiveness. Surfing behaviour can be classified as follows:

- *Exploratory surfing*. Low purposiveness, low specificity. The surfer is almost playing with the Net. This is common when an individual is killing time or just seeking amusement by finding out what's new.

- *Window surfing*. Medium purposiveness, low specificity. Here the surfer will follow up on interesting items – for example, visiting a website that has details of a new sports car – without necessarily having a specific purpose in mind.

- *Evolved surfing*. Medium purposiveness, high specificity. The surfer is looking at a particular category of information – for example surfing the travel pages. Even though no purchase is intended, the information sought is highly specific.

- *Bounded navigation*. High purposiveness, low specificity. The individual has determined the search boundaries in advance and is looking for any available information about the search object. For example, a student might be looking for any information concerning the alcoholic drinks market.

- *Targeted navigation*. High purposiveness, high specificity. Here the person conducting the search is looking for specific information about a specific product or product category. For example, a potential car buyer might go straight to the BMW homepage to find out what models are available, what the prices are and where they can be purchased.

The issues for marketers implicit in this analysis are that the information offered to each type of surfer will vary according to the stage of information gathering the individual is at. Exploratory surfers are likely to respond to new or at least interestingly presented messages. Window surfers are more likely to respond to messages that direct them to more detailed information, but at this stage they are not in purchasing mode; they are very much at the information-gathering stage of the buying process. The purpose of the messages must be to turn window surfers into evolved surfers. Those engaged in bounded navigation and targeted navigation know what they are looking for and will prefer not to be distracted by spurious sales pitches or persuasive communications. The distinction between sought and unsought communications is particularly appropriate here (see Chapter 3).

In addition, the type of information supplied will determine (in conjunction with the surfer's characteristics and purpose) whether the effect is primarily on the consumer's awareness, knowledge or liking of the company's products. Liking can be enhanced considerably by the amount of fun the surfer has when visiting the website; conversely, hard information supplied to the evolved surfer or targeted navigator will greatly increase knowledge and awareness.

Using the Internet effectively

Figure 12.1 shows some of the steps on the road to online success. Some steps are more important than others, depending on what the firm is trying to achieve and on what the market conditions are. Each part of the diagram is discussed below.

Traffic-generating techniques

Several techniques are available for companies to generate traffic to the homepage, many of which are off-line (for example TV ads, newspaper ads and billboards).

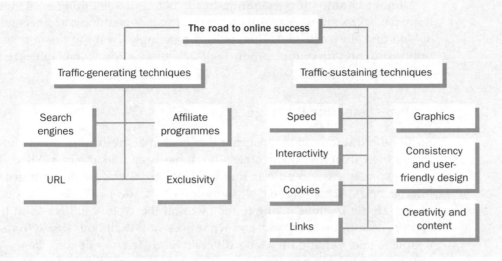

FIGURE 12.1 The road to online success

Online techniques are used to convert casual surfers into visitors to the website, or to encourage those who are seeking something specific to visit the website.

Submitting the company's URL to various search engines is considered by Sellers (1997) as being the single most important step a company can take in order to promote its homepage. Customers will tend to visit the first few sites listed and are unlikely to go beyond the first 10 or 15 sites before either finding what they want or giving up the search. There are several search engines on the Internet and it is not possible to optimise the company's position on all of them since the search engines use different techniques in order to rank a site (Sellers 1997). It is therefore best to focus on a small number of search engines since this will produce the best result in the end. There is no magic formula that can always make a site appear in the first 10 results, and many companies are therefore satisfied if they can produce a good match within the first 30 results (Sellers 1997).

Affiliate programmes were launched by Amazon.com in 1996: Amazon pays its website partners a commission for every customer they send to Amazon's page. Affiliate programmes are effective but are relatively little-known and are under-used (Bove-Nielsen and Ørsted 2000). Bove-Nielsen and Ørsted assert that what makes affiliate programmes so effective is that companies pay only for results and not for exposure, hence both partners are likely to be interested in helping each other to get the most out of the deal.

Benzon (1997) asserts that having a URL which is easy to remember, short, relates to the company and can be written in English, also helps to generate traffic to a homepage.

A final technique for generating traffic is to put something exclusive on the homepage (Procknow 1998). An exclusive offer is something customers will not be able to find anywhere else. This could, for example, be up-to-the-minute pricing, online ordering discounts, product specials or even downloadable screensavers with company logo.

Traffic-sustaining techniques

Sustaining traffic is about ensuring that customers return to the site and spend longer there than they do on other sites. It has been said about HTML code that it is gruesomely easy to do – so many people are therefore doing it gruesomely (Sterne 1995). According to Coldsborough (2000), no principles of good website design are set in stone owing to the fact that the Web is still new, but there is a consensus about what works and what does not. It all boils down to respecting people's time, valuing the Web's diversity and striving for consistency and creativity. Breitenbach and van Doren (1998: 569) argue that a homepage should provide users with an experience which cannot easily be replicated by traditional media. On top of this it should provide users with added value so that they have a reason to return in the future.

The main priority for any Internet user is speed, and until availability of high-speed Internet access becomes widespread, companies should not overdo the graphics as these take a relatively long time to download (Procknow 1998; Coldsborough 2000; Monti 2000). Most users want instant gratification and they should therefore be given smaller file sizes since size equals time. Ten seconds is a long time for users to wait, according to Procknow, and if a homepage loads slowly many visitors will quickly move on to another homepage that will deliver similar information faster.

Sometimes pictures are necessary in order for the user to see what he or she is actually buying, and this can be a problem if the picture is too small (Amire 2000). To overcome this problem, Coldsborough (2000) suggests that companies should supply the visitor with a smaller version of the picture, called a thumbnail, which can be downloaded quickly but which can be enlarged if the visitor is interested in what they see. If a company is selling experiential products like holidays, a vivid display on the site can be advantageous because it can make the consumer imagine what it would be like to own or use the product or service (Briggs 1997; Shih 1998). However, Shih argues that vividness must not be provided at the expense of interactivity. A study by Dholakia and Rego (1998) found that the number of clickable pictures, the total number of pictures, Java applets and gif animations on a homepage are positively correlated with the hit rate. In other words, the more interesting and lively the graphics are, the more likely it is that the user will return to the site or recommend it to friends.

Homepages can also be made interactive so visitors can communicate with companies. This can save customers the costs of a long-distance telephone call (Breitenbach and van Doren 1998). Dialogue on a homepage keeps visitors involved; hence they are more likely to stay longer (Sterne 1995; Gillespie *et al.* 1999). Schwartz (1997) asserts that offering people the opportunity to post messages to a homepage is a good way of getting visitors to return because they are curious to see how other visitors responded to their message.

Some companies have realised the importance of interactivity and have therefore moved away from first-generation homepages, which were mostly characterised by one-way communication (Mejlvang 1999). So far, e-mails are the commonest medium for interaction but, with the continuing development of the Internet, real-time communication with company representatives is likely to become more common (Breitenbach and van Doren 1998). Gardner *et al.* (1999) found that more people would buy online if human interaction was possible: recent research shows that websites are unlikely to replace the salesforce (Moen *et al.* 2003).

In order for the user to feel a sense of interactivity, company feedback must be instant because, for every second it takes to respond, the site becomes less interactive (Shih 1998). The worst thing a company can do, according to Monti (2000) and Schwartz (1997), is to indicate that it is willing to communicate with customers via e-mail and then not have the time or the capacity to respond. If a company cannot respond quickly to all e-mails then Monti (2000) suggests that it should install an automated acknowledgement that will assure the user that the company will respond as soon as possible.

The travel industry has made extensive use of websites, and consequently some travel suppliers find that the public availability of their e-mail address leads to large numbers of general information queries from consumers (Sheldon 1997). Since these e-mails need a response, personnel costs are likely to increase. One way round this is to set up an FAQ (frequently asked questions) section on the site (Benzon 1997).

Consistency and user-friendly design are other basic attributes of a successful website. New Web design programs have made it easier to create a more professional-looking site (Coldsborough 2000). They can help to provide a consistent style for headlines, text, navigation aids, and headers and footers. A site map is also helpful, especially for first-time users to a site (Procknow 1998). A site map is like a table of contents, and if it is designed like an organisational chart it will give a good overview. A search index can also provide help for the user, but the study by Dholakia and Rego (1998: 733) found that there is no correlation between search indexes and hit rate. This does not mean that designers should leave search indexes out: they do provide a lot of help even though they might not generate traffic. If search buttons and help buttons are used often, it probably indicates that the site is frustrating to navigate (Monti 2000).

A cookie is information that a website saves on a user's computer in order for the website to be able to recognise the user in the future. This makes it possible for companies to personalise their site for each user, which means that the user can easily find what interests him or her the most (Baagø 1999). There is also a bonus for companies because the cookies can be used for targeted marketing since they contain information about a user's movements on a site (Hancke and Snitker 2000). If the user's preferences are monitored, the company can offer products which are likely to be of interest to the user. One problem, however, is that some users feel that they are being watched when cookies are used (Hancke and Snitker 2000), so some authors advise that any website that collects data from visitors should state how the information is going to be used (Schwartz 1997; Amire 2000).

Besides consistency, a homepage also needs to be creative or else it is going to be boring to look at. However, creativity can be overdone – for example, coloured or textured backgrounds can make the main text difficult to read. No matter how attractive a homepage looks, it is the actual information provided on the site which is the key to success; hence what is said is more important than how it is said or presented (Kalakota and Whinston 1997; Coldsborough 2000). In the off-line world, 'location, location, location' are the key words, whereas 'content, content, content' are the key words in the online world. However, too much text will be counterproductive (Amire 2000); in other words, online information about a company is good, but it is the value-added content that is ultimately going to make the sale. Consumers often find value in how-to sections, product comparisons, expert sources and testimonials (Crockett 2000).

By contrast, Dholakia and Rego (1998) found that there is no relationship between the content of a homepage and the hit rate – meaning that the content does not seem to matter that much anyway. This seems surprising in the light of the statements above. A reason for this counter-finding could be that Dholakia and Rego's research is from 1998: at that time, simply having a nice-looking homepage meant having a lot of visitors. Today there are many homepages which look nice, so more attention has to be given to the actual content of the site in order to make it stand out.

Dholakia and Rego (1998) found that the number of links to a homepage is positively correlated with hit rates. In practice, many firms enter into agreements with other organisations in the same business to set up mutual hyperlinks to each other's sites. For example, a firm which sells light aircraft might have links to owners' clubs, flying schools, aerodromes and maintenance organisations; the same organisations would reciprocate by having hyperlinks back to the aircraft dealer. However, when a company exchanges links with another company there is a downside, because it gives the visitors an opportunity to leave the homepage (Sellers 1997). There are some techniques available which can reduce the possibility of this happening. A company can either bury links in the middle of the homepage so users are forced to explore what the site has to offer before leaving, or make target tags in the HTML which will open link destinations in a new window, keeping their own homepage in the background. Dholakia and Rego (1998) found that the number of links from a homepage is positively correlated with hits – so maybe links from a homepage are not as bad as they immediately seem to be.

A major problem for website owners is that the Internet is worldwide and can be accessed from anywhere. Normally, marketing communications need to be culturally sensitive, so marketers adapt the communications for different countries and cultures. In the case of the Internet, this is virtually impossible, but some firms (for example, Amazon) set up different sites for different countries or cultural zones. The evidence is that most site owners adapt their sites but keep a number of basic features as standard. At the same time, standardisation of websites for durable goods (such as books, DVDs and CDs) is much higher than for intangible goods such as software and services (Okazaki 2005). Because of this high propensity to standardise, the evidence is that companies do not pay much attention to cultural issues: most websites are firmly rooted in their countries of origin (Singh *et al*. 2005). Japanese firms seem to be better at adapting their websites for local target audiences (Okazaki and Alonso 2003).

Internet trading can be instrumental in developing customer loyalty. Customers will tend to return online much more if the after-delivery satisfaction is high: this is a more important factor than after-checkout satisfaction (Jiang and Rosenbloom 2005). There is also evidence that technology-mediated communications tend to increase future propensity to buy (McDonald and Smith 2004). Visiting a website even has a positive effect on bricks-and-mortar businesses – perhaps because people can undertake an information search in advance of visiting the store (Muller and Chandon 2004). Since many people are nervous of purchasing online, they are likely to use the website to find information, but make the actual purchase in a physical shop. This may partly explain why the so-called **clicks-and-mortar** businesses, which have both an online and a physical presence, have done better from the Internet than firms which exist only in cyberspace.

Service quality is improved by using the Internet as a communications tool. There are five dimensions of online service quality (Jayawardene 2004):

- *Access*. The site needs to be easily accessible and quick to download.

- *Website interface*. The site itself needs to be engaging and effective.

- *Trust*. The website should give an impression of solid reliability.

- *Attention*. The site needs to be engaging and interesting to use.

- *Credibility*. The site needs to be truthful and authoritative.

Interactive information kiosks

Interactive kiosks use touchscreen technology to allow consumers to access information in-store or, in some cases, in public locations. Typically, these kiosks are used to provide tourist information or 'how to do it' information in DIY stores. Kiosks can achieve the following (Lord 1997):

- Extend the brand presence beyond the existing retail sites and reach more potential customers.
- Create a non-intimidating environment in which customers can make their purchasing decisions.
- Free up staff from answering basic enquiries.
- Relieve staff of the pressure to make recommendations that they might be ill-informed to cope with.
- Provide a greater range of information than most human beings could offer.
- Provide customers with a hard copy of the information they need.
- Allow customers to work within a budget and compare prices easily.
- Increase awareness of complementary products, thus increasing average customer spend.

Kiosks can provide customers with stock information so that they can quickly see whether the product they want is in stock, which can save a great deal of in-store search time and staff time in checking. Also, customers are able to ensure in advance that they are buying the right product for the job, which saves time, money and wasted effort.

Kiosks can be seen as the automated sales assistant; given the increasing cost of using human staff, and the increasing availability of relatively cheap technology to replace them, it seems likely that the use of kiosks will greatly increase in future.

Non-computer technology

Although much of the emphasis on technological change focuses on computer technology, there are other technological changes afoot that will alter the communications scenario.

The increase of satellite, cable and digital TV means a proliferation of channels. This means more hours of programming with audiences spread across a much wider range of stations. On the one hand, this leads to greater segmentation and easier targeting of audiences, but on the other hand it will mean greater pressure on TV stations' revenues as the advertising spend is spread more thinly. Reductions in the quality and quantity of advertising are likely to result, and certainly reductions in the cost of TV advertising are likely to lead to greater access to the medium for small companies.

Improvements in print technology allow the production of the following new types of advertisement:

- *Heat-sensitive*. Inks can be used that change colour as a result of heat or light.

- *Scratch'n'sniff*. These release the smell of, for example, a perfume when the advertisement is lightly scratched with a coin or fingernail.

- *Double-image*. These create the illusion of movement.

- *3D*. These use an apparently random, complex pattern to show a three-dimensional image by means of an optical illusion.

It is only a matter of time before talking adverts become commonplace in print advertising.

Light-sensitive supermarket displays can be triggered by passers-by, and shopping trolleys can carry video displays that could be triggered by sensors in the store to inform the customer about special offers.

Hologram technology allows advertising materials to be projected in three dimensions. The technology is in its infancy, but improvements in this approach could mean that goods on display in shop windows could be replaced by holograms, and the window itself could be dispensed with so as to allow customers a clearer view of the products on display.

Laser projection of images on to clouds and buildings is spectacular but also still in its infancy. The technology itself is fairly well established but is expensive and requires bulky equipment for its operation. The images can be distorted by the patterns of the clouds, and although the technique works fairly well in a country like the UK, where cloud cover is common all the year round, it would be less useful in countries where cloud appears only when accompanied by rain. Once the technical problems are overcome, the medium has considerable merit, since it is relatively cheap and yet has an immediate impact and is visible over very large areas.

Telesales and telemarketing are also undergoing considerable transformation. For example, although it is known that people are more likely to buy from a salesperson whom they perceive to be similar to themselves, this knowledge has been difficult to put into effect until recently. It is now possible to match up inbound telesales customers with similar salespeople by using the computer's database. The technology is in its infancy, but already some telemarketing firms are able to match customers with salespeople from their own part of the country, for example. Eventually it should be possible for a car insurance company to link the customer with a salesperson who drives a similar car, or who is of the same age and has the same family circumstances.

Telemarketing is undergoing further transformation as a result of the proliferation of telephones. Even twenty years ago a substantial number of homes in the UK were without telephones; now it is rare to find an individual with no telephone. Partly this is the result of falling subscription prices owing to competition in the market, and partly it is owing to the proliferation of mobile telephones, which for some users replace the landline telephone altogether. At the same time, there has been a huge increase in the amount of unlisted telephone numbers – to the extent that telephone directories are much smaller than they used to be. The growth in the number of telephones has increased the possibilities for telemarketing in general, but the ongoing desire for privacy evidenced by the number of ex-directory numbers reduces the opportunities for outbound teleselling. The trend for consumers to seek control of the process is likely to continue as individualism gains strength.

Increasing ownership of mobile telephones will eventually lead to more person-to-person contact rather than the current person-to-place contact. Provided the individual telephone owner has released the number to the marketing company, outbound telesales direct to the consumer will become possible. This places a heavy emphasis on establishing a trusting relationship with the consumer.

SOCIAL CHANGE

Shifts in social attitudes will lead to shifts in the style, content and acceptability of marketing communications as well as the methods of delivery. A current ongoing change in the social structure of western countries is the increased emphasis on individualism brought about by increasing wealth. Those familiar with Maslow's hierarchy of needs (Maslow 1954; see Chapter 1) will know that as individuals become wealthier and more secure in their economic and social lives, they tend to seek self-actualisation and become more individualistic in their behaviour. Social security, increased leisure time to pursue social fulfilment and increased financial wealth mean that approximately 40 per cent of Europeans are now self-actualising (McNulty 1985). Many of these people are seeking self-actualisation through social campaigning, raising the profile of ethical issues in marketing as well as elsewhere. Appealing to self-actualisers is much more likely to work on an individual basis; not only do such people not wish to be included in a segment (pigeonholed), but the prevailing social paradigm is shifting so that the remaining 60 per cent who are not yet self-actualising also want to appear to be individualistic and thus prefer individual appeals (Evans and Blythe 1994).

Demographic shifts mean that the youth market is shrinking and the grey (or even elderly) market is increasing. Communications will need to reflect this shift, particularly in terms of modelling and types of appeal made in advertising. There is an expected increase in the number of one-person households due to the rising divorce rate and greater mobility of the workforce. This means that the traditional appeal to the typical family unit is becoming irrelevant. In the 1960s, the typical UK family consisted of a husband who earned the money, a wife who stayed at home and looked after the home, and their 2.4 children. In the twenty-first century, the typical family is more likely to be a divorced husband who lives with his new partner and pays maintenance to his working ex-wife who juggles her career with looking after their 1.8 children.

This is reflected in advertising. Already advertisements show men shopping for themselves, or taking their children to hamburger restaurants on their 'access' days; some advertising shows teenage children helping their (single) mothers with the housework. Advertisers need to reflect the behaviour of their target consumers as well as shape it if the communication is to be seen as relevant. In future, this will also need to be reflected in other forms of communication; for example, tele-sales calls fixing appointments for salespeople to visit householders usually insist that both partners are present for the presentation. This is rapidly becoming obsolete as a marketing practice, since single-person households are the biggest single category of household in most of northern Europe and the USA.

Some social changes have effects on individuals that can be relevant to marketers. For example, although many women feel that they should have careers as well as families, there is evidence that most of them feel guilty about this and have negative feelings about leaving their children to go to work (Smith 1998). Communications that assuage these guilt feelings are likely to be more effective than those that increase them.

Much of this social change is one-way. Although change is popularly seen as swinging back and forth like a pendulum, there is no evidence for this; for example, if increased individualism is coming about because of increased wealth, conformity would arise only if there were a sudden reduction in wealth. Although this might well happen at some time in the future, there is no logical reason for it to be seen as a pendulum effect since the average material wealth of western Europeans has been steadily rising for most of the last five centuries.

The twenty-first century marketplace

Schultz and Schultz (1998) theorise that marketing has gone through two distinct phases in the past 40 years and is about to enter a third. The first phase was domination of markets by manufacturers, who were able (through intensive promotional campaigns) to control markets or at least to have the strongest influence in them. The second phase is domination by the retailers, who (because they are closest to the market) have been able to determine which products are offered to consumers and which are not. The third phase, brought about by the increasing use of IT by consumers, is consumer domination of the marketplace.

In some ways the role of marketing is shifting from a strategic function to a tactical one as consumers become more powerful in the relationship. The strategic role of marketing has sometimes been seen as patriarchal, the powerful, all-knowing marketers providing consumers with what the research says is best for them. This model has been breaking down for some time, in the face of unpredictable consumer responses, fragmentation of societies and increasing individualism. This means that market research findings no longer act as truly effective predictors in many cases, and marketers are therefore left to respond as effectively as they can to consumer demands as expressed through interactive media.

This set of circumstances will lead to a change in the way marketing communications operate. Of course, the traditional manufacturer domination will continue in some markets and the retailer domination of major store chains will also continue, but the growing ability of consumers to make their purchases almost anywhere in the world and to access information from almost anywhere will increase the pressure on marketers to integrate their communications to maximise effectiveness and efficiency.

Firms go through four levels of integration of communications, as follows:

- *Level 1: Tactical coordination*. In the historical marketplace there were relatively few ways of communicating with consumers. The past two decades have seen a massive increase in the available tools. The Level 1 response is to create 'one sight, one sound' by consolidating communications planning. Often this leads to attempts at cross-functionality, where teams of specialists from different areas of expertise are formed to increase synergy and cross-fertilisation of ideas.

- *Level 2: Redefining the scope of marketing communications*. Rather than viewing marketing communications as a series of outbound activities, the firm begins to consider all the points at which the consumer and the brand are in contact. This often leads to new ideas on communicating, and indeed one of the most important results of Level 2 thinking has been the inclusion of employees both as targets for and as proliferators of marketing communications. Internal marketing thus becomes one of the driving forces of Level 2 thinking.

- *Level 3: Application of IT*. IT is both driving the changes in marketing communications and providing the solutions. The key ingredient in Level 3 thinking is the use of databases to capture individual transactions. This enables the firm to market to groups of individuals rather than to the average customer at the middle of a segment, the approach that typifies traditional marketing.

- *Level 4: Strategic and financial integration*. Two issues are paramount: the ability to measure the return on customer investment, and the ability to use marketing communications to drive organisational and strategic directions. Rather than measuring, say, extra sales resulting from an advertising campaign, the firm would now measure the returns from a specific group of customers against the costs associated with all the marketing communications directed at that group. Under this approach, financial directors would have sufficient information to be able to compare investment in communicating with a particular group of customers with, for example, investing in new manufacturing facilities.

There are definite problems in integrating marketing communications, not least of which is that the medium becomes part of the message. As we saw in Chapter 1, messages do not necessarily arrive as a 'magic bullet': people think about the message, the medium, their existing knowledge of the sender and so forth so that the message sent by the firm is greatly transformed by the time it is analysed by the recipient. Messages sent by different routes are therefore unlikely to be perceived in the same way by each recipient; for example, someone who dislikes television might respond unfavourably to a TV advert for a brand while being favourably disposed towards a radio advert for the same brand. Complications of this nature are likely to make fully integrated communications difficult to achieve.

Overall, marketing in the twenty-first century presents many new challenges. Shrinking markets, green issues, runaway advances in communications technology and rapidly changing public attitudes to consumption and communications predicate major changes not only in communications techniques but also in communications strategy. Marketers will need to re-examine their models of marketing communications many times; in an era where change is the only constant, marketing communications cannot afford to stand still.

CASE STUDY: West Country Violins

West Country Violins was set up in 1999 to supply local violin students in rural Devon with good quality violins. The violins themselves were often antiques, from the nineteenth century, but the market quickly became saturated and West Country Violins needed to look further afield.

The key to West Country Violins' business approach is that each violin is individual to its owner: the company does not deal in mass-produced, cheap instruments, but in high quality instruments from well-regarded manufacturers. The obvious solution for this tiny company was to use the Internet – but how could it maintain its personal service when using such an impersonal medium?

Realising that it is the sound of the violin more than anything which sells the instrument, West Country Violins decided that having pictures and descriptions of the instruments on the website was insufficient. The company therefore created recordings of each and every violin in the store, and put these on the website. The recordings are not mere soundbites, either – each violin is named, and the recording lasts for thirty seconds, more than enough to make a judgement about the sound quality. The pictures and descriptions of the violins are detailed and comprehensive, and in fact some customers have even said that the company tries to make the flaws in the violins look as obvious as possible; but it is the recordings that make all the difference.

Customers can place their orders over a secure encrypted link, so that credit card details are safe, but this is standard practice for online purchases. Where West Country Violins scores is in the way the company maintains contact with its customers. Each customer is regularly contacted with an update on the progress of the order, and the company prides itself on being accurate about delivery dates. The violins are delivered set up ready to play, the customers have a guarantee that they can return the violin free of charge if it does not match to the description, or indeed for the shipping costs only if they simply change their minds. Customers from all over the world buy from West Country Violins, and the company has added a Japanese page to the website to facilitate purchases from customers in the Far East.

West Country Violins applies the same standards whether the customer is buying a violin for £200 or one for £4,000. When one Australian customer visited the store in 2002, the managing director, Brian Ward-Smith, collected her from the station and dropped her off again afterwards. This level of customer service has generated amazing loyalty – a layperson might imagine that few violinists would buy violins regularly, but many of West Country Violins' sales are actually repeat purchases, as students upgrade or as professional musicians add to their range of instruments. Everyone from beginners to virtuosos, from classical concert violinists to country fiddle players, has been able to find a suitable instrument at West Country Violins. As one customer wrote: 'Brian is more than a seller of violins, he is a friend to those who are looking for the right violin.'

Brian Ward-Smith comments: 'Customer satisfaction must remain at the heart of overall business strategy and we've endeavoured to keep this in mind as we build our website and integrate e-commerce with our business operations.'

Questions

1 How might West Country Violins build on its success?

2 What role does new technology have in building customer relationships?

3 What lessons might be learned by other companies selling musical instruments?

4 To what extent is Brian Ward-Smith's approach transferable to other companies?

5 To what extent is West Country Violins' success due to its being a small firm?

SUMMARY

The future of marketing communications is, like most other things, uncertain. What is a certainty is that the world in general is changing rapidly, the pace of change is increasing, and marketing communications must reflect those changes if it is to remain relevant in the twenty-first century.

What needs to change is not merely the tools of marketing communications, although the impact of IT and rapid broadband communications networks will cause changes enough. Marketers must also change the way they plan for communications and recognise the strategic implications of the shift in the power base that underpins communication.

Here are the key points from the chapter:

- The World Wide Web operates as a virtual marketplace, with buyers, sellers and competitors operating in the same virtual environment.

- The Net is independent of governments and big business, so the users set their own rules and exercise most of the control.

- Interactive information kiosks empower customers as well as save on staff costs.

- Social changes are not on a pendulum; most changes are one-way.

- Technological change encompasses more issues than IT: cellular phones, new print technology, holograms and new media will also have a major impact.

- Change is the only constant and must drive strategic thinking as well as providing new tactics.

CHAPTER QUESTIONS

1 What might be the key success factors in website design?

2 How does the Internet empower consumers?

3 Why might an online storefront be more successful than a presence site?

4 What are the main strategic issues that arise for marketers in the twenty-first century?

5 What effect will the rise in individualism have on marketing communications?

FURTHER READING

The problem with predicting the future is that it is upon us before we can finish writing about its possibilities. For this reason there are few textbooks that look into the future.

Wang, R. and Jackson, R. (1993) *Strategic Database Marketing*. Lincolnwood, IL: NTC Publishing. This covers some of the strategic issues involved in database marketing, but is probably already out of date. Ultimately, it is journal papers that are likely to be the most up to date; better still, surf the Net!

REFERENCES

Amire, R. (2000) 'Web design pitfalls: what not to do', *Candy Industry*, supple. *Harnessing the E-commerce Boom*, May: 5.

Anderson, C. (1996) 'Computer as audience: mediated interactive messages in interactive marketing', in Forrest, E. and Hizerski, R. (eds), *The Future Present*. Chicago: American Marketing Association.

Baagø, H. (1999) 'Småkager i cyberspace', Tænk, no. 3: 10–12.

Bailey, A.A. (2004) 'Thiscompanysucks.com: the use of the Internet in negative consumer-to-consumer articulations', *Journal of Marketing Communications*, **10**(3): 167–82.

Benzon, S. (1997) *Virksomhedens 5 grunde til at gå på Internettet – en vejviser til et nyt medie*. Copenhagen: Copenhagen Business School Press.

Berthon, P., Lane, N., Pitt, L. and Watson, R. T. (1998) 'The World Wide Web as an industrial marketing tool: models for the identification and assessment of opportunities', *Journal of Marketing Management*, **14**(7): 691–704.

Bove-Nielsen, J. and Ørsted, C. (2000) *E-Business – digitale forretningsstrategier*, Copenhagen: Børsen Forlag A/S. www.digitalestrategier.dk

Breitenbach, C. S. and van Doren, D. S. (1998) 'Value-added marketing in the digital domain: enhancing the utility of the Internet', *Journal of Consumer Marketing*, **15**(6): 558–75.

Briggs, S. (1997) *Successful Tourism Marketing: A Practical Handbook*. London: Kogan Page.

Carson, S., Peck, J. and Childers, T. (1996) 'Preliminary results on the determinants of technology assisted shopping: a model, measure development and validation', *Proceedings of the AMA Winter Educators' Conference*, pp. 229–39.

Coldsborough, R. (2000) 'Stickier sites: A primer', *Restaurant Hospitality*, **87**(7): 86–8.

Crockett, R. O. (2000) 'Keep 'em coming back', *Business Week*, 15 May, p. EB20.

Dahlen, M., Murray, M. and Nordenstam, S. (2004) 'An empirical study of perceptions of implicit meanings in World Wide Web advertisements versus print advertisements', *Journal of Marketing Communications*, **10**(1): 35–47.

Dholakia, U. M. and Rego, L. L. (1998) 'What makes commercial Web pages popular? An empirical investigation of Web page effectiveness', *European Journal of Marketing*, **32**(7/8): 724–36.

Drennan, J.C. and Cornwell, T.B. (2004) 'Emerging strategies for sponsorship on the Internet', *Journal of Marketing Management*, **20**(9/10): 1123–46.

Eng, T-Y. (2004) 'The role of marketplaces in supply-chain management', *Industrial Marketing Management*, **33**(2): 97–105.

Evans, M. and Blythe, J. W. D. (1994) 'Fashion: a new paradigm of consumer behaviour', *Journal of Consumer Studies and Home Economics*, **18**: 229–37.

Gardner, M., Karoulina, E., Mullen, R., Ridoux, C. and Valen, G. (1999) *Filling the Gaps in Online Retailing: Analysis and Recommendations on How to Improve the Online Retailing Environment.* Owen Graduate School of Management, Vanderbilt University, USA. www2000.ogsm.vanderbilt.edu

Gillespie, A., Krishna, M., Oliver, C., Olsen, K. and Thiel, M. (1999) *Online Behaviour. Final Project: Stickiness.* Vanderbilt University, USA, 5 May. www2000.ogsm.vanderbilt.edu

Gorn, G.J., Chattopadhyay, A., Sengupta, J. and Tripathi, S. (2004) 'Waiting for the web: how screen colour affects time perception', *Journal of Marketing Research*, **41**(2): 215–25.

Hancke, J. and Snitker, M. (2000) 'Mere om cookies'. www.forbrugersikkerhed.dk

Hoffman, D. and Novak, T. (1996) 'A new marketing paradigm for electronic commerce', *The Information Society*, **13**(1).

Jayawardene, C. (2004) 'Management of service quality in Internet banking: the development of an instrument', *Journal of Marketing*, **20**(1): 185–207.

Jiang, P. and Rosenbloom, B. (2005) 'Customer intention to return online: price perception, attribution-level performance and satisfaction unfolding over time', *European Journal of Marketing*, **39**(1/2): 150–74.

Kalakota, R. and Whinston, A.B. (1997) *Electronic Commerce – A Manager's Guide.* Reading, MA: Addison Wesley Longman.

Lord, R. (1997) 'Death of the car salesman', *Revolution*, July: 38–40.

Maslow, A. (1954) *Motivation and Personality.* New York: Harper & Row.

McDonald, J. B. and Smith, K. (2004) 'The effects of technology-mediated communication on industrial buyer behaviour', *Industrial Marketing Management*, **33**(2): 107–16.

McNulty, W. K. (1985) 'UK social change through a wide-angle lens', *Futures*, August: 331–49.

Mejlvang, M. (1999) 'Skræddersyet til Nettet' 21 April. www.jp.dk

Moen, O., Endresen, I. and Gavlen, M. (2003) 'Executive insights: use of the Internet in international marketing: a case study of small computer firms', *Journal of International Marketing*, **11**(4): 129–49.

Monti, R. (2000) 'Better Web design boosts sub sales', *Folio: The Magazine for Magazine Management*, **29**(2): 54.

Muller, B. and Chandon, J-L. (2004) 'The impact of world-wide web site visits on brand image in the motor vehicle and mobile telephone industries', *Journal of Marketing Communications*, June, **10**(2): 153–65.

Muylle, S., Moenart, R. and Despontin, M. (1998) 'World-Wide-Web search behaviour: a multiple-case study research', *Proceedings of the 3rd Annual Conference of the Global Institute for Corporate and Marketing Communications*. Glasgow: Strathclyde Graduate Business School.

O'Leary, C., Rao, S. and Perry, C. (2004) 'Improving customer relationship management through database/Internet marketing: a theory-building action research proposal', *European Journal of Marketing*, **38**(3/4): 338–54.

Okazaki, S. (2005) 'Searching the web for global brands: how American brands standardize their websites in Europe', *European Journal of Marketing*, **39**(1/2): 87–109.

Okazaki, S. and Alonso, J. (2003) 'Right message for the right site: on-line creative strategies by Japanese multinationals', *Journal of Marketing Communications*, **9**(4): 221–39.

Procknow, S. (1998) 'The Web essential check list', *Industrial Distribution*, **87**(9): 88.

Ray, N.A. (2003) 'Cyber surveys come of age', *Marketing Research*, **15**(1): 32–7.

Schultz, D. E. and Schultz, H. F. (1998) 'Transitioning marketing communication into the twenty-first century', *Journal of Marketing Communications*, **4**(1): 9–26.

Schwartz, E. I. (1997) *Webonomics: Nine Essential Principles for Growing Your Business on the World Wide Web*. Harmondsworth: Penguin.

Sellers, D. (1997) *Getting Hits: The Definitive Guide To Promoting Your Website*. Berkeley, CA: Peachpit Press.

Sheldon, P. J. (1997) *Tourism Information Technology*. Oxford: CBA International.

Shih, C. F. (1998) 'Conceptualizing consumer experiences in cyberspace', *European Journal of Marketing*, **32**(7/8): 655–63.

Singh, N., Kumar, V. and Baack, D. (2005) 'Adaptation of cultural content: evidence from B2C e-commerce firms', *European Journal of Marketing*, **39**(1/2): 71–86.

Smith, P. R. (1998) *Marketing Communications: An Integrated Approach*, 2nd edn. London: Kogan Page.

Sterne, J. (1995) 'What makes a world class business to business web site', www.commerce.net

Traynor, K. and Traynor, S. (2004) 'A comparison of marketing approaches used by high-tech firms: 1985 versus 2001', *Industrial Marketing Management*, **33**(5): 457–61.

Ward, S., Bridges, K. and Chitty, B. (2005) 'Do incentives matter? An examination of on-line privacy concerns and willingness to provide personal and financial information', *Journal of Marketing Communications*, **11**(1): 21–40.

Glossary

ABC (Audit Bureau of Circulations) The UK body responsible for verifying the circulation figures of periodicals.

Above the line Advertising, any paid insertion in a medium.

ACORN (A Classification of Residential Neighbourhoods) A method of classifying people according to the area in which they live. Very useful to retailers and to billboard site planners.

Activity management A management style that concentrates on the behaviour of salespeople rather than on the outcomes of the behaviour.

Addressability The capacity for sending a communication to an individual.

Advertorials Advertising which is made to look like a news story.

Affect The emotional aspect of attitude.

Agricultural show A temporary event which combines an exhibition with competitions and demonstrations of agricultural produce and farming skills.

Aided recall Testing which advertisements a consumer can remember from a given list.

Alliteration Use of similar-sounding first letters to create impact.

AM (Amplitude modulated) A technical term meaning that the broadcasting system has low sound quality but long range.

Ambient advertising Non-traditional advertising in which the message is built into the surrounding environment.

ASA (Advertising Standards Authority) A voluntary regulatory body in the UK.

Aspirational groups Groups which the individual would like to join.

Assonance Repetition of vowel sounds to create impact.

Attitude splitting The ability to acknowledge the truth of a dissonant stimulus, but still reject as being inapplicable to the individual.

Audience fade-out The practice of leaving the room when the adverts are on.

Banners Brief advertisements run on a website to point the way to other websites, possibly through a hyperlink.

BARB Broadcast Audience Research Bureau.

Barrier to entry A factor in the production or marketing of a product which makes it difficult for competitors to enter with a competing product.

Below the line Any marketing communication which is not advertising.

Benchmark To use the best individual performances of competitors as targets to aim for.

Big-book catalogues Mail-order directories which contain a very wide range of products.

Billboard A large advertising sign, usually by a main road.

Blimp An unmanned helium-filled balloon.

BRAD (British Rate and Data) The directory which contains details of virtually all periodicals in the UK.

Brand architecture The process of structuring brands in order to transfer brand equity from product levels to corporate levels.

Brand extension Marketing new products under an old brand name.

Brand extension offers Promotions in which the gift offered has the brand name on it.

Branding Applying a name to a specific product in order to improve its recognition among consumers.

Brand name A term, symbol or design that distinguishes one seller's product from its competitors.

Bulletin board A website that allows subscribers to add comments and to debate issues via e-mail.

CAP (Committee of Advertising Practice) The watchdog body responsible for maintaining standards of decency and honesty in British advertising.

Card decks Direct-response communications from several firms, printed on reply-paid cards and mailed out in a group.

Chunking The collecting together of similar types of information.

Circulation The number of copies of the periodical sent out or sold to the public.

Classified adverts Advertisements which appear within a set classification, along with others advertising similar products.

Classroom training Training conducted at the company's offices, away from customers.

Clicks and mortar A business which combines a substantial online turnover with a physical presence on the High Street.

Closed questions Questions to which there is only a yes or no answer.

Closers Salespeople who develop solutions to customers' problems and win the order.

Clutter Excessive advertising which overloads the audience.

Cognition The intellectual aspect of attitude.

Cognitive dissonance The holding of two opposing attitudes at once.

Cold prospects Potential customers who have no previous relationship with the firm.

Colour-blocking Arranging same-colour packs together on the shelf so that the group stands out from surrounding products.

Comparative parity Setting promotional budgets according to the level of expenditure undertaken by competitors.

Compositioning Grouping products under a single brand name with a single position in the consumer's perceptual map.

Conation Intended behaviour resulting from, and part of, attitude.

Connotative That which is understood by the individual alone.

Content site A website containing an actual product, for example online publishing or software that the subscriber can buy and have delivered to his or her home computer.

Copy The words in an advertisement.

Core benefits The aspects of the product which are like those of its competitors and which would be expected as a matter of course by consumers.

CPT (Cost per thousand) The cost of advertising to a thousand readers; a way of comparing periodicals in terms of value for money.

Customer holding The effect of rewarding existing customers through a sales promotion.

Customer intimacy The act of getting close to the customer; obtaining and using detailed information about customers.

Customer loading The effect of encouraging customers to stock up on a product line.

Customer usage The ways in which a product is used by a customer.

DAGMAR (Defining Advertising Goals, Measuring Advertising Results) An approach to planning and executing advertising strategies which includes the measurement of the effectiveness of the advertising, often in terms other than merely sales.

Database Customer details held on computer.

Database marketing Segmenting and targeting consumers whose personal details and shopping habits are held on computer.

Decoding The act of extracting meaning from signs and symbols.

De-duping Removing duplicate entries from a database.

Defensive PR See reactive PR.

Delayed discounts Promotions that offer a benefit at a later date or with a subsequent purchase.

Denotative That which is common to everyone's understanding.

Denouement The revelation of new information at the end of a teaser campaign.

Direct marketing A cybernetic marketing process which uses direct response advertising in prospecting, conversion and maintenance.

Direct response Any advertising that elicits a response direct to the advertiser rather than through an intermediary such as a retailer.

Display advert Advertisements which appear at any place within a periodical and which are paid for according to the area of the space they occupy.

Double-crown Standard size of poster measuring 20 by 30 inches.

DRTV (Direct-response television) TV advertising which includes a response mechanism.

DTP (Desktop publishing) A computerised system for producing documents which include varied typefaces, graphics and sometimes colour printing.

Effectiveness Sales leads generated or other objectives achieved.

Efficiency Effectiveness compared with other media.

EFTPOS (Electronic funds transfer at point of sale) This allows payment by credit card, and even cash dispensing from supermarket tills.

Encoding The act of translating ideas into signs and symbols.

Endorsement Recommendation of a product by a prominent person.

EPOS (Electronic point of sale) This allows the rapid throughput of goods through checkouts, and also the collection of detailed purchase data.

Ethnocentrism The belief in the superiority and universal applicability of one's own cultural norms.

Exhibition A temporary event at which customers, sellers and competitors are brought together.

External PR Public relations exercises aimed at those outside the organisation.

Eye camera A camera used to record movements of the eye; it is often used to record responses to advertisements.

Family branding Grouping products under a single brand.

Field training Training conducted in the presence of prospects.

FM (Frequency-modulated) A technical term meaning that the broadcast system has high sound quality but short range.

Font The typeface used on packaging.

Foregrounding Bringing particular aspects of the ad to the forefront; for example, making the voice-over louder than the music.

Freesheet A periodical which is distributed door-to-door for no charge.

Free-to-air TV Television that is broadcast through the airwaves without the need for a subscription payment on the part of the viewer.

Frequency The number of times an advertisement is seen.

Galvanic skin response The reduction of electrical resistance in the skin due to interest in a stimulus, e.g. an advertisement.

Gone-aways Customers who have moved house or died.

Graphics The visual element of an advertisement or packaging.

Hacking Gaining illicit access to a database.

Halo effect The belief that if one aspect of a product is good, then all aspects are.

Hierarchical database A database which holds customer details under one access method, e.g. a name.

Homophones Words which sound alike but have different meanings.

Hook A few words which attract the reader's attention.

Hot prospects Potential customers who are almost certain to have an interest in buying the product category.

Hyperlink A quick way to access further information through a website.

Icon A visual image directly connected with the object of the communication.

Image reinforcement The effect of enhancing the image of a product or of fixing it in a customer's mind through sales promotion activities.

Inbound telemarketing Telephoned marketing communications originating with the customer.

Index A sign which is indirectly associated with the concept being communicated.

Infomercial An entertainment programme which contains, in a documentary format, information about a new product.

Inserts Loose leaflets inserted into magazines or newspapers.

Inside transport advertising Advertisements on the insides of buses, taxis, trams and trains.

Interactive kiosk A computer and screen, usually in-store, that provide the customer with an interactive information source.

Interactive systems TV or computer-based advice systems used by consumers in-store to explain the use of the available products.

Interference Intelligent, planned distractions from a communication.

Internal PR Public relations exercises aimed at those within the organisation.

Internet The global linking of computers to create a single information environment.

Intonation The rhythm of the sentence; this can be deviant in order to create impact.

Involvement The degree of personal importance attached to the attitudinal object.

IVR (Interactive voice response) A computer-based system for handling routine enquiries without human intervention.

Joint promotion Sales promotion undertaken by two or more companies in order to take advantage of synergies and economies of scale.

Junk mail Indiscriminate marketing communications delivered through the postal system.

Kinetics Movement.

Lead Someone who is prepared to see a salesperson.

Linage Advertisements which are charged for by the line of copy. They do not contain any graphics.

Line family branding Grouping related products under a single brand name.

Livery A whole vehicle painted to advertise a product.

Logo A stylised image used on packaging to denote a particular brand or company.

Lookalike branding Packaging a product in such a way that it looks similar to the brand leader, without actually making the pack or brand name identical.

Loyalty card A card issued by a retailer that allows the customer to collect points or obtain discounts whenever he or she shops at the retail outlet issuing the card.

Mail order Ordering and delivery of goods via the public mail system.

Major account Any customer who represents, alone, a significant portion of the firm's turnover or has strategic importance.

Manufacturer promotion A promotion that is aimed at consumers, but that originates with the manufacturer.

MEAL (Media Expenditure Analysis Ltd) A company which provides statistics on the advertising spend of UK companies.

Mechanics The activities a consumer or customer has to undertake to obtain a promotional benefit.

Media event A publicity exercise aimed at arousing interest in the organisation from the news media.

Medium The periodical in which the advertisement is displayed.

Missionaries Salespeople who do not directly take orders, but who spread the word to those who do, for example pharmaceutical salespeople who persuade doctors to prescribe new drugs.

Modelling The use of actors to demonstrate the use of a product.

Multilevel marketing A system of personal selling in which recruiting new salespeople is the responsibility of the salesforce, and where promotion is dependent on the number of recruits found.

Narrowcasting Accurate targeting of a specific audience.

Network database A database in which the records can be sorted by any of the factors held in the records.

Nielsen ratings A system of calculating audience sizes used in the USA and some other countries.

Noise Non-intelligent distractions from the communication.

Objections Problems raised by prospects in the course of presentations.

Off-the-screen selling Advertising products on TV with a hotline number for customers to order the goods directly.

Off-the-shelf A promotion that offers a service from a third party.

Omnibus surveys Market research exercises which include questions from a number of different firms.

Online storefront A mechanism for virtual shopping on the web; a medium through which web subscribers can buy goods using credit card payments.

Open questions Questions to which the answer is not limited to yes or no.

Order takers Salespeople who collect orders after the buyer has made a decision to purchase.

OSCAR (Outdoor Site Classification and Audience Research) The research arm of the outdoor advertising industry.

Outbound telemarketing Telephoned marketing communications originating with the marketer.

Outside transport advertising Advertisements on the sides of buses, trams, taxis and trains.

Outsourcing Buying in from outside the firm.

Override Commission paid to managers based on the sales made by their subordinates.

Party plan A system of selling based on inviting the host/ess's friends to a party at which products are demonstrated and sold.

Perception The development of the individual's world view.

Phantom partnership Implying a connection with a prestigious event or company without actually saying so, or having such a connection.

Point of purchase The place at which the customer makes the final buying decision and commitment to pay.

Positioning The place the product occupies in the consumer's perceptual map.

Post-testing Experimental trial and evaluation of advertising or other communications after they have been made public.

Pre-bid sessions Meetings which take place with prospective TV commercial producers to explain the brief for the commercial. The production companies are then invited to tender for producing the commercial.

Premium promotions A free gift with each purchase.

Presence site An advertisement on the web that establishes a company's presence, but little more.

Press conference A meeting of journalists at which an item of news about the organisation is released.

Pre-testing Experimental trial of advertising or other communications prior to making them public.

Private exhibition An event organised alongside a mainstream exhibition, usually at a nearby venue.

Private responses Complaints which the consumer makes to friends or family about products or services.

Proactive PR Anticipating and meeting threats to the organisation's reputation.

Product placement Arranging for the firm's products to be featured in films or TV shows, usually (though not always) in exchange for payment.

Profiling The act of dividing the database into segments and categorising the customers on it.

Prospect Somebody who is prepared to listen to the salesperson's presentation and is able to buy the product.

Publics Those groups with whom the company wishes to establish a favourable reputation.

Pull strategy Promoting heavily to end customers and consumers in order to pull products through the distribution channel.

Pupil dilation response The increased diameter of the eyes' pupils when the respondent sees something interesting.

Push strategy A set of activities aimed at encouraging members of the distribution channel to stock and sell the product.

Qualitative research Research designed to find out why consumers respond in the way they do; research which cannot be expressed numerically.

Rackjobbing Placing a display stand in a retail store and taking responsibility for stocking it: the retailer retains a proportion of the sales from the stand.

RAJAR (Radio Joint Audience Research) The UK body responsible for researching the size and composition of radio audiences.

Ratchet effect The process by which sales, having risen by means of sales promotion, are maintained at the higher level by other promotional tools.

Rate card The price list for the medium.

Reach The number of people who see an advertisement.

Reactive PR Responses to outside threats to the organisation's reputation as they arise.

Readership The number of people who read a publication.

Redundancy Sending the same message via different routes to overcome the distorting effect of interference and noise.

Reference group A group from which a consumer takes guidance, directly or indirectly, about purchase decisions.

Registration Filing a brand name with a government department to ensure exclusive use of the name.

Relational database A database in which records are stored in two or more dimensions.

Reliable The quality of a research measure which is free of random error.

Retailer promotion A promotion that originates with the retailer.

Road show Mobile exhibition organised by a single exhibitor or a small number of exhibitors.

Role model An individual who demonstrates the use of a product.

Rooky New, inexperienced salesperson.

Roughs Draft advertisements produced by the creative team for the client's approval.

Sales cycle The series of activities a salesperson undertakes in the course of making presentations and selling products.

Sales promotion Short-term activities designed to make a temporary increase in sales.

Salient beliefs The most important beliefs about a product.

Scamps See Roughs.

Scratchcard A promotional game that involves scratching off an opaque layer on a card to reveal a set of symbols. Winning cards have matching symbols.

Search engine Software that enables the web subscriber to locate the desired information or websites.

Selective perception The process by which individuals reject information which is not relevant or which conflicts with existing ideas.

Self-liquidating offers Promotions where the cost of providing the promotion is covered by payments made by the customer responding.

Shooting The actual production of the TV commercial.

Sign Anything which stands for something to somebody in some respect.

Silent seller Folder of press cuttings, advertisements, brochures, price lists etc. which a salesperson uses to show prospects features of the product and company.

Skywriting Using a smoke trail from an aeroplane to write an advertising message in the sky.

Smart card A credit-card sized card containing a computer chip which holds customer and purchase details.

Sought communication A communication which the consumer actively searches for as part of the information-gathering process.

Specialogues Mail-order catalogues which are aimed at a specialist or niche market.

Sponsorship Funding of arts, sporting and cultural events in exchange for publicity.

Stimulus rejection The act of ignoring a specific stimulus which does not conform to the receiver's previous experience and attitudes.

Storyboard A set of drawings which depict the outline of a TV commercial.

Subjectivity The interpretation of information according to the individual's previous experience.

Sugging Selling under the guise of market research.

Surfing Searching the Net without having any particular purpose in mind.

Symbol A universally agreed sign which stands for the concept being communicated.

Tamper resistance Making packages (particularly of food) difficult to open or contaminate without making this obvious to a subsequent purchaser.

Telephone canvassers People who make appointments for salespeople over the telephone.

Territory The area allocated to a given salesperson to work within.

Third-party responses Complaints which the consumer makes through a third party such as a lawyer or consumer to the supplier.

Trade promotion A sales promotion aimed at members of the distribution channel.

Trial impact The effect of a promotion aimed at encouraging first-time purchase of a product.

Ultravision A billboard made up of rotating triangular slats which allow three separate advertisements to be carried on one site.

Unaided recall Testing which advertisements a consumer can remember without giving any prompts.

Unsought communication A communication which the consumer is not currently looking for, but which may become part of the internal search at a later stage.

USP (Unique Selling Proposition) The factors that differentiate the product from its nearest competitors.

Valid The quality of a research instrument which measures what it is supposed to measure.

VFD (Verified Free Distribution) The equivalent of ABC, but applied to freesheets.

Voice responses Direct complaints from the consumer to the supplier.

Warm prospects Potential customers who have had some previous contact from the firm.

Webcasting Delivering specific information to web subscribers who have requested the service.

World Wide Web A division of the Internet that carries most of the commercial and public-access material.

Zapping Using the remote control to switch channels or switch off the sound when the adverts come on.

Zipping Using the fast-forward or cue button on a VCR to skip past the commercial breaks.

Index